A Turbulent Priest

JEMAHL EVANS

In Memoriam

For Maureen Toomey (nee Brennan) who always welcomed me with a smile.

CONTENTS

Becket: Warrior
Chapters 1 – 8
Historical Note
Becket: Rebel
Chapters 1 – 8
Historical Note
Becket: Martyr
Chapters 1 – 8
Epilogue
Historical Note

BECKET: WARRIOR

1.

The County of Toulouse in the Kingdom of France, August 1159.

Osbern ran as hard as his short legs could roll in the hot noon sun. His head was thumping and heart bursting as he sprinted. His very life, and the King's, depended upon speed. The scrawny little freeman could hear the pursuit behind, hooves pounding thunder in his ears, but dared not risk a glance.

The trees were only thirty yards away.

If he could make them before the knight stuck him with his lance, he was away. The woods would stop the horseman and he could find the Chancellor. Osbern's lungs felt as if they were fit to explode and his legs were as heavy as lead, but he pushed himself ever on. The King's life depended upon it. His life depended upon it; he kept repeating it over and over as he ran.

Twenty yards.

The snorting horse was on him.

Just ten yards – he was going to make it.

Osbern threw a look behind him. There was a single Toulousian rider on his heels, mail clad with enclosed helm, and with his white ash lance couched to strike.

'God's teeth!'

He threw himself to the floor, scraping his face in the dirt, and the lance whistled over his head, and he rolled on the ground to avoid the destrier's deadly hooves. Horse and rider flashed past in a blur. The French knight yanked on the reins to pull his animal around, but Osbern was back on his feet in an instant and running for the trees once more. As he dived panting for the bushes, a huge figure dressed in a mail shirt and holding a great battle axe stepped out of the cover.

'Worry not, Rabbit, the Bear is here.'

It was a young English hedge knight. Osbern knew him – Reginald FitzUrse. The knight's moniker was well earned: tall and broad with muscular arms, wild brown beard and long hair, and a temper to match his ferocious reputation. Osbern scrambled into the trees whilst FitzUrse faced down the French knight with a wide grin on his face.

The Bear showed no fear as the French knight steadied his steed and saluted FitzUrse with his lance. He just waved his axe menacingly in response. The knight began to trot towards him, slow at first and then picking up the pace; he lowered his lance, couching it in his armpit to bear the force of collision. Osbern watched on aghast. The power of mail clad Franks had shaken the very walls of Jerusalem, but the young Bear simply stood like a mountain facing down the charging horseman.

At the last moment, just as the lance was about to skewer him, and faster than Osbern's eye could catch, FitzUrse stepped to the left and lance point whipped past him. The Bear swung his axe at the horse as he moved, striking a great blow at its head. There was a loud crack as the axe smashed into the side of the equine skull. The animal screamed as it toppled on its forelegs, stunned and dying. Its rider was pitched over the head, somersaulted in the air and landed with a great crash. He lay sprawled on his back, knocked senseless by the fall. The man had lost his helm in the collision, and Osbern could see that the French knight was barely more than a boy. The Bear did not wait for the lad to rise, or take his parole as was customary and expected. Instead, he swung his axe once more and hacked at the Frenchman's exposed neck in a fountain of blood. Once FitzUrse had despatched him to God, he turned back to Osbern covered in gore, grinning, and with his battleaxe dripping.

'I must see the Lord Chancellor,' said Osbern, gulping at the horror. 'The King is under attack and sent me to find him.'

'Come along then, Rabbit.'

The Bear led Osbern quickly along a narrow animal track to the Chancellor's encampment. It was a bustling hive of activity hidden in the woods: blacksmiths at work hammering away, sharpening weapons and shoeing horses. Cooks toiled and broiled at steaming cauldrons to feed the hundreds of men gathered around the white tent. Thomas of London travelled in style. When the army had come to Toulouse from England, the Chancellor had made certain that his host was the greatest and best equipped of all the King's barons. Thomas had spent coin like water, even borrowing some from the king to build this force.

My master tries too hard to make up for his common birth, thought Osbern. He always has to be the best, but also to be seen to be the best. It is an obsession and it makes others jealous. The King's favour is ever a double edged sword.

Osbern had served the Chancellor for nearly ten years. Thomas was but a petty clerk in Canterbury running errands for the Archbishop back then, and Osbern little more than a boy. Now, Thomas was the Lord Chancellor of England and second only to the King, but his common birth in Cheapside haunted the man.

He is ashamed of his birth.

Thomas's pavilion was set up in the centre of the camp. A leather canvas bleached white and glistening like a jewel in the summer sun. The Chancellor's banner of three Cornish crows on a white field fluttered above the tent. It was pristine perfection surrounded by the dross and dirt of the common soldiery.

'Over there,' said the Bear. 'He will be at his bath; he's always at his bath. I will wait.'

Osbern ignored the warrior's jibe and ran to his master's tent. There were guards at the entrance, but they recognised the Chancellor's manservant and allowed him to enter. It was dark inside, cool away from the sunlight. The slender dark-haired Chancellor was seated at a table with his mercenary officers. They looked up as Osbern entered. Thomas smiled at him, but the captains looked irked at the scrawny servant's interruption.

'What is it Osbern? Have you come from the King?'

'The King is under attack, Lord. He sent me to find you.' Osbern blurted out the words. 'Through the woods, about a mile that way.' He gestured vaguely in the correct direction. 'There are at least two companies out of Cahors attacking him and his household knights.'

'Then we must respond immediately,' said Thomas quietly. 'He turned back to his captains. How quickly can you be ready?'

'In moments, Lord, at your command,' said Hywel, a grizzled grey-haired veteran who claimed to be a prince among the Welsh.

'So be it.'

The captains called for the alarum and begged leave of Thomas as they made ready to ride. There was haste but no panic among them. Thomas had chosen his officers wisely, and made sure that they were very well paid and very well equipped.

'You can help me into my arms, Osbern.'

'Yes, Lord.'

'You are going to fight?' came a voice.

John of Salisbury appeared with a jug of wine in one hand and a scroll in the other. His chubby face was already flushed from the grape, and his shaved tonsure burned red from the French sun. It gives him the countenance of a strawberry, thought Osbern. The churchman looked disappointed with Thomas.

'Why else are we here?' replied the Chancellor.

'I am here because Archbishop Theobald sent me to watch over you. You do not know how to fight. You will only get yourself killed, and then where will we be? You are not a warrior, Thomas.'

'I can learn, John. I have been learning.'

The chubby scholar sniffed. 'Well, I am staying here with my books and wine. Books are proper learning. The grape around here is exceeding good, you know.'

Thomas smiled at his old friend. 'I shall tell you all about it when we return.'

The chubby priest waved his hands dismissively. 'I have no time for tales of battle, but if you find any interesting books bring them to me? There are rare manuscripts in the university at Cahors, and I know that the students and masters will try to sneak them away.'

'Books, books, books, it is ever books and wine with you, my friend.'

'Each to their own station.' John sat down on the cushioned chair brought from Poitiers, poured himself a cup of wine and began cutting a quill. 'My next treatise must be ready soon, you know.'

'I look forward to reading it,' said Thomas.

Osbern helped the Chancellor pull on his leather hauberk and excruciatingly expensive mail coat, tying the buckles as his master spoke with the old scholar. Finally, he took out the white surcoat from the chest where it had been packed. It was emblazoned with the three crows that Thomas affected for arms, embroidered by the Chancellor's own sister. Surcoats were a new fashion brought from the Holy Land by the crusaders. There, the sun was so hot that white linen was a necessity to a metal clad man else they would boil alive in the armour. In the damp summer of Western France, it was considered an expensive vanity. Few of the barons and knights wore the new surcoats. Worse, Thomas's was not made from linen but from the purest silk brought from Cathay and excruciatingly expensive. It singled the Chancellor out in the armed host, which was exactly what the Chancellor wanted.

The camp was in uproar as men scrambled for their weapons and animals. Thomas's mercenary captains beat their best companies ready for action. In the time it took the Chancellor to arm, three companies (nearly five hundred men) were assembled for battle. Two hundred horse, knights and men-at-arms, and the rest were veteran spearman.

A groom brought Thomas's white steed (another expense), and the captains waited for him to mount the animal. Osbern could hear some sniffs and sly comments from the common levy, but their betters sat in stony silence as the Chancellor took hold of the reins and swung himself into the saddle. Osbern smiled at the shock on some of their faces. Thomas had a good seat; he may have been unused to the ways of war, but he could ride as well as any of these knights and warriors. The Chancellor had spent his dissolute youth hunting and hawking before becoming a clerk to the Archbishop, and he had to keep up with the King's coursing.

Osbern also knew of the secret weapons practice Thomas had undertaken back in England. The Chancellor had spent his early mornings after prime prayers sparring with Hywel. John of Salisbury was still snoring with a hangover whilst Thomas had trained. People were going to be in for a surprise, thought Osbern. His master liked surprising people.

Osbern handed Thomas the thin ash lance and his shield emblazoned with three crows.

'Thank you, Osbern,' said Thomas. 'Stay close in case I need to send a message, but I do not want you to fight.'

'Have no fear, Lord. I have no desire to fight in a battle.'

FitzUrse had mounted up with the other troops, and he led the companies through the rough tracks that criss-crossed the woodland. They passed the body of the killed French knight and his dead horse that had chased Osbern down. The Bear laughed and pointed at the two corpses with his comrades. Thomas was sure to reward the brute; the Chancellor was always generous in his gifts and praise. Overly generous some said, and where the coin came from was an oft whispered question at court.

The Chancellor always travelled in style, always spent coin lavishly, but whose coin was it?

Once through the woodland, the three companies reformed and rode at a trot towards the King's retinue. Osbern was forced to run with the spears to keep pace with the horsemen. Such a huge army and such poor roads meant that the English companies were spread out over a vast area as they marched towards Toulouse. His Majesty had been caught with only a small company of household knights and men at arms at a small village near the town of Cahors.

'Faster, faster.' Thomas urged haste as they rode towards their King's rescue. If Henry was killed it would be a disaster for England.

As the company crested a rise, Osbern could see the King's embattled household in the vale below. There were nearly two hundred attackers, knights and men at arms as well as spear levy, swarming around Henry's small company of perhaps fifty mailed warriors. The red-haired monarch was in the middle of a cluster of knights, on foot and swinging his sword, but the battle looked desperate. They were outnumbered four-to-one in the fighting. Thomas's arrival had turned the tables.

Thomas did not wait for his captains to issue their commands; instead, he rode to the front of the host on his white steed so that all could see he was leading, and ordered his horns to blow the charge. The trumpets were another vain expense, no other in the army had them even the King, but the sound brought precious relief for Henry.

The knights under the Chancellor's command started at a trot towards the fight in the vale. Some of the Frenchmen had seen the relief arrive behind them and were already turning to run. Thomas and his knights began to pick up speed, rolling towards the battle in a wave of metal and beast.

Osbern watched from the hilltop and his master led the warriors as if he had been born to the task. The spearmen followed on behind in a rush to keep up.

'Don't get yourself killed,' he prayed.

The trot became a charge, thundering down towards the enemy. The Englishmen held their discipline, lances lowered as one and couched as they hit the French rear at full tilt and smashed through them. Thomas was first among the attackers; his lance shattered into splinters at the first clash, but swinging his sword left and right at the enemy. Osbern could see him clearly emblazoned in white and standing out from the crowd around him. Thomas always wanted to stand out in a crowd, but in a battle it made him a target as he fought his way to the King.

'Please don't get yourself killed.' Osbern repeated it over and over.

King Henry was on his feet wearing a rusty mail coat with no helmet, swinging a long two-handed blade, decapitating and maiming his enemies as he slashed at them. The King was tall, red haired with a barrel chest and muscular arms like a smith, and fearsome to behold in battle. Henry shouted at the Frenchmen, taunting them as he cut them down, grinning from ear to ear and covered in blood. He was enjoying himself, even in such dire straits. This King was born to battle, not like old King Stephen. It was tale well known that Henry's Angevin ancestors were descended from the devil. Osbern believed it; the King could be wild.

The French were running back towards Cahors. Those who were too slow were quickly cut down. Neither the King nor Chancellor showed any mercy to their enemies. Rich knights with rich ransoms were butchered instead of taking parole, although some baulked at the lost coin, but the common spear levy were slaughtered with no thought. Their bodies were stripped of clothes and purses and cast naked to the side of the roadway. The English host (English, Norman, Aquitainan,

Angevin, Breton, Irish, and few Welsh) cleared away the dross of battle and paused on the road south. Cahors was only a few miles distant, and beyond that the army's ultimate destination and glittering prize: the city of Toulouse and its scheming Count Raymond.

'Time for me to get back to work,' muttered Osbern to himself, and started to run down the slope to attend to his master.

Thomas was already dismounted when Osbern arrived, enveloped in a bear hug from the King. The slender Chancellor was a touch taller than the broad shouldered monarch. Henry was laughing and joking, despite the danger of his previous situation, and the older man joined in with his young monarch's merrymaking. The two of them were as close as brothers. Thomas handed Osbern his shield and sword to take away, as the King called for wine to celebrate the victory.

Where the buggery do I put these? thought Osbern, as he took the weapons. He noted there was no blood on the blade.

'I was worried the Rabbit might not get to you in time,' said the King looking at Osbern.

The manservant kept his head down and his mouth shut. Everyone at court had learned that Henry's bluff joviality could turn in an instant to a black tantrum. Saying nothing was generally the best policy.

'He can scuttle fast enough,' said Thomas with a smile at his servant. 'What now, Lord?'

'Now we take Cahors and march onto Toulouse. When we get there, I am going to shove this broken spear up Count Raymond's fat arsehole.'

The watching knights laughed at the King's jest, and not just from sycophancy. Henry was popular, beloved even, by the rough fighters that served him. In return for their loyalty and love they were well rewarded in turn.

2.

The town of Cahors is situated on a horseshoe bend in the Lot River and protected on three sides by the water. A rickety wooden bridge (that the town's dignitaries were always promising to rebuild in stone) was the only way into the town from the western approach. A stone gatehouse, nearly thirty feet in height guarded the entrance; the final obstacle to the attackers. The King settled down and made ready for an assault as soon as English companies started arriving at the town. Henry did not want Cahors free behind him as they advanced on Toulouse; it threatened his supply lines and retreat should they be forced to withdraw. Once Cahors had fallen, it would be a jewel to gift a baron whose loyalty Henry wished to secure or reward.

'Order the crossbows to keep the gatehouse defenders worried,' Henry told one of his captains. 'When the ram goes in I want you with me.'

The man nodded to his king and hurried to make ready.

The crossbowmen were all from Bordeaux and Poitiers; Aquitanian subjects of the English King. They were professional and well drilled, and expensive. Their captain made them wait for marks to appear on the battlements about the gatehouse, sending their deadly bolts at any who dared to poke their heads up. The town's defenders were not mere passive spectators, but there were few armed men in Cahors and none had more than hunting bows to return shafts. Henry stood alone out of arrow shot and studied the town's defences.

'It is mostly scholars and students left in the town.' Thomas told Osbern as they watched the King from their pavilion. 'They will not make for much of a fight, wastrels and delinquents all.'

Osbern did not mention the irony of his master's own past schooling in Paris – where the Chancellor had most assuredly been a wastrel delinquent by all accounts. Instead, he watched as the men carrying the ram came up towards the wooden bridge and halted just out of arrow range. The tree had been felled and trimmed to batter at the stout town gates once the attackers were readied. They would have to charge across the wooden bridge and hammer the stout oaken gates at the far end, all the while the enemy would be loosing arrows and throwing rocks and any other projectiles to hand down at them. The Bear was with the ramming party. Osbern could see his huge frame bullying the levy.

'The casualties will be high in the first assault,' Hywel said to Thomas.

The Chancellor merely nodded. He fully intended to join in the attack regardless of his personal safety.

The mercenaries are somewhat more circumspect, thought Osbern glancing at Thomas's Welsh captain. They see it as a prize to be taken and looted. He had expected his master to urge restraint upon the King and to protect the innocent townsfolk caught up in this game of kings and princes, but Thomas was just as bloodthirsty as the rest, just as caught up in the fiery passion of war.

He is a man obsessed with his new role.

It had surprised Osbern, who had served the Chancellor for years, but disgusted his friend John of Salisbury who had known Thomas even longer. The Chancellor had taken to war as if he had been born to it (which delighted King Henry, of course). Thomas supped ale with his mercenary captains and loyal knights like some petty warlord, and laughed at their coarse jests. He always has to be the best, be it clerk, or Chancellor, or knight errant, or general; he always has to be the best. The Chancellor was a good master but demanding. Osbern was expected to be the best manservant. It was a height he oft failed to attain and Thomas's disappointment was like a barbed weapon, but he could rage too. The Chancellor had just as black a temper as the King when defied.

'Bring me my sword, Osbern.'

'Your sword, Lord?'

'I am away to see the King.'

Normally men did not bear arms in a King's presence, but Henry was typically lax about such securities. Thomas, among other privileged barons, wore their swords with him in court, but only Thomas's display caused complaint among the others. Osbern retrieved the sword from its chest and buckled it on his mail-clad master. A gaudy jewelled hilt, but the blade was made with fine tempered steel from Damascus. He picked up the helm and shield and followed on as Thomas strode down to the men gathering around Henry before the town.

Out of arrow shot of the town gatehouse and bridge, the English companies made ready for an assault. There was no element of surprise to the preparations; the defenders could see what was coming. Men drew straws to see who would carry the ram over the wooden bridge to batter away at the gates. The chosen few stripped off their leather hauberks (those that possessed such) and made ready to heft the ram. Some prayed quietly to themselves, others jested and japed loudly to cover their nerves. With them were the hardened men-at-arms who would lead the attack into the breach. Old veterans who quietly checked their weapons and made sure the edge was sharp. Osbern thanked God that he would not be involved in the fighting.

'Do you think they will surrender, Lord?'

'I think they will put up a token resistance. Otherwise Count Raymond would hold it against them, but there are not enough warriors in the town to defend it for long. Once the gatehouse falls the town will be ours.'

'The King will be pleased.'

'Keeping the King pleased is why we are here, Osbern.'

'Yes, Lord.'

'When the fight happens, I want you to remain with John and stay out of trouble.'

'Happily, Lord.'

Thomas smiled at his manservant. The Chancellor was clearly enjoying himself.

King Henry directed the preparations for the assault personally. He had a wide grin on his face, as Thomas and Osbern arrived. The young King was delighted that the town had refused to surrender. It gave him the chance to display his martial prowess to his men. He was also canny enough to know that word of his valour and strength would be whispered in the courts of Franks and Latins. The King had already earned a fearsome reputation; Cahors would help to build it even higher.

'Have you come to join us, Cheapside?' Henry called over to Thomas.

'Yes, Lord, I will be at your side.'

None other than the King would dare mention Thomas's common London birth (although the city's townsfolk and aldermen were delighted at their native son's meteoric rise), the Chancellor would have cut them dead with cold fury, but Thomas just gave a wan smile at Henry's taunt. The King was always bluff with his jesting and it did not do to complain. The King was also prone to tantrums and histrionics.

The companies were assembled ready for the assault: crossbowmen from Aquitaine, heavily armed Saxon footmen and men at arms, and dismounted knights from the King's own household. The spears that had drawn the short straws would carry the ram, whilst others would protect it with wickerwork shields from the defenders missiles.

'There is no hot sand, no boiling water, and no machines; we have water and food enough. Did I tell you about the fall of 'Edessa, Osbern?' said Hywel.

Thomas's Welsh captain had been to the Holy Land and often regaled the Chancellor and his retinue with tales of the boiling hot sun, untrustworthy Greeks, and merciless Saracens, as well as the women and wonders of the Kingdom of Jerusalem.

'Edessa was not part of the Kingdom of Jerusalem, you know,' Hywel continued. 'It was an independent fief, but it fell to the Saracen's in only a week. I was there.'

Osbern knew all that, word of it had resounded through Christendom, but saw no need to point it out. Hywel had spent nearly a decade in the East and enjoyed telling his stories; Osbern enjoyed hearing them, he dreamed of the Holy Land. There was no need to doubt the Welshman's words, no matter how fantastical the tales he sometimes told.

'My helm and shield, Osbern.'

Osbern helped Thomas buckle on the heavy enclosed helm, flat topped with only a narrow slit to see out, and fixed his shield on the left arm. The Chancellor and Welshman made to stand with the King ready for the assault.

The manservant retreated to a small rise to watch the action. John of Salisbury came out to join him and see what the fuss was about.

'Is he really going to fight again?'

'So he says.'

'Pathetic.'

John turned away from the siege and went back to his books with a look of disgust. Osbern turned back to the fight.

Once the levied men were readied, Henry ordered the crossbows to fan out and send their bolts at the walls and gatehouse. Then he sent the rammers across the bridge to the gate. The men charged over the wooden bridge, their boots pounding out a beat on the planks. Arrows from the defenders whistled down at them. Men groaned and fell as they were struck, the metal barbs piercing leather and cloth, disabling and killing. Once at the gates they hammered the ram into the wood. The sound boomed out with each stroke, echoing across the sun parched fields.

'FitzUrse, Now! Go now!' Henry shouted at the Bear who was leading the assault party.

FitzUrse led his party across the bridge to help with the ram. There were less missiles coming from the defenders now; the King's crossbowmen were doing their job well. Anyone who poked his head above the battlements was gifted a bolt in the face. There were few who dared after the first casualties.

FitzUrse's men hacked and hammered at the gates with small axes once they arrived, reinforcing the spears and rammers battering with the log. A groan of tearing wood, like a dying man's last gasp, could be heard across the field as the gate broke open. Osbern heard it from his vantage point. Henry and Thomas could hear it as well. The King's household knights were ready to attack; they looked to their lord expectantly. There was urgent fighting at the gates with FitzUrse's men and the town's defenders.

'Charge!' The King shouted.

His household pounded across the bridge the broken gates weighed down in mail and helm. They were the best, the most loyal, proven warriors; their training and years of combat gave them strength in battle. Alongside them and the King ran Thomas of London. The slender Chancellor kept pace with them all, despite the unfamiliar weight of his armour, and arrived at the gate by the King's side. It hanged, torn half off its hinges. FitzUrse and his men battled their way inside as the enemy tried to hold the gatehouse. The defenders were poorly equipped and only a few had any sort of armour to face the best of the English army. The King and his men rushed to join the fight.

Henry cut a swathe through the defenders, wielding his great sword as if it were a stick and scything down enemies in the enclosed space. Beside him, Thomas stabbed and slashed, keeping to his Lord's side. The King prized Thomas's loyalty above all else, but valued his other talents: his sharp mind and obsessive ambition. Thomas's need to be the best made him a perfect royal weapon at court, and the Chancellor was now proving his ability as a warrior and battle lord as well. The King laughed as the enemy fled from the two of them, falling back in terror at their shining swords.

'Are you enjoying yourself, my Chancellor?' Henry asked, voice muffled in his helm.

'Inordinately, serving you is ever a pleasure, Lord.'

As they overwhelmed the last defenders and burst into the town itself, Henry stumbled over a broken cartwheel. Two Frenchmen finally saw their chance and turned to strike the English King down in the mêlée. It was Thomas who stepped forward and stopped them.

The Chancellor moved between the prone King and the approaching warriors. Both of the Frenchmen were dressed in leather hauberks with open faced pot helmets, but their swords gave a bloody testimony to their fight. They were grim faced and the first one struck out at the Chancellor. Thomas parried the blow with his shield, sending a shock right up his left arm like it had been struck with a hammer and almost dislocating his shoulder, but he grimly ignored the pain. The other man moved to cut him down, but Thomas did no wait for the killing blow. He barged into the first enemy with his shield, knocking him to the floor and yelling as pain shot up his arm. The watching

Henry, still lying prone on the floor, was surprised at Thomas's strength and speed. The Chancellor slashed at the other warrior's chest as he charged. His sword did not pierce the leather coat, but the blow snapped the man's collar bone. The Frenchman screamed in agony until Thomas struck another great blow on his helm and knocked him senseless. Then he stabbed down at the fallen man before him. Thomas had beaten both of the attackers in his charge. The other enemies nearby were swiftly despatched by Henry's bodyguard, as Thomas leaned on his sword and panted from the exertion.

'You have been practicing,' said the King, as he climbed to his feet helped by a flunky.

'So as best to serve my lord,' said Thomas. He looked at the two defeated Frenchmen 'But these were only peasants, not real warriors.'

The attackers had broken into Cahors as the last defenders at the gate were overwhelmed, and rapine and pillage soon ensued. Henry had not given his men the right to loot the town but when a city falls there is always violence, there is always murder, and there is always theft. The common levy, mercenaries, and coarsest of knights would take what they could from the town. The King meanwhile withdrew back to his tent and summoned the town's leaders to formally surrender.

***

They could hear the sounds of revelry and drunkenness outside as they searched through the library. Nearly a hundred books and countless scrolls and treatise' were stored in an antechamber to the church. John of Salisbury had led the way there as soon as Cahors had fallen and was declared relatively safe. Thomas, with his shoulder bound up, with Osbern and some guards accompanied him. The stone building had been abandoned by the priests and scholars, broken dross left discarded in their flight. Precious books and documents, parchments and vellum, lay scattered on the flagstones. The warriors who had looked to loot the church had taken any gold or coin, ripping off expensive jewelled covers, but dismissed the writings as worthless.

'If only they knew the true worth is in the words not the

bindings,' said Thomas, sadly.

The Chancellor was as interested in the discarded papers as his friend, but Osbern was singularly bored by the whole process. He could read the Latin catechism and understood the alphabet. Osbern could even write his name, but he took no interest in books or learning. He was after all but a manservant and messenger. All of these papers and parchments were meaningless to him. It was a point he made to his master.

'The man who can read but does not, has no advantage over the man who cannot read,' Thomas told him.

'I have little time to spend in a scholar's cell, Lord. You keep me too busy.'

'We both serve the King, Osbern, and he is a most demanding master.'

That is true enough but so are you, thought the manservant.

Henry was already preparing to march on Toulouse. In a day or so the army would take the old Roman road south towards the city. It was like the King's very own summer pilgrimage. There was no time to waste as far as Henry was concerned. He was all drive and energy, an explosion bubbling away just waiting for a spark to fire. Thomas matched the King in his pursuits and pleasures (excepting women where the cleric was unusually pious), but whilst the King slept, his Chancellor ordered the Angevin realm.

'I have found it,' cried John.

Thomas and Osbern both looked at the small tome the cleric had found on a shelf: a leather bound booklet with pages made of thin parchment. The words inside were plain and unadorned Latin but it had been beautifully inscribed. The cost of the sheepskin parchment alone would have fed a village for a year.

'That is one of your works, John? Why on earth do you want that? Surely you have your own copy?' asked Thomas.

'Well, it is always good to see your own name in a library,' said the cleric, going red at the vanity he regularly chided his friend for.

Osbern and Thomas both burst out laughing.

'When you write your own book you will see,' said John. 'It is a petty vanity I grant you, but I cannot help but feel some pride. You will write one day and understand. The Pope himself has studied this, you know.' He waved the booklet at them.

'I fear my lord the King keeps me too busy to spend writing in a scribe's cell,' said Thomas, echoing his manservant. 'I have neglected my studies for too long.' Unlike Osbern he actually looked guilty over that.

'He will get you killed fighting,' said John.

'We all serve the King to the best of our abilities.'

'I serve the Lord God first and foremost.'

'And Pope Hadrian and the Archbishop who both give you succour.'

'Archbishop Theobald is doddering and Nicky does not have the King's tantrums.'

Osbern was taken aback at John's familiarity which verged on insolence. Not just to the King but also the Pope in Rome. John took no notice of the servant's surprise; the cleric had known Pope Hadrian for years before he was enthroned on the papal see.

'The Lord God won't get me killed doing something foolish like storming a town,' the cleric continued.

'You serve your master as best you can; I serve mine the same.' Thomas took the small book off him. 'It takes a special kind of individual to write a book – a watcher, not a doer. Has the King read this?'

'He told me that it was impudent but kept his copy.'

The book stated that monarchs were absolute in everything but the church, which they should revere. It was the kind of argument most nobles would merely nod along too, but Henry was well read and educated – all of them knew that – and the King also had a piercing intellect that was hidden under his coarse bluff exterior. Henry constantly surprised Thomas with his depth and breadth of understanding, and he had an amazing grasp for detail. The King had read the book in a night, digested it, and dismissed it.

Thomas will hammer out the flaws and make Henry a great King, thought Osbern. That was the old Archbishop's plan from the outset; it was why Archbishop Theobald had placed Thomas in Henry's court and Osbern with Thomas. What worried John of Salisbury was that Thomas, instead of taming the young king, began to ape him.

'May I be dismissed, Lord? If you have no use for me here?' asked Osbern.

Thomas nodded. 'Stay out of trouble; we do not want a repeat of the incident in Dover.'

Osbern winced. He had been drunken and disorderly, but considered it his family's fault. His father was in Dover and had there had been a celebration when Osbern returned to the town in Thomas's retinue. It had ended with fists and broken crowns as so many of his family's celebrations seemed to.

'It is small beer for me from now onwards, Lord. I promise on Saint Arnold's bones.'

3.

Osbern wandered through the fallen town. Most of the locals were in hiding or had fled, a few remained in despair at the destruction of the town, as the English army had free rein inside the enclosed walls. He paused outside a small taverna near the bridge gatehouse. The rude wine shop was filled with drunken and belligerent English warriors. A bewildered and bedraggled innkeeper watched in horror as the plague stripped him of food and wine. When the army moved on, Cahors would be left a broken wreckage of the prosperous ancient city it had once been.

'And the King urged restraint,' muttered Osbern to himself. 'I would not like to see what would happen had he given them free rein.'

He paused on the cobbles outside the tavern. The smell of the wine and food was enticing. He loved the grape too much. Thomas said it was his fatal flaw (whatever that meant), and it had caused him no end of trouble in the past. Since the incident in Dover he had sworn to moderate himself and take only small beer, but, but, but… The smell was delightful. One cup would not hurt, would it?

'Rabbit!'

Osbern looked over: it was the Bear down a side alley, leaning and pissing against the tavern's wall. He was drunk. Everyone was drunk.

'Are you coming to drink with us, Rabbit? There is good wine.'

Osbern loved good wine but he had promised the Chancellor, he had promised to only take small beer.

'There is good food too, but the sausage makes you fart.'

Osbern could smell the food. Someone had butchered a pig and set it to roast. He could almost taste the salted crackling on his tongue, crisp and crunchy. Thomas kept an austere table unless he was entertaining (then the fare had to be the most extravagant) and Osbern had not had pork meat since the last feast day. He nodded to the young warrior. One cup would not hurt.

'Come along then,' said FitzUrse.

As if in a trance Osbern followed the coarse young knight into the tavern. He had not yet thanked the Bear for saving his life, but the man had not taken offence. FitzUrse had a renowned temper and his size and skill made him feared, but in general he was happy and hearty and overly familiar. He reminded Osbern of the King himself. When FitzUrse had joined with Thomas's companies he had taken a liking to the manservant. Osbern had not yet determined if the man's friendship was a blessing or a curse.

'More wine, Innkeeper.' He pushed Osbern to a seat in the corner. 'Take that table, Rabbit. Over there with Di Condi.'

Di Condi was manservant to Humphrey Bohun, the Lord of Caldicott and Trowbridge: a cheerful blonde-haired lad from Wiltshire who moved up so Osbern could sit beside him.

'Your master is proving people wrong,' said Condi.

'How so?'

'The barons all said he could not fight or lead men and he would be a disaster on campaign, now the Chancellor does both with success.' Condi have a wry grin. 'Most of them seem strangely upset that their honest concerns have proven unfounded.'

'Even your Lord?'

'My Lord keeps his head down and tries to win back the King's favour, but he bears the Chancellor no will.'

Osbern recalled that Bohun had annoyed the King during the campaign in Wales the year before.

Men cheered as a Breton minstrel started up with his songs on a lute. The atmosphere in the looted tavern became even more festive at that. Boots stamped out a rhythm, and they clapped and bellowed along to the popular bawdy ballads. Di Condi happily sang along as Osbern waited for his wine. The Bear arrived with a young lad who brought over a jug of the grape and set it on the table, along with a platter of pork and bread.

'Here is the wine for you, Rabbit,' FitzUrse boomed out and slapped Osbern on the back.

Osbern licked his lips as the Bear poured out a cup for him and passed it over. Di Condi and FitzUrse watched as Osbern quaffed his in one deep gulp.

'More?'

'Yes please.'

He had broken his vow to Thomas but the wine tasted so good, sweet and thick and heavy. He savoured this second cup, swilled it around his tongue and breathed in the thick aroma. The Bear poured out cups for himself and Di Condi.

'The vineyards in this land are delightful,' said FitzUrse. 'Perhaps the King will reward us with lands here.'

'I shall be happy to go home,' said Condi. 'The wine and women are comforting enough, but the food gives me the shits. I miss Wiltshire.'

Osbern agreed with the Bear about the quality of the grape, but he knew that the rich fiefs of Cahors would be picked off by powerful barons not impoverished household knights. There would be no rich estate for one as raw as FitzUrse, and certainly not for petty menservants like himself or Condi, freemen or not. Osbern helped himself to some pork and bread, stuffing his face and squealing with delight at the fatty meat. The young knight did the same, wiping his greasy fingers on his wine-stained tunic.

'How old are you now, FitzUrse?' asked Osbern.

'Sixteen, I am Seventeen at Michaelmas.' He belched.

My God, thought Osbern. He is already huge. When he is full grown he will be terrifying. Men already feared the Bear, he wielded his battle axe like it was a stick and Osbern had seen for himself how deadly the boy was. Yet, there was something about him that Osbern liked. He had an easy smile and was more than loyal to King Henry. It was an obsession. Thomas too appreciated the Bear's absolute dedication to the King. FitzUrse had been at Henry's court in Anjou as a pageboy, and the bluff Henry had happily cultivated the young warrior. Osbern poured himself another cup of the wine. The Bear sat back and belched again.

'The pork is better than the blood sausage,' said Condi. 'Too much garlic, it gives you wind.'

Osbern liked garlic, so said nothing, and wondered where he could find some of the sausage. A rough man-at-arms, face flushed and nose red and clearly worse for the drink, addressed them from the next table.

'You two serve the Chancellor, the cleric who dares to bear arms like a real man?'

He had some friends with him, all from one of the companies that had stormed the town. They wore no livery or badge, only Thomas and some of the more fashion conscious lords had such fripperies, so Osbern could not tell which band it was. He said nothing at the insult; he had heard the taunts about his master before and knew that it was best to ignore the bait. FitzUrse of course took offence.

'I saw Thomas the Chancellor save the King's life in the assault. He killed two men with his own hand. What did you do, simpleton? Where were you? I do not recall seeing your ugly face there.'

The man gulped. FitzUrse was not to be riled, everyone knew that, and even in his drunken state the man could see the danger he had brought upon himself by poking the Bear.

'I meant no offence, FitzUrse.' He spluttered out his apology.

The matter could have, and should have, ended there and then, but FitzUrse had drunk too much wine and decided not to accept the apology. Without getting up, he hammered his fist into the man's crotch, causing him to bend over in his seat, doubled and gasping in agony. FitzUrse grabbed the groaning man's hair and hammered his forehead into the table knocking him senseless at best, breaking his crown and killing him at worst.

All done without getting out of his seat or breaking a sweat; when he is full grown he will be a monster.

'More wine, Rabbit?' FitzUrse turned back to Osbern.

The manservant nodded and took a cup of the grape; he knew this was about to get out of hand. The man's friends and comrades were not going to stand for their compatriot being beaten senseless, and four or five of them rose up to menace Osbern, Di Condi and the Bear.

'I promised the Chancellor that I would not get into trouble,' said Osbern plaintively to FitzUrse.

'Worry not, Rabbit, I shall keep you safe.'

FitzUrse leaped from his seat and charged into the glowering men, knocking two down in the rush. He grabbed another by the throat and started choking him whilst stamping on one of the prone men. He threw his choked victim into his remaining friends, and knocked another down with a swift blow to the jaw. There was only a single man left standing before FitzUrse, and he looked rather concerned by his friends' sudden fall.

He has only thrown one punch yet four of them are already down, thought Osbern. Thank God he is on our side. We should send him to the Holy Land to fight the Saracens and Damascus itself would fall.

The last belligerent simply turned and ran as fast as he could out of the tavern, better the embarrassment of that than being battered by the Bear. The rest of the tavern's customers cheered and laughed as he left, throwing food after him, and his friends crawled out once they had regained their senses. The troubadour started up his warbling once more and everyone turned back to their drinks as if nothing had happened.

'More wine, Keeper,' shouted the Bear. 'I am always thirsty after breaking some crowns.'

'That was not much of a fight,' said Di Condi to Osbern.

'Thank God, for that,' replied the manservant.

Then he looked over at the Bear again. 'Thank God for the Bear.'

***

The two of them staggered back to the camp outside the city walls from the tavern. The Bear leaned on Osbern for support. FitzUrse was the worst for the wine, but Osbern was not much better. After the fight the pair of them had drunk wine and eaten meat like it was Shrove Tuesday.

'Free food, free wine and a fight. It is better than Paris on a feast day,' slurred FitzUrse.

'I like Paris,' said Osbern, and then started singing about the maids of the Seine and their bountiful bosoms. The Bear joined in and the two of them bellowed out the verses as they wandered through the camp.

The attackers came at them in the darkness: three or four men with daggers. They had been waiting for Osbern and FitzUrse. It was the men from the tavern and they wanted restitution for the fight – restitution in the form of Osbern and FitzUrse's blood. Osbern was grabbed from behind and pulled to the floor by one of them. He rolled as a man stabbed down at his chest and kicked out, his boot connecting with the killer's jaw and knocking him back stunned. Osbern glanced to the side as two others stabbed at the Bear. FitzUrse was drunken but not completely defenceless. He punched one of the stabbers, crushing his nose and spinning him senseless to the ground. He butted the other sending him down and out like he had been felled with a poleaxe. The man who had grabbed Osbern disappeared into the darkness after being kicked in the face, without taking any further part. The killers had thought to take the Bear unawares, but even unawares and soused he had beaten two of them unconscious. Osbern could see blood on the Bear's tunic, a stain of black in the darkness spreading out on the cloth.

'I think the bastards stabbed me, Rabbit.'

They were near the Chancellor's tent, near sanctuary. Osbern had hoped that the evening's events would pass unnoticed by Thomas, a brawl might be missed but a stabbing would be impossible to hide. Best to take him the news myself rather than let him hear it second hand, thought Osbern. Either way I am in for a thrashing.

'Lean on me,' he told the Bear. 'If we can get you to the Chancellor's tent, Master John can tend you. He has understanding of medicine.'

FitzUrse groaned and leaned on Osbern, who almost collapsed under the Bear's weight. Together they staggered over to the Chancellor's white tent. Osbern could feel the sticky blood on his hands. The Bear was bleeding out; if he was not tended soon he would lose too much blood and die. The guards that stood sentinel at Thomas's tent saw the pair staggering in the torchlight and rushed to help. Rabbit and the Bear were both well known to them.

'He has been stabbed,' said Osbern to them. 'Send for Master John.'

'Thank you, Rabbit,' gasped FitzUrse.

The Bear slumped to the ground, white-faced and moaning, blood on his hands and tunic. He looked fit to pass out but John of Salisbury arrived with his magister's bag but with the Chancellor and some other luminaries behind. Osbern winced when he saw the barely concealed fury on Thomas's face.

'Bring him inside where I can see in the light,' said John. 'Let us pray the wounds are not deep.'

The two guards carried FitzUrse inside, cursing at his weight and laid him on the Chancellor's travel table. John cut away the bloody tunic and discarded it. Osbern noted one of Thomas's hounds licking at the Bear's spilled blood dripping on the earth floor. That is a bad omen, he thought.

'Get some boiling water, Osbern,' said John. 'I need to clean the wounds and apply poultices before sewing him up. Throw some vinegar in it.'

Osbern jumped to it, he had sobered up considerably since the stabbing. There was a fire outside and a pan always set to boil even at this late hour. His master put out a hand and stopped him before he could leave.

'You have been drinking wine, Osbern,' Thomas said in a firm voice.

It was not a question but a statement of fact.

Osbern looked to the floor and nodded, ashamed of himself. Thomas was a good lord, but God forbid you embarrassed him.

'We shall speak on this in the morning.' Osbern was not enthralled by that prospect. 'In the meantime you will tend to Master John's bidding and do everything required to save young FitzUrse's life. The King would take it badly if something was to happen to the lad.'

'Yes, Lord.'

He talks as if the Bear is a child instead of a deadly killer, thought Osbern, but he said nothing more. The manservant was certain to be in for a severe punishment and penance on the morrow, perhaps even a beating although Thomas tended not towards physical admonishment. Osbern sighed and rushed to get the boiling water for John to fix up the Bear. The magister worked swiftly to stem the blood flow. He cleaned the open wounds with the water and vinegar. Fortunately the Bear had slumped into a stupor from the wine and blood loss. He passed a small leather pouch to Osbern.

'Grind some of these herbs up to dust in a mortar, and then bring it to me. Find some honey as well.'

Thomas had retired from the operation, drawing curtains across his bunk whilst John tended to the Bear. Osbern went outside to the camped soldiers and stores to find some honey. There was a small clay crock of the nectar with other foodstuffs. Osbern returned with the honey and began mixing up the herbs in a bowl, grinding them away until they were dust.

'When the herbs are a fine powder mix in the honey.'

'Yes, Master John.'

Osbern carefully followed the instructions and then passed the mortar to John. The magister was already sewing up the wounds with a thread and iron needle. Once they were fixed he slapped on the honey and herb mix. The Bear groaned as the poultice was applied but did not come round.

'The herbs will draw out any poison and the honey keeps the wound clean, said John. A Moorish physician showed me the recipe in Rome. It will stop any infection catching.'

'A Saracen in Rome, Master John?'

'He was from Cordoba, in Iberia,' he added when he saw the blank look on Osbern's face. 'An emissary from the Muslim rulers to the Pope.'

The Moors and Saracens had much of the learning of the ancients stored in their libraries. The Latin states in the Holy Land and Moors of Cordoba were the source of so much new knowledge and fashion. Osbern himself dreamed of making the pilgrimage to Jerusalem and Thomas had made no secret of his desire to travel to the city. Even the King had talked of taking the cross on crusade, although Osbern was certain that was more vocal aspiration than committed intent.

'I will speak to Thomas,' said John. 'And promise him that you were not worse for wine and helped.'

'I still broke my promise to him.'

'Yes you did, and I am certain that he will have some kind of penance for you to undertake. Perhaps tending to FitzUrse will be punishment enough. The Bear is not going to be fit to walk for days.'

That was not a condition that would improve the Bear's temper, thought Osbern, but it is exactly the kind of inventive punishment that Thomas enjoyed. He helped John move the Bear onto some cushions and then collapsed himself and tried to get some sleep before facing his master on the morrow.

4.

The Chancellor had been delighted at John of Salisbury's suggestion that Osbern tend to the Bear. Thomas had informed his servant of the penance coldly, and quietly admonished Osbern for his failings and oath breaking. Thomas did not rant and rave as King Henry did when angered, instead it was cold silence and long glares; the withdrawal of the normal consideration and polite requests to his servant, replaced with sullen curtness and sharp commands. He behaves like a spurned maid, thought Osbern. I would rather the King's tantrums to this; at least Henry does not drag out the punishment, and quickly forgets about it.

'Bring me a cushion, Rabbit. My arse hurts.'

Osbern sighed and moved to help the Bear. It was not so onerous a penance; he had expected a beating. As the army left Cahors and marched onwards to Toulouse, the Bear had been loaded onto a cart drawn by two bullocks, plumped with cushions and given a barrel of ale and some bread and cheese. The cart was drawn along by a local man, pressed with his animals into service. The rickety wheels bumped and jumped on the hard sun baked roads, and at every jerk and jolt the Bear would whine and complain.

'What does your father do, Rabbit?'

'He is a wine merchant in Dover,' said Osbern.

'And he put you into service?'

'To the Archbishop,' Osbern pointed out. 'And now manservant to the Chancellor of all England.' He sniffed. 'I am second son. I could have ended up on the midden.'

'Still, I would not like to be a servant.'

Osbern's status was often something remarked upon. His father was not rich, and a Saxon, but he was a free townsman with an estate and industry. He could have put his son in holy orders as a lay brother or scholar. Instead, he had placed him in a position of some lowliness, no matter how exalted the household. Osbern's wit had seen him rise, and as manservant to Thomas he was privy to all the dealings of England. The Chancellor and King had both used him as a petty messenger many times, and the Rabbit was known by all the barons and knights of the army. Generally he was satisfied with his lot, and certainly would not have wanted his elder brother's life or his ugly wife. It was only his love of the grape that caused Osbern problems.

'What about you?' he asked the Bear.

'Me?'

'What do you do here?'

'I serve the King; he is my lord in all things.'

'But for yourself.'

'I have my father's estate, and perhaps the King will reward me with more.' He paused. 'Being laid up in a cart when everyone else is winning lands and honour is not going to do me much good, though.'

'Do you think there will be a battle, then?'

'Hywel thinks so and he is a canny Welsh bugger. Count Raymond will probably try and stop us getting to the city, but he cannot have enough men to force a great fight. We shall end up besieging the city.'

'I have never seen a real battle,' said Osbern.

The Bear frowned. 'God's teeth neither have I. It is damnation that I cannot fight in one if it comes.' He looked accusingly at Osbern.

'Do not look at me like that. You started the brawl.'

The Bear grunted. That was true enough but he was irked by the confinement and enforced rest. The Bear lived for action and lying in a cart was not accommodating his nature.

'Perhaps you can find me a woman?'

'Any woman of worth has long fled before this army.'

That was true as well. The locals had seen what had happened at Cahors and fled in a great wave towards Toulouse, towards Count Raymond's dubious protection. They had driven off their animals and carried everything of value away, but the crops waiting in the dry fields to be harvested were victims to the army's advance. King Henry ordered the land ravaged as they advanced, and Thomas had gleefully set his companies to burn crops, dig up the vineyards, and slaughter any who they came across. Every mile that the army slowly crept towards Toulouse was accompanied by black smoke and the smell of death.

'Perhaps they will surrender when we get to the city.'

'Damn me I hope not,' said the Bear.

They came up over a rise and looked down upon a winding river valley leading to the south. The English army had taken the road towards Toulouse, spreading out on their march as the locals fled before them. Thomas's companies were in the vanguard of the army, the first to advance whilst the Chancellor himself rode with the King and his household. Osbern and FitzUrse's cart took a higher road along a ridge above the river with the other baggage, allowing an excellent view of the marching companies in the parched brown valley below.

'Look there,' said the Bear propping himself up on his cushions and pointing. 'Men out of Toulouse.' There was excitement in his voice.

Osbern shielded his eyes from the sun and followed FitzUrse's gesture. The old Roman road went straight down the valley, but perhaps a mile distant there was a stone bridge and a force of armed men defending it. Osbern could see the sunlight glint off their iron weapons; he could see the dust thrown up by their animals. There were hundreds of enemies at the bridge.

'They are going to make a stand?'

'It looks like it, damn me for being stabbed. This is your fault.' He looked accusingly at Osbern again.

'Hardly. Look there is the King's household.'

They could see the vanguard moving their battle into position. Thomas's companies were joined by the household knights, including the king, in shining mail coats and carrying lances. Osbern could see his master's gleaming white surcoat in the sunlight, but they both struggled to see their royal lord. Henry preferred his old dull, rusty, but eminently practicable weapons over shining and new. Thomas dazzled enough for both of them. As the cart trundled along the road above the battle's advance, the defenders came fully into view.

'They have barricaded the bridge.'

Carts had been pulled across the close side of the bridge to stop the English simply charging over. There were men there with shields, spears and axes. Osbern felt sick to the pits of his stomach, he was no coward but he was not a warrior and the thought of a real battle terrified him.

'Yes, there are rather a lot of them, don't you think?'

The Bear studied the Toulouse army. There were perhaps three or four hundred men there, but most were crude spear levy pressed into service. Men on horseback – knights and men at arms – were behind them in a single unit of perhaps fifty or so. Others armed with hunting bows fanned out along the riverbanks to receive Henry's army, but there were no crossbowmen and few trained footmen. The English army numbered in the thousands.

'It is but some petty lordling putting up a fight, not the Count himself.' He called down to the man leading the cart. 'What is that place called?'

'It is the bridge at Albias,' said the serf sullenly.

FitzUrse turned back to Osbern. 'They are poorly armed but have a good position. It shall be a good fight but they will not hold long.' He cursed again. 'I would have enjoyed the exercise.'

The cart had come to a full stop above the confrontation by the bridge, allowing them to watch the engagement. A frustrated FitzUrse and horrified Osbern studied the opening moves intently.

***

Thomas pulled on the heavy helm over his mail coif when Henry ordered them to move up with the vanguard. It was hot under the sun; he could feel the sweat building on his scalp, and there was only a narrow slit to see out with. He thanked God that he had spent the spring in preparation for the campaign, but he was still not as strong or conditioned as the real knights and warriors. He knew that, he knew it was only his stubborn will that had kept him apace with the King and the others so far. Thomas glanced to the side where the King was sat on his own horse. Henry's face was not visible but Thomas could imagine the wide grin that would be fixed at the prospect of a fight. Thomas prayed to Saint Mary that he did not embarrass himself.

The King ordered trumpets blown and sent a company of heavily armed footmen in to deal with the barricades on the old Roman bridge. The defenders started up with arrow fire, some shafts even falling around Thomas and the King, but only at the extreme range. The crude hunting bows were unlikely to stick any of the household. The King took his helm off leaving just the mail coif; Thomas did the same, gasping for breath in the fresh air. He could not imagine how the Frankish knights endured the heat of the Holy Land in such equipment; it was akin to being boiled alive.

Above them, on the ridge, the sun was in Osbern's eyes and the dust thrown up by the horses and marching men confused the servant. He could not see what was happening and complained to the Bear.

'He is sending in the Saxons first,' said the Bear, pointing. 'They will clear the barricade away.'

'Where is the Chancellor?' It all looked like a mess to Osbern.

'Your lord Cheapside is easy enough to see in his pretty coat.' FitzUrse pointed Thomas out to Osbern. 'The archers are trying to send shafts at him and the King.'

'Has he taken his helmet off? Why would they do that?'

'To show they have no fear, Rabbit.' The Bear shrugged. 'But there is little chance of an arrow striking at that range.'

Henry's Saxon company, in mail shirts and armed with axes like the Roman Emperor's Varangian Guard, moved up to the bridge at a steady pace. As they marched, they beat out the time with their axes on their long kite shields. At the last ten yards, a sergeant yelled an order and the Saxons charged at the barricades screaming their war cry.

'Out! Out! Out!'

It was the same shout they had made at Hastings nearly a century before. Thomas's Aquitanian crossbowmen, hired at an excruciating expense, fanned out on either side of the bridge. They started sending their bolts in at the defenders in a murderous crossfire as the axe men attacked. Osbern could see the defenders falling as the barbs stuck. The hunting bows could not match the crossbow for range or power.

The Saxons smashed into the barricades like a metal hammer

through wattle, cutting and slashing at the enemy spears, dragging away the carts and ripping at the makeshift barricades. Osbern saw one spearman tossed off the top of the bridge by a Saxon, his broken body tumbling down the slopes to the river below. A cart soon followed, crashing to the floor as the bridge was cleared.

The Toulouse spear levy could not stand against the Saxon rage and Aquitanian crossbows. They turned and fled, streaming back to their own side of the bridge. They were happier to face their own lord's anger than the fury of the English king's army.

'Make ready,' Henry called out to his household. 'We clear the bridge on the charge.'

Thomas pulled his helm back on at Henry's command, plunging himself back into sweaty darkness and isolation. The Saxons had cleared away the barricades after the enemy levy had fled the bridge. On the far side there was a flurry of lance points and banners of the French knights, but Thomas could see no identifying badge through his helm's slits. The dust thrown up by the horses made everything confusion. The King, however, knew exactly where his target was.

'Blow,' Henry ordered the trumpeters.

Thomas's four trumpeters at the King's side lifted up their instruments and sounded out a long deep tone at the order.

'Charge,' screamed the King, digging his spurs into his mount's side.

The animal sprang forward in an explosion of power, thundering towards the bridge. Thomas kicked his own beast to keep up with his lord. He had a good seat and was able to catch up with the King as they pounded over the stone bridge towards the enemy knights.

'There they go,' shouted the Bear gleefully as the King's household thundered over the now cleared bridge.

Osbern could see Thomas now, just behind the King in his white surcoat, and at the head of the charging knights with a lance in his mailed hand. The French horsemen on the other side were not waiting passively to receive the King's rush. They had taken up the challenge and thundered towards the royal party.

Just as the King and Thomas passed over the bridge to the far side, the enemy crashed into them. The crashing sound of the impact carried up to the watchers on the ridge. Osbern winced at the sound, but the Bear was elated.

'Oh I should be there. I should be there. Think of the fortune in horses and mail to be won.'

Thomas's lance had shattered in the first impact, and he had struggled to draw his sword in one movement as Hywel had trained him. The chaos of action made his fingers shake, but he finally had the weapon to hand and slashed wildly at a poorly armed French horsemen. A few had mail coats but most were petty hobilars in leather hauberks, with light shields and lance. They could not stand against the heavily armed English knights.

After only a few moments of flurried, and confusing, action, the few French knights fled. Thomas told John of Salisbury and Osbern later that he was not even sure he had struck anyone, and his sword was unbloodied, but he had kept up with the King and had not embarrassed himself. He wanted to defeat a knight or Baron, not a petty soldier, but an equal. It would prove he was a warrior to everyone, but the French were already running. The King had taken off his helm to shout and curse at the fleeing Frenchmen.

'Well, that did not last long.' The Bear sounded disappointed.

Osbern could see that Thomas was still on top of his horse, still safe. He offered a prayer of thanks to the saints for his master's survival.

The French force was streaming away from the bridge in every direction, the levy throwing away their spears and leather shields, but King Henry held off from the pursuit. He only sent a few knights to chase off their enemies with orders not to go too far. The rest of the army would be brought across the bridge before they advanced any further. It had been a swift victory, but the King knew well enough the dangers of a strung out pursuit. There could be more enemies waiting for them.

'The King is setting up camp on the other side. They will not go any further today,' said FitzUrse.

The army had only marched for a few hours and covered barely five miles, but the stragglers and rearguard were still way behind the van. It was going to take a week or more to get to Toulouse.

'We should go down to them,' said Osbern. 'The Chancellor will expect me to be there to wait on him.'

The Bear agreed and told the French serf leading the cart to get them down to the bridge and over. He wanted to hear tell of the fight, whilst Osbern would see to his duties. There was certain to be some sort of celebration or feast.

5.

Whilst the King was delighted with Thomas's action on the campaign, John of Salisbury could not hide his disappointment from his old friend. The Chancellor's tent had been set up as soon as the baggage arrived and John reclined on cushions in one corner as he admonished Thomas.

'You think you are a warrior now? It is undignified.'

'I only do my duty as Chancellor, John. It is no different from any in my position. Odo of Bayeux fought at Senlac Hill and he was a bishop,' Thomas replied. 'I am but a clerk and have taken no holy orders.'

'It was your strength of mind that set you high, not your strength at arms. The Archbishop would not expect you to become a *soldariaus*.' John sneered with the coarse Latin. 'A fighter for coin, and it ended badly for Bishop Odo, as I recall.'

'I do not fight for coin, John. I serve the King. Theobald told me that Henry was to be my master and to do my best. I am doing my best. If that means fighting when the King orders, so be it.'

'Still, it does no good to ape the King's behaviour.'

'I am not a drunk and I do not fornicate.'

The two of them knew that the King was both and that Thomas was neither, although there was a taint of hypocrisy from John given his penchant for the grape.

Osbern had always wondered about the celibacy. Thomas had taken no oath of abstinence, and frankly such oaths mattered little to most priests or mendicants that Osbern knew, but the Chancellor supped his wine with moderation and always retired at the King's more salacious entertainments. He did not seem interested in women at all, nor men or boys. Osbern would know if his master indulged in such. He likes a book more, Osbern said to himself. The queen liked that about Thomas; she liked his studiousness and polite manners, and had even suggested that the Chancellor take their prince and heir as ward. John of Salisbury, on the other hand, was just as fond of the grape as the King and Osbern.

The servant poured another cup of the wine for the scholar.

'Just leave the jug, Osbern,' said John. 'I can serve myself.'

'Thank you, Osbern, you can go now. You have FitzUrse to see to, remember.'

'Yes, Lord.'

Osbern retired and went looking for the Bear. He had left him at the carts, but could not find him there now.

'He is bound to be causing trouble somewhere.'

The Bear had gone looking for tales of the fight and food. He had found both in the baggage train, and Osbern finally discovered the giant supping stolen ale and eating from a pie with one of the carters out of Bordeaux.

'Rabbit, where have you been? I have some ale for you.'

'Serving our master.'

'Is he still upset with you?'

'Yes, and all because of you.'

'Oh, Rabbit, do not take it so hard. He has fought well on this campaign. He is proving everyone wrong, even me.'

'Not the King,' said Osbern. 'The King ever had faith in my master.'

'Who is your master?' asked the carter, suddenly interested.

'I serve the Chancellor, Thomas of London.'

The carter was clearly interested in that. The rank of a servant's Lord always reflected back upon his men, but even Osbern was surprised at the carter's sudden obsequiousness.

'Would you like some wine?' asked Carter.

'No, thank ee,' said Osbern, quickly. 'Just some small ale. Is there any pie left?' he said to the Bear.

FitzUrse passed over a half full crust and Osbern gratefully started digging out chunks of meat. He stayed drinking ale and eating pie with the Bear for a while. Osbern was starting to enjoy the monster's company. There is something perverse in that, he thought, but he is honest and loyal to the King, and as long as I am at his side I am relatively safe.

'Is the King camped here?' asked the carter.

'Aye, somewhere over there, near his master's pavilion.' FitzUrse gestured to Osbern. 'It is all white, you cannot miss it.'

The carter was overly interested in the layout of the camp, and where the King's tent was located. FitzUrse thought nothing of it, happily giving out the information, but it seemed strange to Osbern. The wine was a good enough vintage for a landless hedge knight and a valet, but not a vintage for a King or a Chancellor. As he was taking a piss, Osbern saw the carter sneak off into the darkness. The man was looking over his shoulder in case he was being followed.

Why is he acting so suspiciously, he thought? He behaves like he does not belong here. On a whim, Osbern decided to follow the man through the dark camp. He hurried along as the carter tramped with some speed to the far side of the encampment, near the shit pit dug as the camp's latrines. Osbern could smell the faeces and sour piss on the wind. The carter was clearly in a rush, often glancing behind, skulking and keeping to the shadows. It was not the behaviour of an innocent.

Something pricks at my thumbs, thought Osbern.

Near the edge of the encampment the man stopped and looked around him. Osbern lurched down on his knees in the darkness and prayed that he had not been seen. The carter waited for a few moments, Osbern could barely breathe as he hunched in the night. Then the carter gave out a low hoot, like a barn owl. A few seconds later there was a return call beyond the camp, and the man snuck off into a copse of trees. Osbern got up and half-ran-half-crouched over to the edge of the camp. He could just about see where the man had disappeared into the darkness and he crawled into the undergrowth after him, trying desperately not to make a sound.

'It is not the white tent,' he heard the man's voice.

'Are you certain?'

That was a woman's voice. Osbern had difficulty with the dialect in the south of France, and her accent was thick.

'Yes, that is the English Chancellor's pavilion; the King is in the ruder canvas.'

'The Chancellor is no friend to the Cathars, I do not see how this changes anything. He is the Pope's man.'

'That is not what his men tell about camp, the Chancellor is the King's man now.'

'Neither Henry nor this Thomas can be trusted. They will defer to Rome. Count Raymond has promised us freedoms and liberty. Do you have everything ready?'

'Yes, I passed the potion into the wine. As soon as the King sups at it he will fall ill. There will be no hiding the murder; it will be obvious he has been poisoned.

'Make sure you get out of the camp as soon as the wine is sent.'

Osbern lying in silence in the undergrowth listened as the two killers plotted the King's murder. It was a simple enough plan, and would work given the King's fondness for the grape. Osbern knew he had to get back to Thomas and warn the King. Should something happen to the King it would be a disaster for England. The young heir was barely more than a babe and royal authority only just returned after years of civil war. Henry's death would see the troubles start up again. Regicide was not a crime often practiced by monarchs; they understood well enough that it was a double edged sword that could cut them back in turn. Raymond of Toulouse had no such qualms. He would sacrifice the King of England if it meant saving his city and his title. He might even bend a knee to his brother-in-law the French King, who he despised, if it stopped Henry. Paris and the Occitan combined against Anjou, Aquitaine and Normandy would mean a general war instead of this limited campaign. The whole Frankish kingdom would be torn apart.

Once the killers' plans had been set the carter returned to the camp, walking right past Osbern's hiding place in the undergrowth. He waited a little longer until he was certain that both of them had left, and then ran as fast as he could to the white tent at the centre of the camp.

Thomas and John were still arguing about the relative morality of battle when Osbern rushed into the tent and blurted out what he had discovered. It was garbled at first, as he tried to get all the details out, and Thomas made him stop and start again slowly. He recounted everything the man and woman had said in the trees.

'They were going to deliver the wine here, thinking it was the King's pavilion.'

'I warned you your vanity would come back and bite you,' said John to Thomas.

'I do not think this is the time. Now, Osbern, I want you to find FitzUrse and stop the carter escaping whilst I am away to the King to stop him from drinking.'

Osbern was certain that he had the easier task there. Once he had found the Bear, the Carter's life would be short.

'I want him taken alive, Osbern,' said Thomas, sternly. 'I want to know exactly who is behind this attack.'

'It is Count Raymond, surely?' said John.

'Probably but I would not put it past King Louis to do this and set the blame on someone else. The heretics would help if they thought it meant their freedom to worship.'

Osbern did not understand the Cathars. He had spoken to some in Bordeaux, but they had been utterly boring ascetics. Gnostic dualism was a concept lost on the simple servant, and when John decided he wanted to discuss the theology (instead of attending to the murder at hand), Osbern left to find the Bear. The Chancellor cut the scholar short.

'I hardly think this is the time for theological discussion, old friend. It is a time for action.'

John sniffed. 'You think you are a warrior, but I know better.'

Thomas did not answer but instead called for his guards and strode briskly to the King's tent. He noted that it was not pristine bleached white, and there was only a single banner with the Lion of Anjou emblazoned on it, but there were two men of the household standing sentinel. They nodded to the Chancellor and did not stop him from entering. Henry had given his friend permission to come and go as he pleased. The tent was dark inside, lit only by a few candles, and the King reclined on cushions inside with his gentlemen waiting upon him. There was wine and Thomas noted the two pretty girls drinking with Henry. Was one of them with the poisoner?

'My Lord!'

'What is it, Cheapside?'

There is a threat, my Lord, poisoned wine.

He noted the surprise on all of the faces, even in the shadows; the girls gave no sign of guilt. They were not part of the plot, he decided.

'That's a waste of good wine,' said Henry, and drank the remainder of the cup in his hand. He saw the horror Thomas's face. 'If this was the poisoned vintage would I not already be dead?'

Thomas could not fault the King's logic.

'Who is it? Raymond?'

'I think so, Lord, but there are heretics involved. One of my men overheard the plotters and brought the news to me – Osbern of Dover, Lord.'

'The Rabbit would not spin a spurious tale. Very well, raise the camp and find them.' He turned to one of the gentlemen. 'Try and find me some ale. I have lost my taste for French wine.'

Henry's blasé attitude did not surprise Thomas. The King thrived on people threatening him and causing conflict, he said it made him feel alive. And yet Henry could go wild with anger at the slightest annoyance. Thomas had not yet found himself on the end of one of the King's tantrums, and prayed he never was. They had publicly argued over the cloak Henry gave to that peasant, of course, but it had been a perfect display for the watching Londoners to see their new King, and had been planned by Thomas and Henry beforehand with military precision. Henry knew how to manipulate his audience, be it a court or a kingdom.

'Poison is just the kind of low act that Raymond would try,' said Henry. 'He has always been a snide.'

'We cannot be sure, Lord. Louis of France has been known to…'

'Louis is doddering and he gave me the kiss of peace last month. This will be Raymond's work, you mark my words.'

Thomas did not argue, but he kept an open mind in the matter. The French King was old, but wily, and technically he was Henry's overlord for his French territories. The rise of the young English king had altered the balance in the Frankish kingdoms of the west. We already control more of France than the French king, thought Thomas. We want it all.

Raymond and Louis were not friends, although brothers-in-law through convenience, but France could not afford to see

Henry control the Occitan. It would mean English access to the Mediterranean trade routes, and it would see the French crown ultimately reduced to a petty lordship. Henry understood that, so did Thomas, but so did Louis of France and Raymond of Toulouse. This campaign and the poisoning was just the beginning of a long bitter war.

***

Osbern ran back to the carts where he had left the Bear drinking. The carter was nowhere to be seen. The Bear was still there, still drinking; there were a few other warriors with him.

'Where is he?' Osbern said as soon as he arrived.

'Who?'

'The carter, he has tried to poison the King.'

That grabbed the Bear's attention.

'He was here but a moment ago.' He looked around. 'There, there he is. '

Everyone looked through the firelight. There were a few men in that general direction, but only one of them took off at FitzUrse's shout like a hound from a trap.

'Get him!'

Osbern started up a hue and cry and both he and FitzUrse (and others) rushed after the murderer. There was uproar in the camp. The King had men out and braziers lit as the alarum was raised. The carter was too old to outrun his pursuers. As he sprinted through the tents towards the horse pickets he was tackled to the ground by a soldier. By the time Osbern and FitzUrse arrived there was a crowd of them around him beating him.

'Stop! Stop!' Osbern screamed. 'He needs to be kept alive, on the Chancellor's orders.'

FitzUrse understood that and waded into the crowd with his hams flying, knocking bystanders out of the way and grabbing up the carter.

'We shall take him to the King,' said FitzUrse.

The crowd let the Bear take control of the situation. Young he was, but he was also huge and brooked no argument.

'Where is your accomplice?' Osbern demanded. 'Where is she?'

The carter said nothing; he seemed resigned to his fate. That fate will not be pleasant, the torturers are going to have a field day with this one, thought Osbern. He might not even make it to his own execution.

The crowd followed FitzUrse as he dragged the killer to King's tent. There were others there. The woman had been captured riding away. She had been stopped by a patrol and when the hue and cry started up had tried to escape. The patrol had brought her in. From her bleeding mouth it was clear that they had not been gentle. Even in the shadows, Osbern could see that she was stunningly beautiful – long dark hair plaited back and dark eyes. A Cathar Perfect, a woman priest.

6.

There were three condemned killers brought before the King: the carter and the woman priest, and a local grey-haired servant who had passed the poisoned wine into the royal household. The tainted barrel was discovered among the royal victuals, and it was only good fortune and Thomas's intervention that had stopped it from being served to Henry. They were all Cathars but the two men both deferred to the beautiful black-haired woman. Osbern had expected the King to rage, but he was calm, almost amused, as he questioned them. Thomas observed it all in cold calculation. The camp watched on in the torchlight: a whole crowd of barons, courtiers, soldiers, priests and commoners from the army had gathered for the trial.

'Why did you do it? Who paid you?' The King demanded.

The three said nothing in response. They all knew that their fate was sealed. They were going to die; all that mattered was the manner of their demise. It was within Henry's power to make it swift or terrible. They seem determined to make it difficult for themselves, thought Osbern.

'Was it that arseling, Raymond?' asked Henry. 'What could he have promised you? You are heretics and condemned by the church.'

John of Salisbury, and Thomas, and the other watching mendicants and churchmen all nodded at that. The spread of Cathar teachings in France and Italy was causing consternation in the Basilica of St Peter.

'Perhaps you are the heretics from where we stand, Lord,' said the woman in a soft voice.

There was a gasp from the audience at that. She had spoken quietly but it was a studied insult. The King burst out laughing but Thomas's lips pursed in annoyance. The Bear, watching the scene with Osbern and Hywel, nudged his small friend in the ribs.

'She is as beautiful in speech as in looks.'

Osbern did not respond. The woman was certainly stunning,

had she tried to talk her way into Henry's bedchamber and fed him the wine their plan would have been successful. The King was always a fool to his passions. She was clearly some sort of noble lady, of higher birth than both the Rabbit and the Bear. She had been the one who had directed the plan, the carter and the grey-haired serving man were but pawns on her board. Despite further questioning, the three killers remained silent after that. They would not tell Henry who had sent them, and they showed no fear for their fate.

'They are fanatics,' said Hywel.

King Henry clearly thought the same. One of the Lords said that the woman should be sent to the Abbess of Vienne, but Thomas raised his hand at that suggestion.

'Vienne is miles away and the sentence would be the same. We cannot show leniency when it is the King that is threatened, or in matters of heresy.'

Henry unsurprisingly agreed with his Chancellor. Kings tend to take regicide badly. The three would-be killers were taken outside with the court in audience. Ropes were thrown over a nearby tree and nooses tied up. Some of Henry's mercenaries led the three would-be murderers to their fate. Hands were tied behind their backs, but the woman refused a bag over the head. She glared at Thomas and Henry as the noose was put around her neck. Neither showed any reaction to the execution, but neither met her eyes.

The King waved his hand and the stout fellows hauled on the ropes, hoisting the three of them up in the air. The slight woman went up faster and higher than the other two; she struggled, her tongue lolling and kicking out as the noose slowly choked her. The other two did the same, twitching and dancing on the air. Some of the men pulled on the condemned legs and the struggles quickly ceased. It was all over in seconds. Henry turned away from the scene and strolled nonchalantly back to his pavilion, back to the two women and some untainted wine.

'You have done well,' Thomas told Osbern and the Bear. 'Perhaps you can reward yourself with a cup of wine, Osbern. I release you from the vow for this night only, but be careful to be fit for duty on the morrow when we march. I do not want a repeat of Dover.'

Osbern was going to splutter out another pithy promise to take only ale, but stopped himself. It would just be another broken vow if he failed, and besides, perhaps he deserved a cup or two after the evening's events. He left with the Bear and Hywel as Thomas returned to his own tent and a sulking John of Salisbury.

'Your Lord should have been merciful; the woman could have been saved.'

The Bear was also unhappy at the evening's turn. That surprised Osbern. Normally FitzUrse's loyalty to the King trumped everything.

'My Lord? He is your lord too, and the woman was the mistress of the scheme?'

'She was very beautiful, and the King is my lord not the Chancellor.'

'Eve was beautiful when she offered Adam the Apple, and the King is lord over us all, Thomas included.'

'Still, he could have shown mercy. Sent her to the Abbess as Tourney suggested, let her live out her days in service.'

'Some mercy, she would have been tortured and the end result the same,' said Hywel. 'The King and Thomas gave them all a swift end. It was more than any of them deserved.' He sniffed with contempt. 'She was an unrepentant heretic and the Abbess of Vienne would not have been kind.'

'Still she was beautiful,' the Bear insisted.

Osbern realised that the Bear had been smitten with the dark haired killer. A pretty woman can bring even the strongest man to his knees, he thought, and God help you if they are clever. Then they can twist you around their little fingers. The Queen was like that – beautiful and clever. Too clever by half thought the servant. This whole campaign was because Henry wanted to please his wife and give her Toulouse as a gift.

'The Queen has a right, it should have passed to her,' said Hywel.

'The woman reminded me a tad of the Queen,' said Osbern. 'Determined, stubborn, and clever. The Queen is all of these things.

'We have all heard the arguments,' said Hywel. 'Queen Eleanor is not quiet when she is displeased.'

The Welshman was an unrepentant gossip and regaled them with every titbit he had heard of the royal household. Eventually, the three of them found a dark haired wine seller – there was always someone awake and ready to provide food or drink to the marching men, and the camp was awakened after the execution. The new vintner pulled out a table and rough stools for them to sit on and brought out a barrel of wine. Hywel tipped him a coin and they all helped themselves to cups. Osbern threw a log on the campfire for more light as they sat and supped at the vintage.

'In Outremer there is a sect of killers, Ḥashashiyan the people there call them,' Hywel said. 'Their fortress is named Masyaf, in the rocky hills near Antioch, and they are ruled by a Moslem Lord called the Old Man of the Mountains. They say he is a magician over a hundred years of age, but his men are utterly dedicated to him. The old man sends them out to kill, and they do. None are safe. Throughout the lands of the east people fear them.'

'Who do they kill?' asked the Bear.

'Whoever displeases him, princes and kings, bishops, Christian or Moslem. Sometimes it is poison; sometimes it is knives, sometimes strangulation. His men will die to succeed in their missions and they are utterly fearless.'

'Did you ever meet one?' asked Osbern.

'No, thank the Saints. You only meet them before you die. I saw them though; it was the Ḥashashiyan that killed Raymond of Tripoli. I watched it happen from the walls of the city.'

Osbern wondered about these stories. Hywel was not alone in telling them (although his were often the wildest). The west was full of Frankish adventurers returned from the Holy Land who told of adventure and strange tales of the orient, but magicians and supernatural murderers seemed nothing but a fancy.

'They say the sun is so hot that you can fry and egg on the rocks at midday?' The Bear was just as fascinated with the tales, believable or no.

'That is nonsense,' said Hywel. 'But it is hot, terribly hot. I saw one man die in his armour, broiled to death.'

'I would like to go to the Holy Land,' said the Bear. 'To fight the Saracens.'

'The Saracens keep to their own lands these past ten years, and watch as our Lords fight amongst themselves,' said Hywel. There was bitterness in his voice

'What about you, Rabbit?' asked FitzUrse. 'Would you like to go to Jerusalem?'

'Yes,' said Osbern. 'I much desire to see the Holy Land, and to walk in the footsteps of the Lord. Visit Galilee and Bethlehem. It would be an honour. Perhaps one day.' He shrugged. 'For now I serve the Chancellor.'

'Chancellor?' FitzUrse roared with laughter. 'Why he has proven himself a very warrior on this march. Perhaps he will lead a crusade himself and take you along.'

'Perhaps.'

Osbern had been to Rome on the Archbishop's service, but he had not liked it. The basilica was filthy with animals roaming freely and shitting everywhere, and Pope Hadiran himself was not so impressive, even if he was English, but the Holy Land would be a worthy pilgrimage. The march to Toulouse was proving anything but.

*

The army crossed the River Tarn at Montauban. A new town on the road to Toulouse, but it had been abandoned at the approach of the English army. Once they had crossed the river, it was a straight road to Count Raymond's city and the army's ultimate destination. The rickety wooden bridge groaned and creaked at the passage of hundreds of men and animals, but held fast and the army camped outside the Montauban's wooden walls. Henry set up court in a small manor abandoned by its owner.

'They could have stopped us here,' said Hywel as they crossed over the bridge with the Chancellor's baggage. 'Had they the will, they could have made a fight.'

'Raymond does not have an army that can stand against the King's numbers,' FitzUrse asserted. 'And he is a schemer not a warrior.'

'That is all true enough, but pull down the bridge and we would be stuck on the wrong side of the river.'

'It is not so deep,' said FitzUrse.

'It is wider and deeper than the River Jordan, and when you have to charge through it with enemies waiting on the other side loosing their arrows, throwing spears, and rocks, and curses, it becomes a death trap.'

'Is it really wider than the Jordan?' asked Osbern.

The Welshman nodded. 'The Jordan is not so very big.'

Osbern envied Hywel's time in the Holy Land, and certainly dreamed of travelling there one day before he died, but he remained focussed on the matter at hand. Making sure that Thomas's trunks and boxes were ported and unloaded was his main duty on the tramp. His master always insisted upon his pavilion being set on high ground, so that everyone could see the white tent. Osbern directed the carters and porters to arrange everything as FitzUrse and Hywel sat around supping ale. There was no point in asking for assistance from them, they would have scorned the work as warriors not servants. Once he had seen the tent pitched and trunks unloaded, he joined them and took a cup of ale. Everything had been set to his master's perfection. Thomas would be pleased.

'Where is your master, Rabbit? I have not seen him all this day.'

'He is with the King,' Osbern told him. 'They have taken over a manor to the south of the town for the King's rest, but he wanted his tent set up here. There is talk of an army out of Toulouse.

The Bear grunted at that news. 'Raymond will want to parley,' he said. 'His vassals could not stop us in battle; the murderers failed in their task. He either fights or surrenders now.'

'The Count is renowned for his cunning,' said Hywel. 'He will have some twist in the tale for us yet.'

They camped down for the night. Osbern attended on his master but there was little excitement in the white pavilion. It had been a long march for the army from Poitiers, and the Chancellor was exhausted.

'You are not a warrior,' John of Salisbury told him yet again.

'They spend their lives riding around looking fierce and causing trouble with their weapons, you have spent your life with books and a quill. It is why they scorn you.'

'I seem to have done well enough.' Thomas smiled at John. 'My mind is as keen a blade for the king as any of their swords. Help me with my boots please, Osbern.'

'Yes, Lord.'

He kneeled and helped his master out of the high leather boots. French made and a new fashion to protect the legs. FitzUrse said they made the horses uncomfortable, but the Bear was resistant to new fashions at the best of times. Once Thomas had taken off his heavy hauberk and Osbern had put everything away in the trunk, the Chancellor took a cup of wine and sat with John.

'Did you find any good books in Cahors other than your own?'

'Bernard of Clairveaux's letters and sermons, he spoke out against these Cathar heretics.'

'The region is rife with the teachings.'

Osbern brought a platter of candied fruits and nuts for Thomas to eat as he drank. The Chancellor had a sweet tooth and had insisted on the expensive treats in his baggage.

'If Raymond was behind the poison, it is beyond base heresy,' said John.

'Of course he is behind it,' said Thomas. 'He dares not face the King in battle.'

'Are we far from Toulouse now, Lord?' asked Osbern as he topped up their cups.

'At the pace the army marches, perhaps a week still,' said Thomas. 'But it is only fifty or so miles.'

'It feels as far away as Jerusalem.' Osbern was tired of the campaign.

The Chancellor and John of Salisbury both laughed at the Rabbit's comment.

'Fear not, little Osbern. We shall be there soon enough. And then we shall see what tricks Count Raymond still has under the table.'

'It is certain to be something sly,' said John of Salisbury.

'Raymond has always been sly.'

'Oh most certainly,' said Thomas. 'But I can be sly too.'

7.

From Montauban, the army followed the old roman road south. It was dusty and in poor repair with ruts and holes in the paving where the stones had been robbed out. The sun beat down on them, and the pale northern skins got burned. There were complaints and grumbles, blistered feet and parched throats. Count Raymond made no more efforts to halt the advance, but the local population fled at the army's advance, taking their animals and anything that could move with them. The fields waiting for harvest were left in the hope that they would be spared, it was a vain hope. Henry ordered the land spoiled and the fields fired. Thomas and his men, and the other barons in the retinue, took to their task with glee.

After only five days the English came in sight of their destination: Toulouse. The city sat on the east bank of the Garronne, with tall stone walls, round towers and parapets. The square roman tower of the basilica could be seen from their vantage point. Built from red clay bricks as well as white stone, Toulouse shimmered and glimmered in the sunlight with a magical aura. Here was the English army's Jerusalem.

'It is not as big as London,' said Osbern. 'But it is most beautiful.'

'There is a gatehouse keep at the South gate,' said Hywel, 'It is stronger than the White Tower.'

The Welshman was more practical than Osbern.

'A pish on its beauty,' said FitzUrse. 'The walls are in better repair than London but not so tall. How many men do you think he has inside?'

'Too many, and it is still too big for us to invest fully,' said the Welshman. 'We shall have to assault. The pink city will fall but the cost will be high.'

'What does that mean?' asked Osbern. 'It feels like the whole march had been uphill, how long? How high a cost?'

'It shall not be a long siege,' replied Hywel. 'Once the engines are made up, and scaling ladders for the walls, we shall attack.

That will suit the King better; he is not one for waiting on an enemy to starve.'

Not one hundred yards away, Henry and Thomas were having the very same conversation. The slender Chancellor stood with his stocky broad master and dear friend as he surveyed the town. Gentlemen at waiting and household knights stood with them ready for their liege's commands.

'Two assaults,' said Henry. 'One at the Narbonne Keep to the south, one at the eastern wall.' He pointed. 'Between those two smaller gatehouses.'

'Why, Lord?' asked Thomas.

'The wall is not so high, the moat is shallow and filled with dross and the towers are too widely spaced to bring down their arrows. Have men build scaling ladders. We will need to build the towers as well.'

Thomas nodded, they had prepared for that eventuality. There were engineers in the baggage train with machines that could be assembled, and towers could be built, but it would all take time.

'We shall attack the castle gate a couple of times, just to keep them honest, whilst the engines are being constructed. I want horse patrols all around the city. Burn the farms, take the food and animals, and make sure none come in or out of Toulouse.'

'How long?' Thomas echoed his servant's query.

Henry smiled at the Chancellor. 'Not long. A week until the engines and ladders are ready. Unless Count Raymond can come up with one of his legendary schemes to foil us.' He looked up at the city walls. 'Toulouse is ours.'

Thomas was thankful for that, the campaign had leeched the finances of Henry's realms and the army was expensive to keep in the field. Capturing Toulouse would make that all worthwhile. The city commanded the trade routes through the Pyrenees into Iberia, as well as the road to the middle sea and towns on the coast. There were rich fiefs to reward the King's loyal followers; the vineyards and farms were fabulously productive; the land rich and the climate good.

More importantly, with the County of Toulouse in his purse, the King of England would rule over more of France than King Louis in Paris. Henry had taken Louis' former wife Eleanor as his own and now seemed on the verge of stealing Louis' kingdom from under him. All of Henry, and Thomas's, planning had led to this moment of truth. Take Toulouse and the larger prize would come into view. Thomas had arranged the marriage of Henry and Eleanor's son to the French King's daughter the previous summer. Louis had no male heirs, in a decade or so Anjou would rule both England and France. It all began with the fall of Toulouse.

'If I may take my leave, Lord? There is much to do.'

The King waved Thomas away as he studied the city. He would not be in the first assault. The council, including Thomas, had put a stop to that notion. It had more than irked the royal temper but their arguments had been sound and he had been forced to concede the point.

'The royal body was too much of a risk,' they had said.

'Young Henry is but an infant, we have only just got past one civil war,' said one. 'Your death would start another.'

One of them had the gall to say 'Your mother would not be happy.'

That last had caused a tantrum afterwards that only Thomas had been privy to, but he had managed to calm his friend.

At Cahors Henry had led the assault, with Thomas at his side, but Toulouse was a tougher nut to crack. Count Raymond was rich and he had poured gold into buying men for the campaign. The city walls were well defended, not the rough levy of Cahors: crossbows, men-at-arms, free mercenary companies, as well as loyal lords and their personal retinues; veteran knights and returned crusaders. The townsfolk were loyal to their Lord and the surrounding country was hostile. As the rest of the English host arrived, they set up camp on the plain to the south of the city and made ready for the siege of Toulouse. Henry's army was magnificent, the greatest he would ever assemble, but he knew well enough that it could be broken on such a defence.

***

The siege towers rolled towards walls pulled by companies of spearmen. The King and Chancellor watched as they were dragged into place, slowly, excruciatingly slowly. As soon as they came in range of the defenders on the walls of Toulouse, men began falling, pierced with iron bolts from defenders' the crossbows. Hywel and the Bear both ducked out of the storm of bolts behind their tower. The men hauling at the ropes looked for cover behind wicker shields raised by their fellows, but too many were falling from the arrows.

'We have to get closer to the walls,' Hywel shouted at the Bear. 'They are murdering us here.'

FitzUrse nodded and started kicking and beating the spearmen to haul at the ropes, and get the tower moving once more. His side was bound up and he was mostly recovered from the stabbing, and eager to get back to action.

'Move, move, damn your eyes, damn your souls.'

The spears were all veterans; they understood The Bear's concern; they had to keep moving to survive. If they stopped, they were easy marks for the men on the parapets who would pick them off with arrows, pin them down, and the assault would fail.

Hywel and the Bear got their tower moving again, leaving behind the dead and dying caught by the defenders' projectiles to bleed out. There were not enough medics in the army to save them. One of the three remaining towers started to rumble forward as well, following FitzUrse's lead, but the other two wooden beasts seemed stuck fast; their men fallen or crouching from the arrow storm.

'Keep it moving,' Hywel told FitzUrse. 'I am going to see what is happening over there.'

'Do not get them moving too fast,' said the Bear. 'The king will reward the first tower to the wall.'

FitzUrse ducked down as an iron ballista bolt hit the wood above his head. Hywel ran over to the nearest siege tower. The men who were supposed to be dragging it up to the walls of Toulouse were on the floor hiding from the enemy crossbows. Their captain was dead but Hywel soon started beating and kicking them back to their task. The sergeants remembered their duty and got their spearmen into position to haul at the ropes once more, and the tower slowly rumbled forward again. The Welsh crusader was earning his coin.

Henry, Thomas and the household knights watched the scene

from raised platform out of range of Toulouse's walls. Henry had started to go red with pent up fury when the siege towers ground to a halt. He stood gripping the wooden front of his dais, his knuckles turning white and teeth clenched. As Hywel and the Bear got them machines moving again he turned to Thomas.

'Your Welsh captain has earned a reward for that action. If the city falls this day, I shall gift him a fine fief in these lands.'

Thomas smiled and thanked the King, and Osbern knew that Hywel would be delighted with the honour. The question of course was would Toulouse fall?

As the siege towers inched ever closer to the walls, FitzUrse was convinced that it would all soon be over. He was enjoying the battle, the thrill of the fight and the chance to prove his loyalty to his lord. Even as men fell about him pierced through with bolts, or smashed to the ground by great stones, bleeding out with broken bones and cracked skulls, the Bear had a wide grin on his face.

'What are you smiling at?' demanded Hywel when he returned to the trundling tower.

'I always enjoy a fight in the sunlight, it's better than rain for a battle.'

Hywel just shook his head and looked up to the walls; only twenty or so yards left. The ditch before the walls had been filled in with baskets of dirt and rocks to provide a stable platform for the towers to roll right up to the defenders. The towers themselves looked like monstrous wooden hedgehogs, the soaked leather walls were pierced through with arrows, spears, and javelins, but the machines were undamaged. Once they were in position, the men would climb to the top and attack the city's parapets. Henry would send more companies forward and they would clear the walls and breach the city. That was the plan anyway.

The Narbonne Gate was the strongest point in the defence, a castle keep with walls thirty metres high, built upon ancient foundations. Its stout oaken gates were bound with iron and barred and barricaded. It was a castle in its own right, as well as guarding the southern approach to the city of Toulouse. It had withstood Moorish sieges in the past and French kings. Count

Raymond of Toulouse watched from its walls as Henry made his first moves to take the city. A fat man, dark haired and in his mid twenties, he watched with a shark's smile as the towers trundled forwards.

'This is going to send that Angevin buffoon into apoplexy,' he said to one of his waiting courtiers.

The count waved a red kerchief to the men waiting below. The trap was sprung. From four secret doors concealed in the rocks below the walls of Toulouse, Raymond's mail-clad men swarmed out armed with axes, whale oil, and fired torches. The English spearmen hauling the siege towers into place were taken completely by surprise as the defenders overwhelmed them, cutting them down, stabbing at them and trying to burn the siege engines.

FitzUrse had seen the enemies appear in time to draw his sword and swing his shield around.

'Damn! I should have brought my axe,' he said, to nobody in particular.

He took a blow on his shield from one enemy, and then cut down at him with his sword; the shock of the impact ran up his arm. He had connected just at the point the mail hauberk and coif met on the shoulder. There was a loud snap as the enemy's collar bone broke under his sword, and the blade sliced through the leather carving a gash in the man's chest. FitzUrse kicked the screaming man out of the way and looked for more enemies. Hywel joined him, blade in hand, and blood streaming from a cut to his forehead.

'Where is your helmet?'

'It's only a scratch.'

The two of them battled against the firing party, holding their spearmen together. The Bear was a monster in battle, his bloody sword swinging, cutting and maiming. More than one Frenchman tried to kill him, but FitzUrse was invincible against them, brushing away their blows and swatting them down like flies. Hywel was beside him, finishing off any that the Bear missed. The Toulouse party were soon running from the two deadly warriors.

There was a groan and screams, and both of them turned. One

of the siege towers had gone up in flame; the defenders had managed to fire the drenched wood as they battled with its crew.

'My God,' said the Bear, 'There are men in there.'

The screams of the burning victims carried, as did the choking smoke and smell of scorched human flesh. FitzUrse and Hywel had been fortunate, their tower was still solid and functional, and most of the enemies had swarmed the other machines, but over half of their company was already dead or wounded. As another tower burst into flame, Hywel made his decision.

'Fall back,' he called to the few surviving spearmen. 'They have won this day.'

The men started to run back to the English siege lines, carrying their weapons and in good order. The other companies were not so disciplined or led. Most threw away their spears and shields and ran for their very lives. As they ran, the men on the walls jeered and cheered, whilst the other engines were destroyed in short order. The Toulouse raiding party then fell back to the city.

Count Raymond watched from a high tower, as his first move proved successful; the grin on his face growing ever wider.

'I bet that has sent Henry into a fit,' he said. He turned to the tall middle aged man next to him. 'Perhaps it is time we showed our hand, Lord?'

King Louis VII of France looked down at the tubby young Toulouse count and nodded. He did not like Raymond, but he liked Henry even less. The damned Angevins seemed intent on stealing his kingdom county by county. He had been humiliated when his former wife had married the man. Then he saw his best troops beaten in the field by the happy couple's companies and had been forced to betroth his baby daughter to their devil-spawned brat. It was time to reassert his authority over these young upstarts.

'Raise my banner,' he said to the waiting knights.

The French King's banner was a multitude of golden fleur de lys strewn on an azure field. It was known throughout the West as well as the Latin Kingdoms of the Holy Land. Six Feet wide and just as tall, it billowed as it was lifted above Toulouse. In the fields below, the English army, despondent at their first disastrous assault, gave out a great moan at the sight of it. Henry could barely conceal his fury, grinding his teeth and clenching his fists as he stormed back to his pavilion with his retinue, including Thomas, trailing behind him.

'Find the Welshman and FitzUrse and bring them to me,' said the Chancellor to Osbern. 'I must see to the King.'

Osbern nodded and ran to look for Hywel and the Bear. Raymond of Toulouse was a clever bastard, and so was the French King. He was also a vindictive swine, thought Osbern. All of Henry's plans, all of the coin spent, would be wasted if Louis was really inside Toulouse.

8.

The problem for the English King was that Louis was overlord for his Frankish lands. Anjou, Normandy, Aquitaine, and Brittany, were all nominally part of the Kingdom of France, even if in practice they were the possessions of the young English King. Half of Henry's army was drawn from nobles and knights who saw Louis as their ultimate overlord. Had Henry been fighting for England, for English rights, then there would be no issue, but he had invaded Toulouse to please his wife. The claim on the city was the Duchy of Aquitaine's not the Kingdom of England's.

'We should carry on,' Thomas urged the King. 'We have the force to take the city, my spies inside say that Louis brought only a handful of household knights with him. They may have beaten off the first assault, but that is a reverse only, Lord, not a defeat.'

Henry nodded at his friend; he wanted to attack, all of his and Thomas's designs revolved around holding the city and its access to the Mediterranean coast. The King wanted Toulouse, and he was unused to having his desires thwarted. However, some of the other barons looked in disgust at the upstart Chancellor. Thomas would defy all custom and law to achieve his and the King's goals.

'Louis let me make preparations, let me think that he would do nothing,' said Henry, with barely concealed fury. 'His sister is wife to Raymond, could she have arranged this?' He asked Thomas.

'They are estranged, Lord. The Countess despises her husband. I think this is King Louis' design more than Count Raymond's or his wife's, and Louis cannot remain in the city for long. We could wait them out.'

The French King was hardly going to be a passive spectator as Henry and his Chancellor gobbled up the French realm one county or duchy at a time. Until now, he had failed to halt their advance in the field, and only that summer had sworn friendship and betrothed his baby daughter to Henry's infant son. Their marriage could see the two kingdoms united and all of Henry's plans come to fruition. Louis' unexpected appearance at Toulouse had thrown the whole campaign in doubt without a blow, but also that longer design.

'Louis the sly they should call him, Louis the snake,' said Henry, throwing a wooden cup at a dog in frustration.

Osbern poured the King another cup of wine from the Chancellor's personal supply as the hound yelped and slunk away. He handed it to Henry who took it without a word.

'Forgive me, Lord,' said one of the barons. 'Half of the army would refuse to fight as long as Louis' banner flies above Toulouse.' He gave Thomas a withering glare. 'How long can we sit here waiting?'

'Men would desert,' said another. 'Discipline would collapse and we would be beaten.'

'Are you craven?' demanded Henry, going bright red in the face. 'Do you think that we cannot take the city?'

'We can take the city, Lord. But at what cost?' the Baron of Westmorland asked.

Baron De Morville of Westmoreland was new to Court, new to Henry's service. The Chancellor looked at him suspiciously. De Morville had ingratiated himself with the King and the more salacious pursuits that Thomas purposely abstained from. That gave the newcomer influence over Henry that Thomas could not control. The Chancellor did not like situations he could not control. Thomas knew that Henry, despite their closeness, could be fickle in friendship.

'Louis would be our prisoner and the whole Frankish kingdom ours to command,' said Thomas, in response to De Morville. 'The cost is easily outweighed by the prize.'

'The whole of Christendom would turn against us,' said another baron. 'King Louis is a famed crusader. The pope would repudiate us, perhaps even excommunicate us. What use is an earthly kingdom if the Kingdom of heaven is denied?'

There were murmurs of support from watching churchmen at that. Thomas could see that he was losing the argument with the clerics as well as the barons. He looked to Henry. It was the

King's decision to take.

Henry saw the inherent danger in attacking his French lord. He did not like Louis, he had taken the French King's wife which caused bad blood and conflict in the past, but to make war on him with no valid reason was a dangerous risk. It was not simply the foreign implications. The move would give the wrong impression to the English King's own vassals; it made it look as though monarchs could be challenged by their underlings with no due cause. Henry was not so long on the English throne, and not so secure that he wanted to give any of his domestic challengers ideas.

'We shall withdraw,' he said, finally.

Thomas could feel himself going red. He was just as unused to his advice being rejected as Henry was his demands defied. The King could see his Chancellor's discomfort.

'You shall take Quercy as we return to Bordeaux and ravage the county. I shall take men to the north and threaten some French castles in the Vexin. We will meet again in a month and see how the land lies with Louis.' He smiled at his Chancellor. 'I think you have proved yourself a leader on this campaign, friend. Perhaps I shall give the fief of Cahors to you.'

It was an open display of royal favour to the Chancellor, but Osbern noted that not all of the barons and knights smiled at the King's words. Thomas was an upstart, a revolutionary who cared nothing for their rules or customs. The King might praise his Chancellor but there were others at court who despised him. Proposing an attack on Louis in violation of chivalry and honour was just another example of Thomas's determination to upset the natural order of things. The King may love him, but it made him unpopular with the others.

May he never lose Henry's favour, thought Osbern.

***

For three weeks Thomas's companies had ravaged the Occitan, burning, looting and pillaging. The English Chancellor had directed the operations with increasing glee. Raymond of Toulouse had kept his city, but his lands were ruined. Ancient vines dug up and the ground salted, villages left like burn blackened husks, manors torn down and animals slaughtered.

The army ate meat every day: pork, beef, mutton, even venison. Raymond's vassals had paid a heavy price for the Count's argument with the English King. Thomas's army moved slowly back to Poitiers laden down with the spoils of war. The Chancellor himself with a small party then rode north to Caen to meet with the King. John of Salisbury was disgusted with the situation and his friend's behaviour, but Thomas paid his complaints no heed. The Chancellor was enjoying himself, even as his companies ravaged the land about them.

All the way to the edge of Normandy, they were shadowed by some French knights that refused all combat and stayed just out of reach, but watched them all the while from horseback.

'Are they still out there?' Osbern asked Hywel.

'Aye, they will trace us all the way back to Caen at this rate.'

'Why?'

'Who knows what Louis thinks?'

The French king's appearance in Toulouse had restarted the conflict between France and England, by proxy. Vassals on both sides had begun raiding and ambushing the other, stealing cattle and burning out estates. Louis had finally woken up to the threat of the young English King who ruled over more of France than he did.

At the Norman border, there was a single knight in the way of the road to Caen. He was on horseback in full mail with an enclosed helm and kite shield, and a lance in hand. A squire attended to him with spare lances. As Thomas and his companions rode into view, he raised a lance to the skies to salute them.

'Who is that?' asked Thomas.

'He is issuing a challenge,' said Hywel. 'Some French upstart out to make a name for himself I would wager.' Hywel sent a man down to speak with the Frenchman.

'It is Englerame de Trie,' said someone. 'I recognise the horse.'

De Trie was renowned in the lists and the tournament. He made a fortune from unhorsing richer barons and knights who did not have his skill with the lance or his seat with a horse. The English messenger spoke to the knight and returned to Thomas and his party.

'Who is he challenging?' Thomas leaned forward in his saddle.

The messenger looked shocked. 'Why, he is challenging you, Lord.'

'You can refuse him, Lord,' said Hywel. 'He does not have any rank to challenge the Chancellor of England.'

'If I were to refuse him, word of it would soon reach my enemies. They would use it against me.'

'If you lose to him, he will take you horse and arms and demand a ransom. I know De Trie. It will not come cheaply.'

'You trained me in arms; do you have no faith in your own teaching?'

'You have been training with a lance for six months in preparation for this campaign. He has been wielding a lance since he was little more than a babe. I do not doubt your courage or commitment, but De Trie is a master.'

'That is a harsh judgement,' said the Chancellor.

'It is the truth.'

'We shall see. I have shown myself a commander in the field but not yet a warrior. The barons still sneer at me as a pen-pusher jumped above his station and not their equal in arms. I shall prove them, and you, wrong.' Thomas turned back to the herald. 'Tell De Trie that I accept the challenge.'

Hywel groaned as Osbern rushed to get his Lord's heavy closed helm. Thomas took it off him pulled up the mail coif and placed it on his head. Osbern tied up the straps. He wanted to urge his master not to fight, but knew that once Thomas had made a decision not even the Pope in Rome could sway him from his design. *He is too damn stubborn and too damn proud. A lesser man would have laughed off the challenge.* Osbern handed Thomas an ash lance after he had mounted, and the Chancellor took it with his mailed fist and rode down to meet with De Trie.

'If he falls, he will be humiliated at court; all of the summer's trials will have been for naught,' said Hywel watching Thomas ride to the lists.

'And if he wins?' asked Osbern.

'If he wins, he will have proven himself a warrior and everyone else wrong,' said FitzUrse. 'But he will not win.'

Hywel nodded sagely at the Bear's words and Osbern could not help but feel deflated. The two warriors both knew their trade well; they had demonstrated that during the march on Toulouse. Then he remembered why John of Salisbury refused to play chess with Thomas. He is always five moves ahead of the rest of us, the monk would say.

Thomas and De Trie saluted and then charged at each other with little ceremony. Thomas on his white destrier and De Trie on a roan stallion, their lances set and shields held.

'I cannot bear to look,' said John of Salisbury, turning away.

The two of them came together in a great crash. De Trie's lance swept past Thomas's helm just missing him, but the Chancellor's caught the French knight square on the shield, bending at the shock of the blow. The lance shattered into splinters as it bent, showering De Trie and Thomas in shards of wood as they passed each other.

Thomas yanked on his reins to pull his destrier around, frantically trying to locate De Trie through the thin slits in his helm. The Frenchman was turning his own horse and waiting for Thomas to re-arm with lance.

'Take it down to him, Rabbit.'

FitzUrse thrust a lance into Osbern's hands and he ran down to give it to his master. De Trie had his own squire to attend him, but Thomas was no knight. Thomas was no warrior. Osbern reached his master and handed him the new weapon.

'Good fortune, Lord,' he said.

Thomas did not respond, merely turning his horse to face down De Trie once more. The two of them saluted again and Thomas dug his spurs into his horse's flanks. The animal sprang forward and Osbern retreated to the onlookers to watch the match.

Thomas and De Trie clashed again, to gasps from the watching audience. Both of them aimed at the other's kite shield, and both lances shattered in the collision. Thomas swayed back almost horizontal in his saddle through the shower of splinters, but kept his seat. Osbern breathed a sigh of relief when he saw his master had survived another round.

'All the saints be blessed, he is still there!' shouted Hywel.

'He leads the contest?'

'Yes,' said the Bear. 'De Trie must unhorse him on the next pass. Take a new lance down to him.'

Osbern grabbed another lance for Thomas and ran back down to the list, as De Trie's squire did the same.

'Thank you, Osbern.'

Thomas's voice was muffled but he sounded inordinately happy. Osbern retreated back to Hywel and the Bear.

The two riders saluted each other one last time. This was the last pass, if De Trie could not unhorse the chancellor, Thomas had won.

Thomas set his lance straight and level for De Trie's shield as he charged down on the enemy knight. Two shield strikes on two passes was better than he could have hoped, he just had to keep his seat on the last pass. He gripped the horse's flanks with his legs, grimly holding on for dear life.

At the last moment, just as the riders were about to come together, Thomas gave a twitch on the reins and his horse stepped to the side. They had practiced the move over and over with Hywel, rarely succeeding, but it had now worked twice in combat when it mattered.

De Trie's lance glanced off of Thomas's helm this time, stunning the Chancellor, ringing in his ears like a bell and making him sway back, but Thomas's lance caught the Frenchman square on the shield. De Trie was forced up and out of his saddle by the force and thrown from his seat as Thomas's lance straightened. The Frenchman landed on his head with a clatter and lay prone, unconscious or dead from the fall. His horse turned and nuzzled at its fallen rider, as Thomas reined in his own white animal and turned to face the watching company. He had done it.

'De Trie was expecting the move but had no choice,' said the Bear. 'He went for a head strike to win the match.'

'I underestimated him,' said Hywel. 'I taught him to move to the right and twitch the reins before impact, but did not believe he could manage it twice in an actual fight.'

'We all underestimated him,' said Osbern.

Osbern started cheering and rushed down to Thomas. The others all joined in, proud of their lord, and Thomas rode back to his applauding men. He had proven himself as good a warrior as any in the King's service. There was a wide grin on his jubilant face as his helm was removed and the men swarmed around their Lord in delight. Warriors always prefer a fighting Lord to lead them. Thomas had understood that, and he had proven himself to them.

'Will you show him mercy?' asked John of Salisbury when Thomas finally dismounted.

'Mercy is for the weak, John. Not for arrogant knights who lose a joust. De Trie can pay his ransom and I shall take his arms and horse. That is what a warrior does.'

'You are still the Chancellor not a warrior,' John pointed out.

Thomas gestured to the prone French knight, still out cold.

'I beg to differ, my old friend.'

***

At Caen, the King's mood was much improved. He had already heard of the ravaging of the Occitan and word of Thomas's joust had gone through the court like wildfire. Everyone was talking about the Chancellor's shocking success in the field. Some were pleased, all were surprised, but many were surly about Thomas victory. They had hoped that he would fail or fall at Toulouse and Thomas had proven them all wrong – as he so often did. Henry met his Chancellor in the courtyard of the chateau with a wide grin and a hug.

'You unhorsed him with one lance? You have been practicing, have you not?'

'Yes, Lord.' The Chancellor rubbed his back. 'My neck hurts though, from the blow to the head.'

Thomas was still elated at his success in the joust. He now understood the thrill of combat that fired so many of the men around him. John of Salisbury's open disgust had been the only cloud on his horizon afterwards.

'Where is the man you unhorsed?'

'I sent him onto Rouen,' said Thomas. 'He can remain there until the ransom is paid.'

The two friends walked arm in arm to the hall. The castle around them was in uproar as preparations were being made for Henry's return to England. Thomas's arrival had only added to the confusion in the castle.

'There is news from Winchester?' asked Thomas.

'Men from my mother are waiting with despatches,' said the King. 'I kept them waiting on your arrival.'

Thomas sighed. 'The Queen Mother will not be impressed that her men were kept waiting.'

'My mother is never impressed,' Henry replied jovially. 'She is granddaughter to the Conqueror himself, don't you know?'

'She lets none of us forget it, Lord.'

'I shall send her a present to pacify her,' said the King.

The Queen Mother was a power in her own right, and useful regent in England or Anjou if Henry needed it. She was also one of the few people who could command her son. Even Henry baulked at upsetting his mother. Empress Matilda had the same fiery temper as her son. Henry also had a wife just as stubborn and wilful who ruled in Aquitaine. The King was less concerned about upsetting Queen Eleanor, but Thomas had told Osbern that she was more deadly than the Empress.

'Let us see what news they bring then, Lord,' said Thomas.

They entered the wide open hall arm in arm, the slender dark haired Chancellor and the red-haired barrel chested King. The usual petitioners and supplicants that followed the royal train wherever it went all looked expectantly at their arrival but they were ignored. Patiently waiting to one side was the Empress Matilda's messenger. He bowed deeply to the King.

'I bring urgent missives from London and Canterbury, Highness,' he said, keeping his face to the floor.

The man held out two scrolls sealed with wax. Thomas took them off the messenger. The sigil on both was the Queen Mother's. He broke the wax and unrolled it, quickly scanning the words.

'Well,' demanded Henry.

The King could read and write as well as his Chancellor and he was rather proud of that fact, but detested the petty administration of documents. That is what he had Thomas for.

'It is Archbishop Theobald, Lord. He has been taken ill with palsy. He collapsed in the nave of the cathedral. The Empress does not hold out much hope for his survival.'

Thomas was shocked by the news. The Archbishop had been his patron and had placed him in the royal household to serve the King and support the church. Thomas had in turn taken the King's side when the Archbishop and King argued over ecclesiastical courts. Even then, Theobald had not held it against Thomas, and had welcomed the Chancellor warmly ever afterwards and treated him like a son.

'Then there will be a vacancy in Canterbury?' said Henry.

'Yes, Lord.'

The King eyed his Chancellor.

'Oh no,' said Thomas. 'I have seen that look before, Lord. I serve you faithfully but can only bow to one master. I do not want the responsibility of an Archbishop and a nagging pontiff in Rome. It will only end badly.'

'Oh, fret not,' said Henry. 'Theobald will linger on his sickbed for a decade, if I know him. Perhaps you will feel differently when he finally passes over.'

'I doubt it.'

Henry laughed and grabbed his friend in another rough hug.

'We shall see,' he said, kissing Thomas's cheek. 'We shall see.'

Historical Note.

Thomas Becket is perhaps one of the most well documented individuals of the medieval period. After his messy death, the details of his life were written down by numerous hagiographers, but even before the murder in the cathedral Thomas's acts, his argument with Henry II, and his former role as the King's Chancellor were all well known and recorded in letters, court records, and chronicles.

Thomas was born in Cheapside, London, in 1120 to a Norman family. Whilst his father seems to have been little more than a petty landowner in Normandy, the move to London proved successful for the family. Gilbert Beket (sic) became a London merchant and landlord, even serving as Sheriff of the City. Thomas's early education was at Merton Priory and then one of the London grammar schools. He studied for about a year in Paris around 1140, but was not a renowned scholar or student. The death of his mother and reduced family circumstances saw Thomas seek employment as a clerk, and he ended up in the service of Theobald of Bec, Archbishop of Canterbury. It is almost certainly through his father's Norman connections that Thomas achieved the post, but once in the Archbishop's service his talents saw him rise swiftly to a trusted agent. He did not take holy orders and remained a lay clerk not a priest.

England during Thomas's childhood and early manhood was riven by civil war. The sinking of the White Ship only months before Becket's birth had robbed Henry I of his only legitimate male heir. After his death there was a struggle for the throne between Henry I's daughter the Empress Matilda, and her first cousin Stephen of Blois. Whilst Stephen had achieved the crown he was unable to secure it and there was a near constant civil war until Matilda's son ascended the throne as Henry II. Thomas as the Archbishop's agent was intimately acquainted with the Angevin succession, and was placed by Theobald of Bec into the King's household where he swiftly proved invaluable to Henry.

The Toulouse campaign of 1159 was part of the Angevin expansionist policy under Henry II. His marriage to Eleanor of Aquitaine had given Henry a claim on the county that he was determined to press. The records show that Thomas threw himself into the campaign with his typical zeal and obsessive attention to detail. He borrowed money from the King to fund a magnificent force (a later cause of conflict between the two), and the details of trumpeters and lavish baggage is well attested by the sources. His companies mustered seven hundred men in the Occitan, the largest component of Henry's army.

The Cathar Heresy was widespread in the South of France but had not been fully condemned by the church and was growing in popularity despite opposition from Rome. Raymond of Toulouse's son would face an invasion and the fall of Toulouse fifty years later because of his adherence to the heresy. Toulouse itself was well defended and details of hidden doors for the defenders to sally out from and attack siege towers is recorded at the 1211 siege. However, the English army was confident of victory with their overwhelming strength of numbers in 1159. Louis' arrival in Toulouse trumped Henry's military superiority, but Thomas's advice to ignore tradition and oaths of fealty demonstrate just how fiercely the Chancellor was prepared to chase his goals and disregard convention.

Thomas's well attested celibacy was unusual but not unique for the period. There seems to have been no scandal attached to his behaviour at the time, and his enemies would certainly have been certain to expose the merest whisper of a sex scandal if they could. His success as a commander in the field and unhorsing of De Trie were also well recorded at the time, as was his particularly brutal ravaging of enemy territory as they army fell back from Toulouse.

Becket did ultimately acquiesce to Henry's demand he become Archbishop in 1162, a year after Theobald of Bec finally died. He was consecrated a priest on 2nd June 1162 and consecrated Archbishop on 3rd June. Whilst Henry II clearly hoped that Thomas would continue to support royal government from Canterbury, Thomas went through a complete conversion to his spiritual role. The King and his former Chancellor quickly found themselves in opposition.

Osbern was a real individual and probably one of the closest people to Becket in his lifetime. He would serve the Chancellor and Archbishop right up until his death and was present at the murder in the cathedral. Osbern was one of the few who knew of Thomas's hair-shirt and secret asceticism, but was mostly overlooked in the post-murder frenzy for Thomas, which saw everyone and anyone who had known Becket write memoirs, chronicles, letters, histories and hagiographies.

Becket: Rebel

Jemahl Evans

1.

Northampton, England, October 1164.

Archbishop Thomas of Canterbury knelt before the altar in the small dark chapel, bowed his head, and prayed for strength in the coming trial. The previous day had been a repeat of every argument and disagreement he had with the King those past two years. Henry demanded absolute control over the English Church. Royal courts, not clerical courts, would try churchmen accused of crimes. The King's justice would extend to all in England. Nobody was above his law. Once, Thomas would have supported his lord and friend in that desire. The good governance of the realm was paramount when he was England's chancellor, but now he had a different calling. The church was not a mortal monarch's bauble to be played with. It was the House of the Lord. The law of kings could not bind the servants of God.

'I did not ask for this.'

He had begged King Henry to make someone else Archbishop, but the London aldermen were overjoyed that a common lad born on Cheapside could rise to become prelate. Eventually, worn down by others' enthusiasm, Thomas took the oaths to protect the church, to shepherd its flock, and to look to the heavenly realm not the earthly one. He took his oaths seriously. Nobody had expected that.

'Henry thought I would be his chancellor and friend still, he could not see that the two paths are different. He behaves like a spurned lover, but the Lord of all Hosts is now my king not Henry of England.'

Thomas's servant Osbern of Dover, called Rabbit because of his small stature, crept into the lonely chapel. He paused before disturbing his master. Thomas had been ill of late and the Rabbit was worried. The Archbishop's stomach plagued him; always a slender man, he was now thin and bony. His dark hair was thinning and flecked with silver. The arguments with the King had made his master sick and old in only two years. Who would be an archbishop if it does this to you, thought Osbern to himself. Life was easier when he was but a chancellor and not a priest. After a few moments watching his lord pray, he coughed to catch Thomas's attention.

Thomas turned and smiled as he saw the Rabbit standing in the shadows behind him. A loyal servant is a treasure indeed, he thought, and this one is as true to me as the Bear is to his King. FitzUrse the Bear was the King's bully, and had insulted Thomas to his face the day before. The Rabbit and the Bear also had been close friends, just as close as Thomas and Henry once were, but now they too were sundered from each other. This matter taints all, thought Thomas. Who rules, King or God?

'Are you ready?' he asked Osbern.

'Yes, Lord. There is a farrier in the town. He has debts to the abbey, considerable debts. He will do it and keep his mouth shut.'

'Go to the castle first. Inform Hilary of Winchester that I will come to the court after the noon service. I must deal with my other recalcitrant bishop first. Then see to the farrier.'

Osbern nodded, but Thomas could see the fear on his face.

'Do not worry, Little Rabbit. I shall take care of everything with the King.'

That is what I am worried about, thought Osbern to himself, but he did not tell his master.

St Andrew's was set in the north-west corner of Northampton. Osbern left the walled priory compound and hurried through the cobbled streets to the old castle keep at the west gate of the town. He took the port gate into the outer curtain wall, rather than going around the castle to the gatehouse. There was a drawbridge and gates into the inner bailey courtyard and keep. Porters and spearmen watched the flow of servants and animals as they came into the castle. They nodded at Osbern as he hurried past. Everyone knew the archbishop's servant.

The Rabbit saw a monk outside Winchester's chambers and informed him that Thomas would attend the court that afternoon. Then he made his way back to the town to see the farrier. There was a commotion in the courtyard. A crowd had gathered on the cobbles of the inner bailey. It was the Bear.

FitzUrse the Bear parried the axe blow with his shield, but the Dane's weapon carved a great gouge out of his heater and sent splinters flying over the wet cobbles. The match was not turning out the way FitzUrse and the watching courtiers had initially expected. The little weasel Dane was a far more accomplished warrior than he had seemed in the hall, and FitzUrse wondered if he had been played. Both of them were in heavy mail coats and open faced helms, but the Bear was starting to wish he had brought his own huge battle axe to the fight. The man came at him again, swinging his axe low at the Bear's legs and forcing the huge warrior to jump back.

'You are fleet for one so tubby,' said the blonde Dane in barely intelligible English.

The Bear ignored him; he knew better than to get involved in insults and barracking. The two of them had duelled for nearly five minutes and FitzUrse had barely struck a blow. The small Viking was slippery and quick, forcing the Bear to concentrate on his defence. The triangular heater that he carried had already taken some serious damage, another blow would see it split, and his sword was already chipped. Both of the warriors steamed in the wet conditions and puddles on the cobbles made the footing treacherous in their heavy mail coats. The Bear was going to have to make his move soon, or he would be humiliated and then killed before the watching audience.

He stabbed at the Dane's face with his sword, but the man dodged the thrust and hefted his axe at the huge Norman warrior. FitzUrse parried again with his heater, but the blade smashed down and split the wood. The Bear cursed and moved to his right, away from the deadly axe blade. He shook the broken shield off his arm and thrust his broadsword at the foreigner's belly, but the man danced back, light on his feet and out of reach of the Bear's weapon. The Dane was smirking as the Bear panted, the condensation steaming off him.

'You are too big and slow, English, and now you have no shield to hide behind.' He taunted the Bear loudly, so the audience could all hear.

FitzUrse thanked God that his King was not watching. Henry always took it badly when his vassals were humiliated by foreign nobles. The King said it did not reflect well upon the crown.

The Dane stepped forward again and swept his axe low at FitzUrse's knees in a wide arc, but the Bear was expecting the move and leaped forward and up over the blade. That shook the Dane whose eyes widened at the move. FitzUrse had seized the initiative for the first time in the match. With no shield he had no choice. He landed lightly and slashed his broadsword at the Dane's chest forcing the Viking step back.

The watching crowd – men at arms, servants, some of the Dane's friends with their old ambassador, and a couple of other flunkeys from the royal court – gasped at the Bear's sudden audacity and strength. Leaping over a swinging axe in full mail coat and open faced helmet was no mean feat. Neither the Danish warrior nor the watching ambassador had expected the move. The ambassador turned and whispered something to one of his servants.

Osbern the Rabbit watched the battle with a strange detachment. It had been five years since he had seen FitzUrse. The two had become fast friends on the Toulouse campaign, but had then gone their separate ways, as so often happens in life. Osbern served Thomas the Archbishop whilst the Bear rarely left the King's side. Their masters had argued, and the Rabbit and the Bear had been forced into opposing camps in spite of their past friendship. Thomas had been summoned to Northampton to answer the King's charges of embezzlement, and Osbern had hoped that the matter could be settled amicably. Sadly, thought Osbern, neither the King nor my master is inclined to compromise.

The Bear kept pressing at the Dane, keeping in close so the man could not wield his axe to its full effect. He kept stabbing at his face with the broadsword, trying to keep him off balance. The foreign warrior was canny and quick, parrying with the shaft of his weapon or dancing out of reach of the blade. He continued to offer the Bear advice on technique and prowess as they duelled.

'Such a little weapon for such a large man, English, do your women like that belly?' he said loud enough for everyone to hear. 'Can you see your pizzle?'

Osbern shook his head at that comment. Only a fool pokes the Bear, he thought. The more enraged FitzUrse became the deadlier he was to face. The taunting was merely invigorating him.

FitzUrse made a feint with his sword, and the Dane moved to skip away, but instead the Bear swung his left arm around and caught the smirking foreigner square on the jaw with gauntleted fist.

'Now that is what you call a haymaker,' said a soldier next to Osbern.

Osbern nodded. The Dane was stunned by the punch, falling back from the Bear but just about keeping his footing. FitzUrse stabbed at him again, but the man desperately knocked the sword aside with the axe shaft.

It's all over now, thought Osbern. The Dane is finished. I should be about my master's business. He turned to hurry off, but there was a groan from the crowd that made him turn back. FitzUrse had slipped on the wet cobbles. Osbern gasped. The Bear was lying prone on his back as the Dane swung his axe down at him. FitzUrse rolled as the blade struck the stone, sending up sparks. He twisted his legs around the Dane's, bringing the axe man down to the ground and kicking at his face. Both of them struggled to their feet, both blowing from the exertion.

The Danish warrior looked to his master for a moment; the Ambassador nodded for him to get on with it, and the axe man launched another attack on the Bear. Blow after blow swept at FitzUrse, forcing him back and back, until he felt a wall behind him. The Dane yelled in triumph, but the shout died in his throat. As he raised his weapon to deliver the killing strike, FitzUrse rammed the hilt of his sword up under the man's chin. The Dane started to scream in agony, his jaw had been broken by the force of the blow. The Bear silenced him with a lazy swing of the sword that opened his throat and left him guttering out. He fell forward, face down, as a pool of scarlet blood spread out beneath him on the dark wet cobbles.

Some of the watchers cheered for FitzUrse, but the Bear did not seem elated. He knew only too well how close the match had been. He turned away from the bloody corpse and faced the Danish ambassador. People thought that the Bear was simple because of his size and fearsome reputation in battle, but he was not. FitzUrse understood that this was high politics. The Danish King was clearly testing King Henry of England over something. The foreign embassy had arrived suddenly and with little advance warning, and seemingly with little to discuss. The King had welcomed them, but they had caused the drunken fight in the royal hall that had led to this duel. The ambassador had set his man to needle the Bear all day.

'Is it finished?' FitzUrse asked the ambassador.

The white haired Dane nodded shortly and then turned away with his attendants. FitzUrse turned to his friends who rushed to congratulate him. The King would be pleased, they told him. The man he had killed was a champion in the lists.

Out of the corner of his eye, FitzUrse saw Osbern the Rabbit hurrying away. He must have watched the fight. Why does he not come to me? FitzUrse wondered. Are we not friends? Then he looked back to the retreating Danish ambassador. Did the Archbishop have something too with the embassy? Would that explain why the Rabbit had not even bothered to say well met? The Bear felt slighted by his old friend. He was tired of this quarrel between the stubborn, vain Archbishop and his King. FitzUrse strode away from the courtyard after that, set on finding wine and a woman to celebrate his victory.

***

The farrier was surprised that Osbern wanted the horses prepared for travel given the treacherous weather, but he arranged for them to be delivered to the priory later that day. Osbern had strict orders from his master to have the animals' shoed and stabled close at the priory. Ready for our quick exit, thought Osbern to himself.

The argument between the King and his former Chancellor had been tit-for-tat for the past year. Both were stubborn and both convinced they were in the right. Osbern could not help but feel the King was being particularly vindictive over it, but Thomas did nothing to help matters and seemed intent on inflaming the situation instead.

'You want four saddles delivered to the priory as well?'

'Yes.'

'I will want payment on delivery and the debt cleared.'

'You shall be paid by the Abbot,' Osbern assured him.

'You just arrived in Northampton, are you leaving so soon?'

'No, no,' said Osbern. 'We cannot depart until the King gives us leave, but my Master likes to be prepared.'

'They say the King is unhappy with your master.'

'I find it wiser not to listen to gossip and to keep my own counsel. I suggest you do the same, and your debts to the church will be redeemed.'

The farrier sniffed at that, but Osbern cared nothing for his sensitivities. Everyone knew that the King was unhappy with the Archbishop, but the Rabbit was no scandalmonger. More than that, however, he wanted nobody to know of the loan of the horses. The Archbishop's plan relied upon surprise.

'There is a storm coming,' said the man.

In more ways than one, thought the Rabbit.

'Keep your mouth closed on my lord's affairs,' he warned the farrier again.

The man nodded. 'You have my word.'

Osbern's discretion was his greatest virtue as far as the Archbishop was concerned. His small stature and generally retiring nature made him Thomas's eyes and ears about court. Few people ever took much note of a freeman servant, no matter who his master was. Indeed the higher the station the less note of the lowly Rabbit they took. It meant that he was privy to all sorts of secrets. Since arriving in Northampton, Osbern had discovered the King's design to humiliate his Archbishop from half whispered conversations whilst supping in the hall.

Thomas had made these arrangements to escape should the need arise, and the need was now certain to arise. Whilst the

King was vindictive, Thomas was become a mule of stubbornness. Once everything was agreed with the farrier, he walked back to the priory where his master had been forced to take up residence.

It had not been an auspicious arrival in Northampton Town. For over a year the King and Archbishop had bickered and argued. Two of the greatest of friends had become the bitterest of enemies as love had turned to hate. Thomas had arrived with his usual retinue in Northampton, and found his quarters in the castle given over to lowly Danish squires (a studied insult that everyone at court understood). Then the King had denied his Archbishop permission to travel to Sens in France to meet with the new Pope. Osbern had been present when the King had snarled his refusal to that request, but otherwise Henry had studiously avoided his Archbishop. The Danish arrival had caused a minor distraction, but the serious business of the council was to force Thomas to submit to Henry, or declare him traitor.

The King planned to break the Archbishop in the royal court.

Osbern sighed: his master would not submit. Once Thomas had made a decision, nothing would sway his mind – even the King. Henry had found Thomas's fixed purpose more than useful as a chancellor, but as Archbishop it had caused conflict.

When he was chancellor he had to be the best chancellor, when he was a warrior he had to be the greatest warrior. Now he is a priest, he has to be the best priest. It is the constant need to prove himself the best that causes problems.

'Well met, brother.'

Osbern had reached the priory gatehouse and was waved in by the porter. He found Adam of Ely in the refectory. Adam, a young lay brother in the Archbishop's retinue, was one of the few who knew of Thomas's plan.

'Did you arrange for the horses?' Adam asked in a hushed tone.

'Aye, four chargers newly shoed will be delivered this afternoon. Where is the Archbishop?'

Adam made a grimace. 'He is ensconced with the other bishops in the Lady Chapel. They have only just gone in.'

Osbern crept into the chapel from a side door. His master was stood beside the altar, surrounded by a gaggle of priests and bishops. None of them were happy; most were begging Thomas to submit to the King's authority. Thomas would hear none of their complaints. *He has aged these past years,* thought Osbern. *His hair goes grey and he is painfully thin.* The Rabbit stood in the shadows and listened to Thomas's words.

The tall, slender Archbishop towered over the others and spoke loudly and clearly, as if he addressed the congregation in Christ Church.

'Brethren, the world rages against me and mine enemies rise, but do you know what pains me the most?' Thomas paused, fixing the conclave with his piercing stare. None of them answered him so he continued. 'What pains me most is that you, the sons of our Mother Church, fight against me. Future centuries will know you for the baselessness of your faith, even if I leave nothing to posterity.'

There were angry murmurs from the assembled churchmen at that but Thomas hushed their complaints.

'Twice already you have convicted me in a secular court in defiance of church law, and you plan to deny me thrice before this assembly is finished?'

'What would you have us do?' shouted Gilbert Foliot, the corpulent Bishop of London. 'He is our King and you defy convention.'

'John the Marshall's charges are baseless and contrived, you all know that,' said Thomas. 'The King has no authority over criminal clerics, and any outstanding debts from my time as chancellor are long forgiven. This is an attack by the King on the church itself.'

'What would you know of the church?' shouted the Bishop of London back at him. 'You are barely ordained a priest, yet you seek to lecture us in theology?'

Thomas raised himself to his full height at that and gave a commandment in all his authority as Archbishop. He knew that he was only a priest on the King's connivance. He had never wanted the role, but if he was the Archbishop of England then these mere bishops and abbots had to submit to his rule.

'I forbid all of you, on pain of excommunication, from taking part in any further judgement in this court where my person is at stake.'

Thomas said the words quietly, but they were like stones in a pond. There were more gasps from the churchmen. This was an unprecedented command; this was a revolution. It set Thomas and the English Church up in defiance of the English King.

'I shall appeal to our mother church in this,' Thomas continued, not giving them a chance to protest. 'And I order you, should any lay violent hands upon my body, to excommunicate them in turn. Know this, that although the world rages, the enemies rise, the body quivers and the flesh is weak, I shall, God willing, never give in shamefully or commit the offence of abandoning the flock that has been entrusted to me.'

Gilbert Foliot sneered at him. 'I can appeal to the Pope as well.'

'You can,' Thomas smiled, 'but you can do nothing else in the meantime.'

Foliot the Fool flushed red, infuriated by Thomas, but understanding the truth of his words. The laws of the church bound them all.

The bishops and priests all swept out in a gaggle after that. Thomas had made his position clear. He would not submit to the King. This was no personal vendetta; this was a fight for the soul of the church itself. Once the bishops had left him, Thomas slumped to the side and steadied himself on the altar. Osbern rushed to help him.

'I am tired.'

'You must eat more, Lord.'

'It makes the colic worse. I am well enough, sweet Rabbit. Did you procure the horses for the plan?'

'Yes, Lord.'

'Then, it is time to show our King that there is more power in the holy cross than the temporal sword. Have my pallium brought to me, and my ceremonial robes.'

'Yes, Lord.

Osbern hurried to his task. He knew what was coming next.

2.

The bishops and churchmen streamed back to the castle in despair at Thomas' words. Some would go straight to the king like schoolboys sneaking on a classmate. Thomas dressed and returned to the altar in the quiet priory chapel and prayed alone with only the Rabbit watching over him. He remained there for almost an hour in solitude. Then, smiling to himself as if convinced by God of his mission, Thomas made his next move. He walked outside to the priory stables, followed by Osbern, mounted his usual white riding horse and called for his retainers; monks and clerks all. Alexander Llewellyn, a slight lad from the west, took up the archiepiscopal cross and mounted a bay hinny to lead the procession to the castle. Thomas was on his horse, and dressed in his pallium with all the regalia of an archbishop displayed for all to see. He bent down and kissed Osbern on the cheek before leaving for the castle.

'Make sure everything is ready for my return, we will need to act quickly,' he whispered in Osbern's ear. 'Tell Hywel to get himself out of bed.'

'Yes, Lord.'

Osbern thanked God that he would not have to face down the King at Thomas's side. This display of defiance from the Archbishop was certain to send Henry into purple apoplexy, and the King was fearsome to behold in such a rage. Once, Thomas had been the only man who could calm the King in such a fury, now he was the one that infuriated him the most.

'Princes also did sit and speak against me,' Osbern quoted the psalm to himself as he went to wake the Archbishop's Welsh bodyguard.

Thomas led his party of clerks and attendants through the cobbled streets of Northampton to the castle. Alexander Llewellyn held the cross high like a martial banner in battle. The townsfolk watched on, some aghast, some exultant, all of them knew that this was unprecedented: an Archbishop riding in holy orders to spiritual battle with the monarch. Would Thomas dare to excommunicate the King? There were some cheers from the crowd as Thomas and his party rode through the castle gates, but once inside the courtyard the gates were slammed shut behind them by grim faced guards wearing armour and bearing spears.

Thomas dismounted in a nervous energy and took up the cross from Llewellyn. There were only the guards on duty and a solitary porter in the courtyard. A stable boy came forward to take his horse and Llewellyn's hinny to the stalls.

'Follow behind me,' Thomas said to his clerks.

As Thomas ascended to the steps to the great hall, Gilbert Foliot tried to stop him. Foliot barred the Archbishop's path and pointed to the cross that Thomas carried.

'If the king were to brandish his sword, as you now brandish yours, what hope can there be of peace between you?' said the Bishop of London.

He made to grab at the cross and take it, but Thomas, taller than the tubby bishop and ready for a fight, pushed him away. Foliot slipped and fell to his knees before the Archbishop as if a penitent in supplication. Thomas looked down at his prone subordinate.

'The King's sword is an instrument of war,' said Thomas, firmly although he was trembling inside with excitement. 'My cross is a symbol of peace, both for myself and the English Church.' He turned away and led his party towards a small chamber off the great hall to wait on the King's pleasure.

'You are going let him carry his cross?' A knight asked, as Foliot glared at Thomas's back.

The Bishop of London climbed to his feet, brushed himself down, and sneered to hide his embarrassment. 'Cheapside was always a fool and always will be.' He turned and went upstairs to inform the King of Thomas's arrival.

Thomas heard Foliot's parting barb, but ignored it. His common birth in London rankled, but he would rather be a Cheapside rough than a slithering false Bishop.

The sound of running feet and raised voices were heard throughout the castle as everyone waited for Henry to descend from the upper chambers, but the King did not appear. An hour went by and Henry remained in his chambers in the upper storey of the keep. There were some churchmen like Foliot with him, and some of his favourites and barons, all waiting on the King's next move.

'What is he waiting for?' Llewellyn asked a white-robed monk.

'He fears the Archbishop will excommunicate him.'

Llewellyn looked over to his master. Thomas sat silent and stony-faced, lost in thought, as his retainers and monks anxiously chattered among themselves.

'I think he just might as well,' said Llewellyn, half to himself. 'I have ne'er seen him so angry.'

The bishops and churchmen who had refused to support Thomas in the confrontation with Henry were now utterly dismayed by his appearance in full regalia. They had seen a personal argument between two stubborn men become a battle for the soul of the English church itself. At every point the two adversaries had escalated their disputes instead of finding common ground. Henry was vindictive and spiteful, and Thomas was stubborn and arrogant. It left the assembled bishops, abbots, and priests caught between the royal hammer and the Archbishop's anvil. Some of them kept to their own counsel and tried to keep their heads down and safe. Others, like the Bishop of London, sided openly with the King against their Prelate.

The Cistercian monk nudged Llewellyn. 'The Archbishop of York has come to join the party.'

Roger de Pont L'Évêque, the Archbishop of York and one of Thomas's oldest adversaries, had arrived in the Great Hall. Like Thomas his cross was born before him.

'The bishops all come a marching to war,' muttered Alexander. 'I would rather face the Saracens than this flock of harridans.'

The Archbishop of York did not move to wait with the Archbishop of Canterbury. Pont L'Évêque had known and despised Thomas since the two of them had been clerks in the old Archbishop's household. He had certainly not come to support Thomas in his battle with the King. Instead, Roger's party took up the other side of the antechamber, all of them glaring malevolently at Thomas. The various opposing groups: monks, priests, bishops, clerks and assorted servants were all crammed in together, muttering and murmuring like schoolboys at Matins.

Thomas ignored them all, completely lost in thought. His stomach hurt again, twisted around like a knot, and he had barely broken his fast that morning. Every time he ate it just made the fire in his belly worse. All night he had pondered this meeting with Henry. He had questioned whether it was his own hubris or God's will. Only the Pope could decide the matter had been his only conclusion. That itself meant even more conflict with Henry, but his old friend was a different man. Long years in unchallenged power had changed him. Once Henry was young and beautiful, like an Arthur returned. He had brought peace to England, tamed the rebel barons, and the nation prospered. In his victory he had become a tyrant, and it was to Thomas' shame that he had abetted the King's rise.

***

The two of them were laughing as they rode back to the new hunting lodge at Radmore. It had been a good day at the chase. A train of attendants carried a wild boar strung between poles behind them. The King had run down and speared the animal himself, showing no fear as he set the spear. Thomas had watched his friend stick the beast, noting the exhilaration on the red-haired man's face. Henry came alive in action; he lived for the wild hunt. Thomas preferred his falcons but had enjoyed the chase.

'You were fortunate the beast did not gore you with his tusks,' Thomas told the King as they arrived at the lodge.

'Small chance of that, and he will make good eating tonight.'

Thomas winced. Another night of fatty boar meat and wine would give him colic. He would get the Rabbit to make his medicine up if they had a feast. The two of them handed a stable boy their horses' reins and strolled arm-in-arm inside the stone building.

The half built monkish refectory had been turned over to the King and made into a rich lodge set in a picturesque glade in the woods on Thomas's orders. Cannock Chase had good hunting and game, and Thomas had convinced the monks of the King's goodwill should they make a free gift of the place to Henry. They had not been happy about the situation, but Thomas could be quite persuasive when he wanted, and he cared nothing for the churchmen's sensibilities. Thomas was the King's dog.

The fires were stoked up as they entered and servants rushed to take their muddy cloaks and bring cups of hot wine.

'This is the perfect place for a lodge,' said Henry, taking some wine and settling into a cushioned chair. 'Good hunting and FitzUrse tells me there are women in the village. How did you get the Cistercian monks to hand it over?'

'I asked for their accounts,' said Thomas, taking the seat beside him. 'At that point they bent over backwards to gift this petty place.'

Henry laughed. 'Not so petty. I like it. They way you dealt with the Cistercians as well. It tells me that you would do well, if I made you prelate.'

'Not this again, Lord?' Thomas held up his hands in mock horror. 'I would make a terrible Archbishop.'

'You are not so riddled with vice that the priests could complain, and with you as Archbishop and me as King we can remake this land.'

Thomas had heard the arguments before. Henry had been pestering him since Toulouse to take the See of Canterbury. Since Archbishop Theobald's death, the nagging had become incessant. Thomas did not want to let his friend down, but to be Archbishop of all England was something else. That was a responsibility that Thomas did not want, but the King could not see it. Henry thought only of the advantage a subordinate bishop would give the crown. He thought nothing of the heavy duty for a servant of God.

'I can serve you better at your side,' said Thomas.

'You would still be at my side,' the King retorted. *'We can order this land like brothers in arms. Think on it some more. The barons and bishops would be cowed before us.'*

'Oh, I do think on it,' said Thomas with a smile. *'It terrifies me at night and stops me from sleeping.'*

Henry laughed again at that. He thought it nothing more than a jest.

FitzUrse brought the conversation to an end, arriving from the nearby village with some women and more wine. The hog was being butchered but the sweetmeats were thrown on a griddle and fried by one of the servants. Henry took a platter and picked at the fried kidney as he eyed the women. Thomas refused the food.

'This is good, do you not want some?'

'No, Lord, my belly is already too hot. I shall leave you to your entertainments. I have despatches to write and the Rabbit to find.'

'Work, work, work,' said Henry. *'It is ever work with you. At the least, we had a good day's hunt today.'*

'A very good day indeed, Lord.'

'Think on what I said, my friend,' said Henry, and waved him away.

Oh I will, said Thomas to himself and hurried to find his servant Osbern. His old friend settled in for an evening with wine, women and roasted boar.

*****

I did not want this, Thomas said sadly to himself. I did not want any of it. Now only the Pope can decide.

A young herald, but a small boy, came to summon the other bishops upstairs. He was dressed in oversized red livery, and his voice cracked as he issued the call. The requested churchmen trailed upstairs to resume the court, leaving Thomas to await the sentence and his fate. Gilbert Foliot and Pont L'Évêque both shot Thomas a vindictive glance as they stalked out, but he studiously ignored them.

'The King plans to convict you of embezzlement,' said a black robed monk to Thomas. 'From your time as chancellor and the Toulouse campaign.'

Thomas nodded at his words but said nothing. The charges were trumped up and he could produce documents to prove that if he was given time. He had already secured indemnities for any debts unpaid, but he did not believe Henry would grant him the time. The King was not interested in justice; he planned to break him here and now. He could see no reconciliation with his old friend. He doubted Henry would forgive him now.

I am Archbishop, ordained by God, and only the Pope can judge me. The church is my shield against this unjust King. I have no choice.

There was shouting and arguments upstairs. The King was shouting. Thomas sat back and smiled quietly to himself. The court was not turning out how Henry had expected. The power of excommunication terrified the King; it terrified the assembled churchmen, and the very real fear that Thomas might use his power gave everyone pause for thought.

Henry forgets that I know him too well, but I do not think he ever truly knew me.

Thomas had discussed the step with his confidantes like Herbert of Bosham and John of Salisbury. He had the power to deny heaven to any man, to sever him from the church and from God's grace for eternity. There were some of course that always would choose earthly power over spiritual salvation. They would stick limpet-like to Henry, even most of the bishops, but some would not, and ordinary priests and clerics would not defy the interdict, nor would their congregations. The whole of England would be in uproar.

The English bishops could not judge him, Thomas had forbidden it, and the King dared not risk excommunication. When push came to shove, only the Pope could decide the matter.

***

Hywel was laid on a pallet snoring, dribbling from the side of his mouth as he lay face down on the blankets. He was a broad shouldered warrior who had served Thomas as a bodyguard since his time as chancellor. He had spent the previous night in his cups. Osbern shook the old Welshman awake.

'Get up you lazy drunk. Our master has work for you.'

The grey-haired warrior's eyes snapped open; they were still bloodshot from the night before.

'Do you have to be so loud? I found a vintner in the town last night with wine casks from Poitou.'

'He wants us ready when he comes back from the castle. I think he is actually going to do it.'

That made Hywel sit up, his hangover forgotten.

'Truly?'

Osbern nodded.

'Well best I get up then. Did you arrange for the horses to be delivered?'

Osbern nodded. 'This afternoon.'

Their plan was not at all sophisticated, but it relied upon them doing the unexpected. Once the matter in the castle was settled, Thomas would return and lead prayers as was usual. Osbern, Hywel, and Adam of Ely would saddle the horses and make sure they had provisions ready for a week's travel. They would leave Northampton in the dead of night whilst another party would leave openly at first light. The second party would go directly to Canterbury whilst Thomas and his three companions would take a more circuitous route to avoid capture. The four chargers Osbern had procured earlier would be perfect for the escape.

'As long as the farrier keeps silent the plan will work,' said Hywel.

'He will keep silent,' said Osbern. 'He owes the Abbot of St Andrews more than his life is worth. And anyway, should the King find out he aided us after the event, his life won't be worth much at all. He will keep silent.'

'Did I tell you how I escaped from Damascus? I climbed down the walls with a hemp rope rolled by naked maidens in the Caliph of Baghdad's harem.'

'Last time you told me it was a silken rope spun by giant spiders in the lands of Cathay?'

'Ah well, yes, it could have been too, you know.'

Osbern smiled. 'You grow more incorrigible by the day, Hywel. I saw the Bear at the castle.'

'Did you?' Hywel brightened up at that news. 'I like FitzUrse, how was he?'

'In a killing mood.'

Hywel looked quizzical and Osbern described the duel with the Dane that morning.

'He has grown huge this past five years, a boy no more, but not an ounce of flab upon him. He is not a bear - he is a mountain.'

Hywel laughed. 'As long as he is on our side it does not matter.'

Osbern shot him a glance. 'The Bear is the King's man. After today he will be on our side no longer. Do you think he will hold it against us?'

'Oh, most certainly, but only as long as the King does. You know FitzUrse; he does as his lord desires and has no thoughts otherwise. He is quite simple in that respect at least.'

'Still deadly though.'

'Most certainly.'

The farrier brought the animals to the priory not long after noon, as he had promised. Osbern and Hywel ran their eyes over them. The man had provided good beasts, mounts that could run all day and carry Thomas far away from Northampton and the King.

'Now what?' asked Hywel.

'Now we wait for the business at the castle to be settled.'

***

Thomas and his party sat in silence as the arguments in the royal court upstairs continued. They could hear the raised voices and slap of feet on the flagstones above their heads. Another hour passed, and another. The clerics with Thomas growing were ever more worried, until finally a deputation was sent down by the King. Henry himself dared not face his Archbishop. He was terrified that Thomas would wield his spiritual sword against him and excommunicate the King.

Instead, Henry sent a small group of senior bishops, but not of London or York, to question Thomas. Did he have his accounts from his time as chancellor? Could he produce them?

The monks and clerks with the Archbishop started muttering nervously amongst themselves, but Thomas silenced them with a cold glance and answered the deputation confidently, without bothering to rise to his feet. His answer was comprehensive and detailed, to the dismay of the churchmen.

'As for my accounts for my time as chancellor.' Thomas stood as he came to a finish and pulled himself to his full height; his slender frame still taller than most of his accusers. 'I was exonerated for all my debts by Prince Henry and the King's brother upon my ascension at Westminster. The King may deny it now, but you all know the truth of the matter because you were there. I have appealed to His Holiness the Pope in these matters and forbidden any churchman from judging me in this secular matter. I place both myself and the Church of Canterbury under the protection of God and our lord, Pope Alexander.'

There was stunned silence from the clerical deputation at first. A couple of them shook their heads sadly, as if Thomas was gone insane. Others scowled at the affront to their King. A few recognised it for what it was: a declaration of war between church and crown. They began to shout at Thomas as he sat back down but he studiously ignored them. Alexander Llewellyn stepped forward, and held the cross between them like a shield to remind the priests of the power behind Thomas's words.

'Behold we have heard the blasphemy from his own mouth,' said one finally.

They all turned away at that and trooped back upstairs to deliver Thomas's speech to the King. Henry had been waiting anxiously, nervous in case he had gone too far. When he heard of Thomas's response, he went wild at the words, going puce in the face and kicking a dog. He screamed at the court that his will was being denied.

'The conqueror knew how to deal with his priests,' said one Baron to the King.

'Let's take him outside and cut off his balls,' said another.

'Stick him in a pit till he submits,' advised a third.

FitzUrse said nothing. He was not so high in rank that his counsel mattered, and he did not have the wit to care about weighty church matters. He was simply affronted by the insult to his master, and he would take Henry's lead in the matter. The King was full of bile and fury, which meant the Bear was also. However, the priests present were not prepared to sanction any physical punishment against Thomas. Some like Pont L'Évêque were, but most balked at such a sin. They were well aware that the royal blade could catch them in turn, and Pope Alexander would most certainly condemn them for it.

'You are all snivelling cowards,' shouted the red-haired King at them.

Thomas's words had had the desired effect and sown division among his enemies. The Barons called the bishops cowards and dissemblers, the bishops demurred and dissembled, and all the while King Henry raged. For over an hour it went round and round, getting nowhere. Eventually Henry let the bishops retire. He did not want to drive any of them into Thomas's arms. He had brought peace to this kingdom after two decades of anarchy. His law; his justice, and now it was flouted by frocked priests.

'You bishops may not judge him in a secular court,' the King declared. 'But the barons of my realm still can. Go back to him and await our judgement.'

The Bishops all trooped miserably back down to Thomas in the small antechamber muttering to themselves. The Archbishop ignored them once more. The Barons court above did not take long to come to a decision. The King summoned some knights and the Sherriff of Northampton to add weight to the sentence, but it was merely a legal fig leaf. Roger of Beaumont, an old friend of Thomas' from his time as chancellor, was sent to deliver the King's verdict. Beaumont was a middle aged man, tall but out of condition, with his dark hair receding and beard shot through with white. He was clearly unhappy that he had been chosen for the task, but dared not defy his king. He started speaking almost as soon as they entered the antechamber.

'You know, Thomas, we have been good friends, and the King has always been kind to you. He raised you up to the highest position, fed you, clothed you, and gave you succour…'

'I have heard all this before,' said Thomas, interrupting Beaumont.

'It is with unhappy heart that it has come to this…'

Thomas stood up and took the cross off Alexander Llewellyn. He held it up high above his head.

'It is not for you to judge your Archbishop for a crime,' he proclaimed loudly for all to hear.

Beaumont faltered at that. He had not wanted the task in the first place and now it was all getting out of hand.

'Perjurer,' shouted one of the barons.

'Traitor,' shouted FitzUrse.

'You have to hear the judgement,' said the Bishop Hilary of Chichester.

'No, actually, I do not,' said Thomas. 'Because the judgement has no weight.'

He strode out past them using the cross as a staff with his few monks trailing behind. There were more catcalls from the barons of coward and traitor, but not one dared place their hands upon him. At the doorway to the Great Hall Thomas turned back at their taunts.

'If I were a knight, my fist would prove you all liars.'

He stormed out of the keep into the cobbled courtyard and mounted up on his white horse. The porters were absent, but one of the monks found the key to the gates and opened it for his Archbishop. There were guards there but they did not dare stop an Archbishop. The King would not thank them for it later. Thomas rode out on his white horse bearing the cross and rode back through the town to the priory. Word of the confrontation had spread through Northampton, and the townsfolk flocked to the sight of Thomas on his white horse, calling out Hosanna and cheering the rebel archbishop on.

Henry watched Thomas flee from the open window of the court chamber. He was calm now, his fury had dissipated. The red hot anger had been replaced by the cold vindictive cunning that his enemies knew and feared. For all his faults, Henry had brought justice to his realms. It was his obsession. Everyone had to be accountable to the King's justice; nobody was above the King's law. If Henry let the church flout his rules, soon the barons would follow, and the anarchy would return. Thomas could spark a civil war with his stubborn mule head, if he was not stopped.

'*Nondum finivimus cum isto*,' he said quietly to himself. 'We have not finished with him yet.'

3.

Thomas was wild with excitement as he rode back to the priory. His heart was pumping and all his senses heightened. The pain in his stomach had gone in the exhilaration of open rebellion. He could hardly believe that they had pulled it all off without Henry stopping him. He could hardly believe he had found the courage to defy the King. Now, the second part of the plan had to be put into action and that was the deadliest act. He ignored the singing of the crowd that followed him, struggling to hold his unwieldy cross and handle the skittish horse.

At the priory, Thomas dismounted and went straight to the Lady Chapel to pray. Beautifully painted icons of saints and a scene of the crucifixion looked over him as he prayed. A few of his clerks knelt in obeisance with him. Thomas was begging for vision and forgiveness for his vanity and pride. There were a few whispers from the monks about the day's events, and once he had finished his prayers Thomas turned to them. He owed them all an explanation.

'Peace, brothers, I leave with you; my peace I give you. I do not give to you as the world gives. Do not let your hearts be troubled and do not be afraid,' he said quoting the Last Supper to the men.

The Archbishop's retinue all knew the words of the Gospel well enough, and they understood the reference to the scriptures.

'What now then, Lord?' one asked Thomas.

He smiled. 'Those matters have already been accounted for and your parts will not be onerous.'

Thomas led his retinue to the refectory to eat their last meal together. There was a melancholic air among the clerks as they trailed behind their master. Sitting on the long benches, already feeding their faces, were the Archbishop's manservant and Welsh guard, and the lay brother from Ely. The clerics nodded politely but said nothing to the three men. Thomas greeted the three warmly.

'It is good that you are here,' he said. 'It is right that you are here.'

Osbern, Hywel and Adam of Ely stood at Thomas's words. All of them had been stuffing themselves with food for the journey ahead. The priests and clerics, including Thomas, had no idea of the hardship that lonely travel would mean at that time of year, but these three were more worldly wise. It was the very reason Thomas had chosen them for his companions on the flight. Monks and clerks would give him away, but those three common reprobates will keep me safe, he thought to himself when he saw them waiting.

He sat and ate sparsely; his stomach was a tight knot once more. The colitis had been forgotten in the confrontation with the King's justice. Now the excitement had subsided, the pain in his abdomen had returned. He moved the food around his platter and pondered his next move. With his three companions, he would flee to a Kentish port and take a ship for France. The pope was in Sens and Thomas planned on throwing himself on the pontiff's mercy. At the same time Herbert of Bosham would take some monks directly to Canterbury and find as much coin and plate as possible, and then take his own ship to France with the funds. Thomas would need coin if he was to become an exile.

Some of the clerks came to him when they had finished eating their supper and begged to be released from their vows of service. They had no desire to be caught between Archbishop and King, to be caught between spiritual and temporal power. Thomas granted their request happily enough and with no remonstrations, but his loyal servants were not so kind.

'Faithless,' muttered Osbern.

'A friend is someone who happily eats your food, but seemingly then disappears in your hour of need,' said Herbert of Bosham, only half jesting after they had left the refectory.

'I shall spend the night in prayer,' declared Thomas to the remaining clerks and monks, but he beckoned for Osbern and Herbert to come to him.

'Is everything ready for our travel?'

'Yes, Lord,' said Osbern. Herbert nodded.

'You know your task, Herbert?'

The priest nodded. 'I will put Brother Matthew on your white horse; he is about the same height as you. It will be enough to have them pursue us.'

'You take a risk, my friend.'

'We stand for our mother church against a tyrant,' said Herbert, defiantly.

Zealot, thought Osbern. I remember the Anarchy before Henry.

The monks of the priory made a place in the chapel for Thomas to spend the night in prayer. Word came that the King had refused him safe conduct back to Canterbury, demanding his presence at the court as and when Henry required. In Northampton, Thomas would be left unmolested but at the King's pleasure. Thomas had no intention on waiting for Henry. He knelt before the altar with his three companions and a couple of lonely monks, and prayed for guidance. The candle light behind his head cast the illusion of a halo to Osbern's eye, but the Rabbit blinked and it was gone.

'Let us all pray for success in our endeavours,' said Thomas quietly, making the sign of the cross. 'Let us pray that God's providence shines down upon us.'

Failure is not an outcome that promises longevity, thought the Rabbit.

It was raining heavily when they left the priory, in the darkness before dawn. The foul weather was their greatest ally in the escape, Hywel told them cheerfully. Thomas had dressed himself in a black monk's robes, cloaked and hooded in rude commoners garb, and mounted his borrowed destrier. The three others did the same. Only Herbert of Bosham was in the priory courtyard to say farewell to his Archbishop. Herbert and the other Canterbury monks and priests would embark on their own journey south at dawn.

'May the saints preserve you all,' said Herbert, with tears in his eyes.

'God go with you, my friend', Thomas told him, and then kicked his horse into a canter out of the priory courtyard and turned north. The other three followed as Thomas led them through the streets of Northampton in the darkness. The downpour muffled the clatter of their horses' hooves on the stone cobbles, and they reached the gates with no surprises.

'It is locked, Lord.'

The north gate was locked, but left unguarded. The night porter was absent from his duties, and the keys to Northampton town were left hanging on a nail by the gates.

'They should hang the porter for his dereliction to duty,' said Hywel.

'Thank the Lord for his providence,' said Thomas. 'If the porter was here he would tell the King where we went. Why are we going to the north when the boats are to the south?'

'We shall head into the fens to avoid pursuit, Lord,' said Hywel. 'Adam knows the way. The King will send men after Herbert first. We shall hide out and then make our way slowly by night to Dover. There are some safe houses, friends that will keep us hidden as we travel. Once they catch up with Herbert, they will realise what we have done but by then it will be too late.'

'Poor Herbert,' said Osbern. He did not like the overly zealous cleric, but would not wish the King's rage upon anyone.

'I have every faith in him to succeed,' said Thomas. 'As I do you three. Come then, let us make haste and get away from here as quickly as possible.'

They spurred their horses up into a canter, and rode hard through the darkness to put as much distance between themselves and Northampton before dawn.

***

When the King rose the next morning, he called his advisors to him to decide on their course of action: how to bring the rebel Archbishop to heel? Henry was calmer after his tantrums the day before. He sent the old Bishop of Winchester to find out what Thomas was about.

'Test the waters, see what his plans are, find out if he will submit,' Henry told the old man. 'I do not want a war.'

The Bishop was rolled up to the Priory to speak with Thomas, with some clerks in tow, but when he got there and tapped on the gates they remained shut. A hatch opened and the porter peered out.

'I have come to inquire on the Archbishop,' said the Bishop, somewhat affronted to be kept outside the religious house.

'The Archbishop is doing rather well,' said the porter. 'Since he left late last night, to only God knows where.' The porter slammed the hatch shut in the stunned bishop's face.

Winchester sighed, remounted and turned his horse back to the castle. The King was going to be apoplectic with fury. He did not hold out much hope for Thomas's survival when he was caught, and the King was bound to set the Bear on his trail. The Bear was a relentless hunter and killer.

It is a shame, thought Winchester to himself. He liked Tomas and agreed with him on the legality of his arguments, but that had to be balanced against royal favour and patronage.

'We live in the earthly realm with earthly kings, after all.'

The red-haired King was calmer after the previous day, but the news that Thomas had escaped Northampton in the storm did not improve matters. He did not rant and rave or chew the rugs in a fury, as the Bishop of Winchester had expected. Instead, he plotted his counter moves with the same cunning that his former friend had shown to escape.

'Get you to France and see the Pope,' Henry told the Gilbert Foliot and Roger the Archbishop of York. 'Plead our case with him before Cheapside gets there. Take gifts of coin and lavish it on His Holiness's court. That is where the rebel will be going.' He turned to FitzUrse. 'You, Bear, get after him. They will be going to Canterbury to steal coin and fund their treason. Find his party and bring him back here in chains.'

The Bear nodded and turned to go.

'Do not harm him or any in the party,' Gilbert Foliot said. 'It would not sit well with His Holiness.'

'Leave the others be,' said the King. 'There is no need to antagonise the Pope over this. It is only Thomas I want...' Henry paused. 'Alive and unharmed.'

The Bear left the King and his Bishops and magnates in the court chamber. He knew his dark reputation as the King's bully, but his devotion to Henry had only grown over the years. As the King had become capricious and grasping, so had FitzUrse. He would hunt old friends and bring them back in chains to face royal justice, and would act on a whim to please his royal lord. The Bear gathered together his followers, all rough hedge knights and lordless mercenaries that thought nothing of honour and only of advancement. They saddled up their horses and rode south out of Northampton in pursuit of their quarry.

***

'Where do we rest tonight?' The Cistercian asked Herbert.

Herbert almost didn't answer; he did not like the portly white robed Cistercian monk. The man was always questioning, and he had no respect for his rank or his closeness to the Archbishop. The Cistercians were always too damn cheerful.

'Tickford Priory,' he said, eventually.

'They are Cluniacs at Tickford?'

Herbert nodded.

They had taken the road south from Northampton, but struggled with the muddy track and had to take to the fields instead. The cart with the archbishop's possessions had been dug out of the quagmire twice by lay brothers, delaying them even further. After only ten miles, they abandoned it with the black robed Augustinian monks from Thomas's Canterbury retinue. Herbert told them to make their own way to Kent and await word from the Archbishop. He and the others with horses rode on. If they stayed with the cart they would be quickly caught and questioned, and Thomas's ruse would be quickly discovered. The Archbishop's escape depended on them laying a false trail for as long as possible.

'They will have word of the Pope in Sens at Tickford,' said the Cistercian. 'Most of them are French.'

Herbert nodded again but said nothing. The man seemed determined to engage him in conversation. He hoped his silence would be infectious.

'I wonder where the Archbishop is?' said the Cistercian. 'I wonder if he got away.'

'Keep silent about the Archbishop,' snapped Herbert.

'Oh I know that,' the Cistercian waved his hand airily. 'Do you think he has got away?'

There was a crash in the undergrowth and everyone turned in their saddles. Herbert gave a silent prayer of thanks for the distraction and turned himself to see what the commotion was. It was the Bear and his men on horseback bursting out of the undergrowth. The monks and priests all started praying for deliverance.

The Bear and his men were covered from head to toe in mud from the road, all in mail coats and open helms, and they looked terrifying to the churchmen. Only Herbert felt no fear. He knew his task. Herbert was a loyal and willing disciple of the Archbishop and the church. He would sacrifice himself to the cause and his Archbishop, if needs be. Thomas had a way of inspiring devoted loyalty in his close friends.

'Now, the King's most devoted dog comes to hound us,' said the Cistercian quietly.

'Not a dog but a bear,' said another in a terrified tone.

'Halt,' shouted FitzUrse, holding up his hand. 'Where is he?' They could all see that the servant sat on Thomas's horse was not the rebel archbishop. 'Where is he?' the Bear repeated.

FitzUrse was furious. He had been outwitted and sent after a false trail by the churchmen. Thomas could be anywhere by now. They had ridden south all day, soon finding the abandoned cart and black robed monks guarding it. FitzUrse had bullied and threatened them for information, and quickly overtaken Herbert and his party on the Tickford road. He had expected to catch Thomas and drag him back to the King with ease. Now, the realisation he had been fooled befuddled him further. His orders were to bring the archbishop back, not some upstart theologian. He did not know what to do next. The King had been quite clear about not harming the priests.

'What now?' asked one of the mercenaries.

'We take this lot back to Northampton,' said the Bear.

Herbert did not protest; he had expected this. He was excited by it, just as determined to make his stand against a tyrannical king as Thomas. The monks said nothing as FitzUrse and his men led them back to Northampton. FitzUrse took them straight to the castle to see the King. The Bear had refused to answer any of Herbert's questions, but had made it clear he would not be gentle if they resisted. The King and court were already abed and their royal audience would have to wait, but Herbert was still confident that the King would not harm him.

'The King will not dare offend the Pope when he needs the Pope's judgement against Thomas,' Herbert told the monks.

'I do not think the King cares who he offends,' said the smug Cistercian. 'Can His Holiness afford more royal enemies with the Emperor of Rome already set against him?'

Herbert did not respond to that. He was growing to heartily dislike the man.

The next morning the Canterbury monks were taken before the King and Bishops and Barons of the realm in the vaulted hall of Northampton Castle. Henry was in no mood to be kind, but he understood that Thomas had outwitted him. The King had to bring some semblance of control back to the situation before it got out of hand.

'This vain upstart Archbishop must be dealt with,' said one of the court sycophants as Herbert was brought in for questioning. 'Do not be kind to his servants, Lord.'

'Thomas has always been guilty of vanity and pride,' Henry told them, with no hint of irony. He turned to the captive Herbert. 'Where is he then? Where are you supposed to meet with him?'

'I do not know the answer to the first and am forbidden to answer the second, my lord King.' said Herbert defiantly.

'You refuse to answer me, priest's son?' said the King. 'That is brave.'

"I am no more the son of a priest than you are the son of a king,' Herbert pointed out. 'My father came to the church after I was born.'

There were gasps from the court at that statement. The only child of a King in the court was the Bishop of Winchester, son of old King Stephen, whose line Henry had usurped. Henry's own father had been a petty count of Anjou until he married the Conqueror's granddaughter. The tubby Bishop of Winchester allowed himself a sly smile at that. Herbert knew that Winchester secretly supported Thomas, which was precisely why he made the point.

'Get out,' said the King, finally, struggling to control his fury.

'I am free to go?'

Henry wanted to break the man, punch his face in, smash his teeth and snide smile, but he could not. If he started arresting every churchman that displeased him in this matter, soon all the bishops and priests of the realm would be united behind their rebel Archbishop. It was Thomas's head that Henry wanted, this insect could wait. Henry had a long memory. He dismissed Herbert from his presence and let him go about his tasks, knowing full well that Herbert of Bosham's only task was to take coin to Thomas, wherever the archbishop was.

'Have him watched,' he said. 'Thomas cannot have escaped to France yet, and that creature will lead us to him.'

4.

The fens are a wild and lonely country. From Lincoln to Cambridge flat marshes, reed banks, and royal forest dominate the landscape. The rains had swollen the streams and brooks that crisscross the flats, the tracks were turned to muddy quagmires that could swallow a man and horse in one gulp. Thomas and his companions were all cold, wet and hungry, but they had put nearly one hundred miles between them and Northampton in two days. The horses were nearly broken by the journey, and dark clouds above gave warning that more storms were coming.

'We need to get out of the weather and find somewhere warm,' said Hywel. 'The weather is turned foul again.'

'There is a new Gilbertine Chapel not so far away,' said Adam. 'They will help us, I am certain.'

Thomas knew Gilbert of Semringham, the head and founder of the Gilbertine order. He was a conservative old man who would not dare cross the King. Thomas was not certain he would be of any assistance to a rebellious priest.

'Can you be sure they will help?' he asked.

'They had better,' said Adam. 'One of them is my cousin and his mother would take it ill if he did not.' He grimaced. 'My aunt is a fearsome woman when she is in a temper.'

'How much further is it?'

'A few miles, your grace, is all.'

Thomas nodded and pulled his sodden woollen hood up. There was spit on the wind. It was going to rain again.

After leaving Northampton, they had ridden hard for the first day. The farrier had made good on his promise to Osbern, and the horses were well shoed and strong runners. Despite the foul weather, they had made it nearly to Grantham by the time darkness and the elements forced them to halt. Hywel found an abandoned rude hovel in the woods, and he started a small fire to warm them as they camped down. Osbern had brought bread and cheese and some dried fruits, but it was a poor supper washed down with only small beer from flasks. The next morning Adam had taken them deep into the fens. His knowledge of the paths and people were vital to their escape. The few people they encountered had been rough fishermen or fenlanders who spoke in their own strange language. Adam knew their tongue and led them ever deeper into the treacherous marsh. Any pursuit would soon be lost.

'Do you think we have made good our escape?' Thomas looked to Hywel and Osbern.

'Not until you are with the Pope in France, Lord,' said Hywel. 'We can stay with Adam's monks tonight and tomorrow and get some rest, but then we shall travel on by night so word of our passing is not heard.'

Osbern nodded at those words. The last thing any of them wanted was to be caught. Thomas's life might be spared (Osbern was not certain of that given King Henry's capricious temper), but the rest of them would surely be tortured and killed. It was not a pleasant fate to dwell upon. Loyalty has a cost, he mused.

'There it is,' Adam called gleefully.

A small wooden chapel was hidden on an island in the reeds, with a narrow causeway leading up to it over the water. The place was roughly built with a rude shingle roof, and the wooden cross above the doorframe had pitched to one side from the wind. They could see light inside escaping through cracks in the door. All of them dismounted, as Adam went up to the door and rapped at it. The bolts were drawn and door thrown open to reveal a large rotund monk in a dirty wine-stained habit, red-nose, and badly shaved tonsure.

'By the saints' bones,' he exclaimed when he saw them standing on his porch. 'Is that you Adam?'

'Cousin Jocelyn, we need your help. I have the Archbishop of Canterbury with me.'

The words tumbled out in a rush, and the monk's eyes widened at Adam's news. He bowed automatically at the others, and kissed the ring on Thomas's hand.

'Rise, Brother,' said Thomas.

'Come in, come in, your grace,' said Jocelyn. 'There is only me here at the moment. I am being punished with solitude for my repeated transgressions,' he told Thomas quite cheerfully. 'But in all honesty I prefer this place to the Abbey refectory.'

'What were your transgressions, Brother Jocelyn?' said Thomas.

'Persistent tardiness, your grace. I was late for Lauds three days running. I overslept, I am afraid. Abbot Gilbert was most displeased with me.'

'Jocelyn has never been able to get out of bed in the morning,' said Adam. 'It is why the family thought the church would be best for him.'

'It is a curse,' Jocelyn said sadly.

'It is a hangover,' said Adam, with a sly grin.

The red-nosed monk laughed at that and gave his cousin a great hug.

'It is good to see you, Adam. Come in, come in all of you and be welcome.'

The chapel was small inside; a bare room with wooden walls, a small altar, rude cross, and flickering tallow candles and reed lights. Jocelyn led them through into another room at the back. His bedding was thrown into a corner, but there was a stone hearth and chimney, a pot on the fire and the smell of fish stew.

'You must all be hungry. I have plenty of food for you.'

They nodded, taking off their wet cloaks and boots. Jocelyn ladled out fish stew into wooden bowls as Osbern hanged their clothes next to the fire to dry. Thomas nearly collapsed with exhaustion but gratefully took a bowl. Jocelyn grabbed a loaf of brown peasant bread and began ripping off chunks and passing them around. They waited for Thomas to say a prayer for their bounty, holding hands together, and then gobbled up the stew without speaking another word. It was simple peasant fare, but warm and easy on Thomas's tender stomach. The pains had been worse when he was riding, now he was settled it was better. The plain food would help, but he only ate sparsely fearful of overloading his stomach and making himself sick. He needed his strength to travel.

'Bread and fishes seems somewhat apt for supper,' said Hywel. 'We will wait here a couple of days before moving on. With your permission of course, Brother Jocelyn?'

'Permission happily granted,' said Jocelyn. 'Would you like some wine, your grace?'

Jocelyn retrieved a small flask of wine from a box and passed the Archbishop a cup. Thomas sipped at the wine. It was a sweet vintage, and pleasant.

'What of your order?' he asked, sitting back on the rude chair. 'Will there be others coming?' Their escape depended upon secrecy.

'There will be some of the women along in a few days,' said Brother Jocelyn.

Thomas knew the Gilbertines were unique in accepting men and women into the order.

'Until then I am expected to spend my time in solitary prayer and self criticism,' continued the monk. 'It is a worry that I have broken another oath to the Abbot.'

'I think I can grant you a dispensation,' said Thomas with a wry smile.

'Oh that is most kind of you, your grace. He tapped his nose. Best we not tell Abbot Gilbert about it though. Let us just keep it between ourselves and the Lord God.'

They settled down for the night after that. All of them fell asleep quickly except for Thomas. He lay staring at the ceiling, wondering if he had done the right thing, and thanking God for the loyalty of his companions. They risked everything in helping him make a stand against Henry, and their families would suffer for it. Thomas felt even more guilt over that than his broken friendship with the King.

***

The soldiers ripped through the small house and work sheds in a storm of anger. These were not the lord's retinue; they were ruffians and scoundrels all.

Richard of Dover watched aghast as his livelihood was destroyed. Not stolen, but destroyed by royal vandals.

Expensive barrels of wine from Aquitaine were smashed open, and the contents just tipped into an open cesspit. Coin was taken from a stout chest hidden in the rafters; the raiders gleefully calling out in joy when it was discovered and broken open. Bedding was torn and cut, straw pallets slashed with blades, blankets ripped and cast aside. The few pieces of good furniture he had were broken. Richard, held at sword point by some of the brigands, screeched out his protests to the Bear.

'I will be ruined!' he cried. 'I have done nothing wrong.'

The Bear turned to face the small wine merchant.

'Where is your traitor son, Richard?'

I have not seen little Osbern in five years or more. He is with the Archbishop's household. Go to Canterbury if you want him.' Richard was still defiant although terrified.

The Bear grabbed the little old man by the throat and held him up against the wooden wall, slowly choking the life out of him. At the point that Richard was fit to pass out, FitzUrse dropped him like a stone to the floor. The old man knelt on the flagstones gasping for breath, and panting heavily like dog.

'I will crush the insolence out if you speak to me like that again.'

'I meant no insult,' Richard gasped. 'I have not seen him, Lord. I swear on all the saints and angels in heaven that I have not seen him. I would tell you if I had.'

Richard's defiance had been crushed out of him. The Bear was a bully, so kicked the old man in the belly and made him double up. FitzUrse left the wine merchant rolling in agony on the floor and turned to his men.

'Come on,' he called out to his bully boys. 'The Rabbit is not here. Have his father taken up to the castle to answer for his transgressions.'

Richard did not protest. His business was ruined, his coin stolen and his home ransacked. He would be left begging for recompense and trying to rebuild his life. He silently cursed the day he had put Osbern into the old Archbishop's household. It had seemed like a good idea at the time, and when the boy had become servant to the Chancellor his business had flourished. Just word of his connections to the great and good had seen his trade boom. Everyone wanted to buy his wine. Even when Thomas became Archbishop, there had been goods bought by the monks at Canterbury just because of Osbern's position. Then the arguments had begun, and fewer and fewer people wanted to trade with him. Now, the Bear had ruined what was left of the industry he had spent his life building. Two of the Bear's soldiers picked Richard up from the earthen floor and carried the weeping wine merchant away to the castle.

'What now?' Guy, the Bear's Sergeant at Arms, asked.

The Bear did not like Guy. He did not like any of the men who served him. They were crude, rude, and landless; freebooters and mercenaries, always on the make. They fitted the dangerous tasks the King gave them in hope of favours or rewards, but they were not very nice, individually or collectively.

'Have men watch the port and all the little village wharfs and jetties. They have to take to ship to France somewhere along the coast. We have people watching the monks in Canterbury, and his friends in London, and there are more at his sister's nunnery. We shall stop him from sailing.'

'What if he has already escaped?'

'He has not. We would have heard tell of it from France.'

The King had been quite clear in his instructions to FitzUrse: stop the Archbishop from leaving England. Henry had already sent a deputation of bishops (including Thomas's sworn enemies - the Bishop of London and Archbishop of York) to attend the Pope in France and put the King's case against Thomas.

There were men all along the south coast watching for the rebel Archbishop and his party. As long as they could stop him from reaching to the Pope, the matter was settled. His Holiness needed King Henry's support in his struggles with the Roman Emperor. Without Thomas in person to press his claims, the pope would be left with little option but to condemn the Archbishop and remove him from his post as Henry demanded. However, if Thomas could get to the Pope in Sens first, then all bets were off. Pope Alexander was in French lands, and King Louis of France would leap at the opportunity to needle Henry. FitzUrse could imagine Henry's temper if that came to pass.

'Make sure to check the little villages,' the Bear repeated. 'That is where they will be hiding, waiting for the wind and a small boat.'

'Yes Lord.'

Guy ran to his task.

***

It had taken them nearly a month of travel, mostly by night and always by lonely paths, to reach the Kent coast. Brother Jocelyn had provided them with provisions and better disguises, and had told them of people who could help them as they travelled. A local fensman had guided the Archbishop and his party as far south as Cambridge. Despite having friends in the city that might help him get a ship to France, they had skirted around London and crossed the Thames at Wallingford in the dead of night. Thomas knew that the King's agents would be watching the London gates and his friends' households.

Osbern could scarcely believe that they had managed to make it to the south coast unmolested. Mostly the four of them had slept in the open, despite the elements and with only a small fire. When fortune had smiled upon them, they had found rest in abandoned barns or hovels that they discovered in the wilds. Thomas was not the best actor and his disguise as a travelling monk easy to pierce, but still they had made it to Kent without incident. Osbern was exultant at that. In Northampton he had feared they were done for, now he could smell the brine on the air and their salvation seemed at hand. It would be a cruel jest to be caught now.

'Will we find a boat in Sandwich?' The Archbishop asked wearily.

'Yes Lord,' said Hywel. 'It is already arranged for us.'

'Do you think they will keep the bargain?'

'They had better.'

Thomas was nearly broken by the journey. He was unused to such long travel with no comforts, and the agony in is belly grew worse by the day. It was a furnace inside him, making his heart burn after eating. So, he avoided eating which only made him tired. Exhaustion dogged his every move; his legs were rubbed raw from days in the saddle. The hair shirt he wore under his robe itched and scratched against his skin. Yet, he endured it all. The trials and tribulations were sent from God to test his resolve in this great matter. Thomas was certain of that.

'The Israelites endured a miserable exile in Egypt, so must I.' He constantly told himself and the others.

'At least there is sun in Egypt,' Hywel replied. 'I am sick of the rain.'

The night before they had stayed, hidden by monks, in the old Roman ruins of Reculver. That morning they crossed the Wantsum ferry and headed down to Sandwich. It was only a few hours travel with their horses, so they hid out for the rest of the day in woodland watching the road into Sandwich. The weather was cold and bright, there had been frosts when they rose.

'Once night falls,' said Hywel, 'we will make our way down to the beach. The boat should be waiting for us; the monks at St Mary's assured me of that, but there have been royal officers watching for us up and down the coast. There was word that the Bear is in Dover. We must still have a care if we are to get away free.'

Thomas and the others nodded at the old crusader's words.

'You will need coin in France, your grace,' said Adam. 'There was no word of Herbert in St Mary's, no word at all if he had visited Canterbury after we left Northampton.'

He did not tell Thomas of the rumours of Herbert of Bosham's confrontation with the King. He did not want to worry his master, and he could hardly believe that Herbert had been so defiant to the King's face and lived to tell the tale.

'John of Salisbury is in Paris,' said Thomas. 'He will be able to find funds and plead our case with King Louis.'

'You will appeal to the King of France?' asked Hywel. 'I am more accustomed to fighting against him.'

'We need all the help that we can find. If our old friends are become enemies, perhaps old enemies can become friends?'

The Welshman said nought to that. He just remembered that Louis of France was almost as vindictive and spiteful as the English King, and just as capricious.

5.

A cold north wind gusted along the sandy beach outside Sandwich, chilling them all to the bone. The dark clouds brooded overhead; another storm was coming. The four fugitives had hidden in woodland all the previous day and long into the night before moving down to the shore. The grey slate waves topped with white foam crashed onto the sand as they waited for the boat. The sound of the breakers roared in their ears. A small boat was supposed to be waiting for them at dawn, waiting to take them to France. Thomas sat, slumped in the sand, saying little to anyone. Osbern was worried about his master, Thomas was unused to such hard travels and Osbern feared the journey ahead would be too much for him. He was also more than worried that they had no coin. It was a situation the Archbishop's manservant was not used to.

'What of the horses?' he asked, eyeing the chargers. 'They were expensive.'

'Leave Adam take them to Canterbury,' said Hywel. 'The boat cannot carry them and we have no time to sell them. It would but draw attention. The church paid for them, after all.'

'Where is the boat?' Thomas voice was weak.

'It will be here, Lord, said Adam. The monks at Reculver assured me of it.'

It had become more and more apparent as they had travelled south, that many in the kingdom supported the Archbishop in his battle with King Henry. The King was not popular with his commoner subjects, and it had been the common sort who had hidden and helped their Archbishop in his flight. Thomas had been constantly surprised by the risks these lowly men and women had taken for him.

Thomas smiled weakly. 'You have been a faithful and true servant, Adam. It pains me to send you into more danger, but needs must.'

Whilst Thomas, Hywel and Osbern would take the boat to France and a semblance of safety in exile, Adam was to return to Canterbury. He was to find Herbert of Bosham (if Herbert had not already departed for France), and make arrangements for Thomas's remaining books and possessions to be taken abroad. Adam would be acting as the archbishop's agent in Henry's lands. The King was certain to take it badly. It was clear to everyone that Thomas was preparing for a long exile.

'I will join with you in France as soon as I can, your grace,' Adam promised Thomas.

'There it is,' called Hywel, pointing out to the sea.

They all turned to look. A small fishing boat appeared in the gloom. It had only one mast and a dirty grey sail and was crewed by three men – one old, two young. A father and his sons thought Osbern. All of them were as dirty as the boat. They jumped out into the water and hauled the boat up the shallow beach. The smell of rotting fetid fish hit the four of them waiting on the sand. Thomas retched at the stink, but stood up to greet them. The ship's grey bearded master waddled up as his boys turned their boat about.

'Best you hurry up, the tide will turn soon and sea rushes out quick. We'd be left high and dry for the day,' he said with no introductions.

Thomas and the others nodded and gathered their few possessions together. They kissed Adam and bade him fare well, and prayed for God's providence to shine down on him. Then they climbed aboard the leaky fishing skiff. It was dirty, it stank, and there were only rude nets to sit upon and no cabin. The two lads in the water helped turn the boat around and into the wind. They climbed back aboard and hauled up the single square sail which billowed as it caught the gust. The boat jumped forward like a salmon leaping upriver, skirting across the waves at the speed of a charging horse. The three of them waved goodbye to Adam who was already leading their horses off towards Sandwich.

'I pray he gets away,' said Thomas.

'You do not have to worry on Adam,' said Hywel. 'It is but a short day's ride to Canterbury. He will be safe with the monks there.'

Once the boat was set on its course across the channel, the old fisherman turned to his passengers grouped at the stern.

'She may not look like much, but I shall get you to France, Archbishop. We shall be there by nightfall, God willing.'

'You know who I am?'

'Oh Aye, your grace. There are people looking for you up and down the coast.'

'And yet you still helped us?'

'The village priest told me that our Good Lord was a fisher, just like me. He said I was to name my boys Simon and Andrew in honour.' The man gave a gap toothed grin.

Thomas reflected that either the village priest had garbled up that story or the Fisher had.

'So I reckoned that it was my duty to help his vicar now,' continued the man. 'Call it the fisherman's bond. And the monks paid me well,' he added as an afterthought.

Thomas felt a wave of pure emotion at that. His struggle with the king so often felt personal, a bitter dispute between old friends who were now the worst of enemies. The townsfolk that had followed him at Northampton singing Hosanna had surprised him. All the different people who had helped their escape - from Brother Jocelyn to these rude fishers and many in between – supported him in his stand against the King. The dispute was so much bigger than Thomas and Henry's petty enmity. Indeed, mused the rebel Archbishop, if it was but an earthly matter I would have bent my head to the King, who I once loved and served. I have a duty to defend the church against a tyrant. That is what he has become. He should never have made me a priest.

'Thank you,' he told the Fisher. 'When I come into my own again; when I have my funds, I shall repay you ten times over for you kindness.'

The Fisher waved away Thomas, telling him to sit back on the nets out of the way.

The crossing to France was hideous. Huge waves tossed the little boat around, throwing the passengers about the deck. The three of them desperately clung onto ropes and nets as the fishers manned the boat. Thomas was constantly retching, his empty stomach producing only sour bile, shooting acid pain in his chest. Osbern tried to mix the powdered cumin and anise that the medics had prescribed for Thomas's colitis with wine, but he spilled most of it over the decks. The Archbishop still gratefully took the drink and supped slowly at it. The wine was supposed to be warmed, but it still soothed the fire that burned inside his stomach.

'How long till we get there,' he asked weakly.

'By tonight we shall be in France, Lord,' Osbern assured him.

***

The soldiers dragged their prisoner before FitzUrse. Adam was bloodied and beaten, his clothes torn and face bruised; his lip had been split by a gauntleted fist and his side hurt from a kicking. The Bear's men had not been kind when he was captured. The four horses had been taken, and he was bound and dragged behind his captors mounts all the way to Dover. The Bear viewed Adam of Ely with naked contempt. As far as FitzUrse was concerned, the man was a traitor who deserved only death for his perfidy to the King. However, Adam was a cleric, even if he was a mere lay brother, and FitzUrse knew he could not simply kill him out of hand. That would just add to the trouble and the King would not thank him for it. He was sick of his hands being tied in this matter.

'Where are they?' he asked.

'Where are who?' said Adam innocently, and then winced at his split lip and bruised face.

'Where is your base common Archbishop who has turned traitor on his own lord?'

'The Lord of all Hosts is my Archbishop's lord,' said Adam, with more than a hint of smugness despite his condition. 'And he is in France by now, FitzUrse, out of your reach and that of our liege King Henry.'

That merely infuriated FitzUrse.

'Do you want to become a martyr?' he growled at the cleric. 'Is that what you seek?'

'*Deus vult*; God wills it.'

The Bear knew he could not simply kill the man and that just infuriated him. Adam knew it as well. That was why he was so smug.

'Take the traitor away and lock him up,' he said, after a long pause.

Two of the local spearmen took Adam away to his cell. There were some stone built stables in the outer bailey turned over to a prison compter. The castle at Dover barely deserved the name. The original wooden stockade and ramparts had been rebuilt in stone during King Stephen's reign, but the rest of the castle was rough and rude, nearly a century old, and falling apart at the seams. The King often talked of rebuilding Dover and making it the gateway to England, but FitzUrse preferred the London palaces and taverns to the cold port and broken down keep.

'You cannot hold him for long,' said Guy. 'He is under the Archbishop's protection, and therefore the Pope's.'

'We serve the King, not the Pope or Archbishop.'

'That is all well and good, but if we harm a cleric the King will not lift a finger to aid us against the church.'

FitzUrse knew that the man was in the right, even if he did not like it. Thomas had turned the fight between two men into a battle between the crown and the church. Henry would not thank him for alienating England's priesthood any further. Still, he could make Adam of Ely suffer first before freeing him.

'You found him near Sandwich?' he said to one of the guards that had brought the cleric in.

They nodded.

'That means the Archbishop has taken a boat across the channel.'

'In this weather?' said Guy. 'If we are fortunate, he may never get to France.'

The Bear agreed. The weather had turned harsh, and a vicious wind came down off the North Sea into the channel, whipping up the waves into mountains and driving the rain in their faces. Nobody in their right mind would take to sea in these conditions, but Thomas had seemingly lost his senses.

'Still, we had best take word to the King,' the Bear decided. 'He will want to know what has happened. Let the priest go free once we have left,' he told the constable of the castle. 'You can keep the horses in payment.'

King Henry was in Winchester with the royal treasury. It was at least three days ride away from Dover. Henry had sent his own bishops to France to plead his case with the Pope before Thomas could get to him. News that the Archbishop had escaped across the channel would incense the King. The Pope would be certain to hear Thomas's testimony, if he could get to him. If the Pope heard his case, then he might just support him. That would leave Henry powerless to punish his rebel Archbishop.

'The King will probably send us to France to chase after Thomas,' mused FitzUrse. 'That is going to be yet another thankless task. Get the horses ready,' he said to Guy, 'and let us pray that Cheapside drowns in the sea and saves us from all this trouble.'

***

Thomas's stomach had started heaving almost as soon as the skiff reached open water. The grey slate waves with foaming tops perversely reminded him of tankards of ale in a London brew house, as they tossed the little boat from side to side. Thomas, Osbern and Hywel huddled together in the stern praying and puking. More than once Osbern thought they would come to disaster as the waves towered over the boat like a castle keep, crashing and breaking over them, soaking them to the skin in brine.

'Please God don't let us drown,' prayed Osbern. 'I swear I shall go to Jerusalem on pilgrimage before I die, if only you do not let me drown.'

'The Lord God will hold you to that, Rabbit,' shouted Hywel over the roar.

Osbern did not listen as prayed over and over, promising to go to Jerusalem.

The Fisher and his two boys were completely unconcerned by the foul conditions, or the overly leaky nature of their tub. Fisher barked out his orders, and the two lads nimbly sprang around the skiff, pulling this sheet or yanking the sail into the wind. Fisher steered the boat through the weather, riding the ridges of the giant waves from one to the other, like a stone skipping across a pond. As his three passengers puked and prayed, Fisher laughed and sang.

'All sailors are madmen,' said Osbern.

Hywel agreed, but Thomas shook his head.

'Are they mad? Or are they perhaps inspired?'

'They are mad, Lord,' said Osbern, firmly.

Despite the stormy weather, they were making good time. The small boat slipped across the channel, as if providence did indeed shine down upon them. Osbern tended to be more circumspect about such things, but as the storm subsided still thanked the saints and swore to keep his promise. By the time dusk began to fall, they could see lights along the French coast. The Fisher took them up to the shore, his boys jumping out into the freezing water to drag the skiff up the rough shingle beach.

Hywel grabbed his weapons and went ashore with them to make a scout of the surroundings. They did not know what sort of reception they would find in France, particularly on some lonely windswept shore, and they needed animals to travel to the Pope. His Holiness was in Sens over one hundred miles inland from the coast. They had little coin and would need help if they were to make it to Alexander. Thomas turned to the Fisher.

'I cannot thank you enough,' he said.

'Your blessing is enough, Lord.'

Thomas blessed the boat, and prayed for the Fisher to succeed in all his endeavours. He bade farewell to the man and his two boys named after the disciples, and climbed down from the skiff.

His boots sunk into the in the soft shingles up to his ankles. The slender Archbishop was broken by crossing and the days hiding out as a fugitive. He had never been particularly strong, always more suited to the cloister or treasury than action, but his health was fast fading. He knew he needed to rest but drove himself onwards. His legs felt like lead as he struggled up the shore, each step sinking deep into the sands. It was like walking through thick mud. Halfway up the beach, he fell to his knees in the shingles. Osbern rushed to his side concern writ across his face.

'I cannot walk,' Thomas whispered desperately.

'Do not worry, Lord, I shall carry you.'

The Rabbit struggled to lift his taller companion up and get him moving, and they had only managed a few more yards before the pair of them collapsed again in a tangle.

'I apologise, Lord, I do not have the strength.' Osbern climbed back to his feet.

'Do you think I would berate you for my own failings, my own weakness, Rabbit?'

The two of them looked set to weep in despair at their condition: lost and broken on a deserted French beach.

'I have found a mule,' said Hywel, finding them huddled together in the shingle. 'Come along, there is a wayside inn not so far away. The town of Gravelines is only a couple of miles. Once we get there we can rest and find out how the land lies.'

'You *found* a mule?' said Osbern

'Yes.'

'Where, perchance did you find it?'

'Tied up outside a house. So we should best get along before they notice it's missing.'

'That is theft,' Osbern pointed out.

'It is but a loan.'

Thomas agreed. He needed to contact John of Salisbury in Paris, he needed funds, and he needed to get to the Pope. All the while he needed to avoid the agents that Henry had most assuredly sent to stop him. The mule would help him to safety.

'I will repay the owners ten times over when I come into my own again,' said Thomas.

Osbern was not so sure how the owners would feel about that, but said nothing more. He helped Thomas onto the beast's back and took hold of the straw bridle. Hywel led the way as they took the road along the coast to Gravelines.

6.

The wayside inn outside Gravelines was a well managed and maintained establishment. Stout white stone walls and red clay roof tiles, not common thatch. Thomas had taken the name and disguise of a wandering mendicant. They were to call him Brother Christian, he told his companions as he dismounted and tied up the stolen mule. There was lights and noise coming from inside the inn. It was full of travellers and locals on a dark winter's night. As they entered the common room, everyone stopped talking and turned to see who the dishevelled strangers at the door were. A jolly innkeeper with white hair, beard, and a pot belly, came to greet them with a smile on his face.

'Welcome, welcome, my lords.'

'Well met, master,' said Thomas, in his cultured accent. 'We need a room for the night and food.'

The man bowed instantly. All innkeepers worth their salt can judge if a customer will be trouble or treasure. In one glance, the man had taken in the large gold ring set with an amethyst on Thomas's soft scholar's hands, his rich if soiled habit, and expensive courtly manners.

'Of course, your grace, if you will follow me this way.'

So much for the disguise, thought Osbern. Thomas would never make a mummer.

The innkeeper showed them to a small table in the corner of the main room. The other customers regarded the interlopers for a moment then all turned back to their conversations.

'Word of us will be all over France by tomorrow,' said Hywel quietly as they sat down.

'We had no choice,' said Osbern. 'None of us could have survived another night in the open.'

Thomas would not have survived another night in the open, perhaps the other two could. His stomach was raw again, tight like a drum, and he was weak from not eating. There were sores on his back and arms from the hair shirt that had become infected during the escape. Osbern had bathed them with vinegar to ease the poison, and Thomas did not complain, but the Rabbit knew his master was at the end of his strength.

'There is good fare here,' said Hywel. 'Let us at least enjoy it while we can.'

The Rabbit nodded at those words of wisdom. It was not a rude London brew house with rushes on the floor and the smell of stale beer. There was wine from Aquitaine served from barrels in the cellars, and the innkeeper's young wife kept a good table. She brought out a warm stew and freshly baked brown bread rolls, and cups of wine for their guests.

Thomas took his companions hands before breaking the bread, and they all prayed together, bowing their heads before eating as if they were in an Augustinian refectory. That just brought even more sly glances from the clientele, but Hywel and Osbern ignored the looks as they gobbled the stew and bread. Thomas ate slowly, only chewing on some of the bread and dipping it into the gravy. It was plain food that soothed the fire in his stomach. He belched.

'Your pardon,' he said, going red.

Osbern and Hywel both burst out laughing.

'Better out than in, Lord,' said the Welshman. 'When I was in Constantinople, I ate so many honey cakes that I thought I would burst but then I farted...'

A shadow fell across them and a wooden club crashed down onto the table, knocking their cups and spilling wine across the wood. Hywel reached for his sword as they all looked up. The intruder was an old woman, short and stout, with a bloodied leather apron, a thick cloak and unbound grey hair. Behind her was a younger woman similarly attired and with a small satchel at her side. Osbern noted with surprise that she was holding a small book.

'Where is my damned mule?' asked the crone, and menaced them with her club.

'I told you so,' Osbern said to Hywel.

'Taken from the house where I was delivering twins. That is theft. We could call the Lord's men out on you, or tell the sheriff.'

The midwife was raging at their impudence. One of the babies had been stillborn, and she had to deliver the last rites and comfort the heartbroken parents only to find her mule had been stolen by runaway priests.

'You gave the last rites?' said Thomas.

'As I am entitled to do, monk,' she waved her club again. 'Or would you damn the babe because our village priest could not get off his drunken arse to do his duty by the child?'

'Please to join us,' said Hywel.

The other customers were all watching the scene, and the last thing the Welsh mercenary wanted was a public confrontation in the common room of an inn. He was already in despair at their failing subterfuge. They would not get to the Pope in Sens if this carried on. The two women pulled up stools and sat, throwing back their cloaks. The young girl sat next to Osbern, saying nothing as her mistress confronted Thomas.

'You took my mule.'

'We meant no offence.'

'Stealing a mule is more than offensive.'

'I will concede that point,' said Thomas with a nod.

'Now I have had to tramp two miles after a long delivery to retrieve it, and two other women are due to birth any moment.'

'I can only apologise, Mistress, and offer you recompense. And I will admonish my servants for their failure to secure permission for the loan of the mule.' He glared at Hywel.

The Welshman winced at that. Thomas could be overly preachy when he had a bee in his bonnet, and he was as stubborn as any stolen mule. It was, after all, what had got them all into this mess in the first place. He did not point out that his master had agreed to the loan.

Mistress Jeanne sniffed at the response but seemed satisfied enough. She called for cups and poured herself some wine from the jug.

That is impudent, thought Osbern and turned to the young girl reading her book.

'You can read?' he asked.

She raised her eyes from the book and gave him a glance of pure contempt. 'Obviously, else I would not be reading. Can't you?'

'Well, yes, but not a whole book. And your mistress gave the last rites. Is that permitted?'

The Rabbit looked to his Archbishop. He was frankly shocked at the audacity of it all. The book the girl read was written in Latin and on vellum, and it must have been excruciatingly expensive. He knew just how much his master had spent on a library in Canterbury. These two women were not noble, nor were they part of any holy order. They seemed unmarried, certainly the old woman was long past mothering, and yet they were giving the sacraments. Women should not give the sacraments. It was forbidden.

The young girl frowned at him, as if it was a tired priestly argument that she had heard many times before.

'The book is part of Physica by Abbess Hildegard of Bingen; Pope Eugenius himself gave her permission to record her knowledge. We are not nuns; we are midwifes. At least my Grandmother is, and I hope to be one day.'

'I know of Abbess Hildegard,' said Thomas. 'She is a remarkable individual, and divinely inspired. John of Salisbury shares correspondence with her.'

John of Salisbury shared correspondence with everybody, thought Osbern. 'He must spend a fortune on the letters,' he said, snidely. His parochial sensibilities still pricked.

Thomas laughed. 'I fear, Mistress, that my Rabbit is somewhat upset that you can read better than he can.'

Osbern went red in the face at that.

'The book must be rare,' Thomas continued. 'And very expensive.'

'It was,' said Mistress Jeanne. 'And it is no sin or crime for us to own it. My son had it copied and brought from the Abbey. The local priest cannot read it either, even when he is sober.'

'I do not condemn you, Mistress,' said Thomas. 'The man who can read but does not has no advantage over the man, or woman, who cannot read.' He was looking directly at Osbern.

It was something Thomas had said often enough before when remonstrating with the Rabbit about his indifference to reading. Osbern recognised the rebuke and sat back in silence, glowering at the midwife and her apprentice.

'You are the rebel Archbishop? Thomas of Canterbury,' said Mistress Jeanne.

Hywel went pale at that question. Whilst they had been lax in their disguise they had still hoped they would be merely regarded as travellers by most people. There was always word of strangers travelling on the road, but news of Thomas's escape had crossed the channel with them. Everyone along the coast knew the rebel Archbishop of Canterbury was fleeing to the protection of the Pope in Sens. Everyone knew that they would have to land on the coast near Gravelines.

'Yes,' said Thomas. 'I am the Archbishop.'

He could see the subterfuge was not working and saw no need to lie to the midwife. The two women knelt before him and kissed his ring, asking for his blessing. Thomas gave it gladly, reaffirming the church's dispensation for Mistress Jeanne to deliver the sacrament to the dead babe.

Everyone in France is going to know we are here, thought Hywel, including King Henry and his agents. We cannot tarry because the Bear will be on our tails before too long.

***

Henry's fury when he was told of Thomas's escape had been a sight to behold: dogs were kicked, tables overturned, servants slapped and punched. The red-haired King was literally foaming in the mouth, raging puce in colour. He ordered FitzUrse to chase the rebel archbishop down and bring him back to England in chains.

'I want him alive,' Henry shouted as FitzUrse left. 'But you do not have to be gentle.'

Henry retired to his private chambers and took a cup of wine. His fury was swift to dissipate and replaced by a cold cunning. The King knew he was feared and not loved. He knew his obsession with royal justice and his imposition of law threatened the power of the church, but the church could not be allowed to defy the King. He did not understand Thomas's change in personality. Once he had supported Henry in this matter; once he had done everything to bring the church to heel on Henry's orders. They had loved each other like brothers. Then he became Archbishop and repudiated everything he had done as Chancellor at his first meeting with Henry two years previously.

'Your chancellor abused church income and encroached upon ecclesiastical privileges' of the Church of Canterbury,' Thomas told him.

Henry grabbed a piece of parchment from one of his clerks and glanced at it. He could see from the seal affixed to the bottom that Thomas was correct. It was Thomas's seal, after all. He was bewildered at his friend's changed attitude and behaviour.

'You do realise that you were my chancellor who did this?'

'Your chancellor did this on your orders.'

'I had no idea that you were doing any of this?'

'You gave express instructions to your chancellor…'

'You were my chancellor!'

Thomas could see he was angering the King, upsetting his dear old friend, but carried on regardless.

'I am the Archbishop of Canterbury.'

'Yes, yes, now you are the archbishop, but then you were the chancellor. You did all of this on your own initiative. Now you are Pontius Pilate washing your hands of it. Is there blood in the bowl, Cheapside?'

Thomas ignored that taunt at his common birth. He did not want this argument, but he had only done as the King had commanded – if only in general terms. He could now only do what God demanded as Archbishop. He stood in silence as his friend went red in the face at the confrontation.

'You are dismissed,' said Henry, clearly infuriated and bemused with his new archbishop. 'We shall discuss these matters again.'

'I do not understand what he has become,' said Henry to himself, as he remembered the confrontation. 'In the last two years he has grown more stubborn by the day.' Henry poured another cup of wine and sat in a cushioned chair to sup at it. 'They did not fear old King Stephen and the world was in anarchy. Now they fear me and my justice, and my realms are at peace and prosper. I am the King and only I can rule in this Kingdom.'

***

The Bear took a ship to France and landed near Gravelines in the territory of Count Matthew of Boulogne. The count was famously devious and sly, offering FitzUrse and his men horses and provisions for their pursuit, whilst secretly sending his own men out to find Thomas. The Archbishop had become a prized quarry for all the royal hunting packs.

'The count will betray us if he sees some gain,' said Guy as they rode to Gravelines.

'Not openly,' said FitzUrse. 'He would not dare defy the King, and he needs Henry's support.'

'He still cannot be trusted.'

The Bear grunted. Everyone knew the tale of Count Matthew's perfidy. The usurper Count of Boulogne had kidnapped Marie the heiress of Boulogne from a nunnery where she had taken holy orders. He had forced her to marry him and then claimed all her titles. It was another matter that the pope was set to decide upon in the council at Sens. A captive Thomas would be a valuable bargaining chip for the count at that meeting. He had sent his own agents looking for the archbishop as soon as word reached him of Thomas's flight.

That the countess was also daughter to old King Stephen of England and sister to the Bishop of Winchester gave added spice to the soup. The whole matter is a Gordian knot of treachery and ambition, FitzUrse decided. Thankfully his task was simple enough in design, if difficult in practice. Find the rebel before he got to the Pope, and before he was taken by anyone else. There was shouting up ahead that shook him from his reverie. One of the scouts came in on a borrowed bay mare.

'There is word of Cheapside and his companions,' Lord.

'Where?'

'Near Gravelines, two local women were with them in an inn three days ago.'

The Bear grinned. 'We are only three days behind? Then we have him. Take me to these women. He cannot have got far.'

The man turned his mount towards Gravelines and kicked it into a canter and the others followed suit. The Bear was more elated by the news. Capturing Thomas before he got to the Pope was all the King cared about. Henry was certain to reward him once the rebel was delivered in chains.

'How far can he have got in three days?' FitzUrse said to no one in particular. 'He has no horses, but must certainly have access to coin. He has not gone to the count, and we have men watching the great abbey and monasteries along the coast. He cannot have got far.'

It took perhaps three hours to get to Gravelines and find the midwife. The Bear had expected the woman to be cowed and submissive. He was not prepared for Mistress Jeanne.

She faced down the armed men with her club. There was a growing crowd of local villagers behind her; all were carrying an assortment of scythes, flails, hoes and there were one or two with small wood axes. The Bear and his men had their swords but none of them wore mail coats, and they were outnumbered ten to one.

'You have no authority here or over me,' said Mistress Jeanne. 'Now bugger off before you taste my stick.'

'Damn you for your insolence!'

The Bear was outraged at the peasant. She should damn well do as told. He moved his hand to the hilt of his sword.

'Move your hands away from your weapon,' shouted one of the peasant men. 'Or lose it.' He waved his scythe at FitzUrse.

'Now you listen to me,' FitzUrse began, flushed at the defiance. He was not used to peasants defying him.

'No,' said Mistress Jeanne.

She struck the Bear's horse right on the nose with her club causing the animal to rear up suddenly and bolt. FitzUrse was taken completely by surprise, his hands were not on the reins and he toppled backwards out of the saddle. He hit the floor with a crash, as his animal took flight. The ten men with the Bear all drew their weapons at his fall, but the hundred or so villagers all made a single step forward waving their farming tools and drawing bows. FitzUrse was shaken by the fall, but not senseless. He could see the situation was beyond his control. If he carried on they were all going to get lynched.

A scythe is as deadly as a spear, he thought.

'Put away your swords,' he shouted to his men as he climbed to his feet. 'One of you go and get my horse.'

Mistress Jeanne put her club up against his face once he had stood.

'There will be no more talk of taking us to the count, and you will be on your way.'

FitzUrse nodded. The woman was impudent and insolent, and if he had the time he would get more men and come back and burn down the village, slaughter the animals, and leave the whole damn lot to starve. However, the King would not thank him for getting distracted from his prey. They had enough information from the recalcitrant midwives and peasants. Thomas and his companions were on foot slowly making their way to Sens. The Archbishop was in disguise as a Cistercian friar and with two companions. The Bear assumed they were Osbern the Rabbit and the old Welsh crusader who claimed to be a prince. Thomas's priests and clerks would be next to useless in this flight, but those two were both clever and sly. One of FitzUrse's men brought the horse back to him and he mounted up. The villagers eyed him warily, still holding their weapons. FitzUrse cursed again internally that he could not teach them the lesson in rank they so richly deserved, and yanked on the reins to turn away.

'Come on,' he shouted to his men. 'We do not have time for this.'

They followed him down the muddy track towards Sens and the Pope.

7.

Thomas heard the high pitched cry of the hawk as they trudged along the muddy track. He turned to look for the bird in the sky. A young man, clean shaven and perhaps only twenty years of age, stood above them on a rise to their right silhouetted against the grey sky. He held out his hand holding a chunk of meat and whistled. The bird swooped down at his call, giant wings outstretched, and landed lightly on his arm. The man hooded the raptor with a leather cap and called for his hound. The huge beast bounded over to him from the bushes where it had been hiding.

'That is a beautiful goshawk,' said Thomas as they passed along the road. 'The master of the King's Muse would pay dearly for such a bird.'

'Keep your head down and your mouth shut, Lord,' said Hywel. 'He is coming over. You are Brother Christian, remember, not a bishop. We have too been recognised by too many people already.'

The knight was dressed for hunting not war: a green tunic that reached down to his knees, dark grey hose and muddy boots. He threw back his rich wine coloured cloak with fur trim, to reveal a long dagger at his belt. Osbern eyed the dog. It was almost as big as him.

'Greetings, brothers,' said the knight. 'Where are you bound on this day and in my lands?'

'We go to the Abbey of Clairmarais, Lord.' Hywel gestured to Thomas in his monk's robes. 'Brother Christian has an appointment there with the Abbot.'

Thomas was studying the falcon, completely ignoring the conversation. The bird was stunning, dark blue-grey with a checked breast and white collar. A small leather hood painted red kept the bird blind and calm. Thomas absently clicked his tongue, as if it were his own hawk and he in his own muse. The falcon cocked its hooded head at the clicking sound, and the knight gave the quiet Brother Christian a quizzical look. Despite the muddy wet robes and grey habit; despite the unshaven face and tired eyes, Thomas's rank was clear. He was no common Cistercian and the knight was no fool.

'You are the Archbishop of Canterbury or his double?' he said.

Thomas quickly bowed his head as Osbern spluttered.

'Think you that the Archbishop of Canterbury would travel in such a fashion, Lord?' said the Rabbit.

'When he is hiding from the mad English King who has set the Bear is on his tail?' said the man. 'Well, have away. I want no part in your business, but it may be of interest that there are other English bishops and priests in St Omer.'

'The Bear is on the Archbishop's tail?' asked Hywel innocently

'Do you know which bishops are in St Omer?' asked Thomas.

The knight smiled. 'The Bishops of London and York, your grace. I hear they have sent a deputation to King Louis in Paris, but most rest there gluttoning on the count's generosity. You are the very scandal of the age.'

The Falconer had a dry wit.

'Will you tell the Bear you saw us?' asked Thomas.

'If he asks me, but I will not seek him out.'

Nobody seeks out the Bear unless they absolutely have to, thought Osbern.

'If you take the left track about a mile down the road, by an oak tree blackened from a lightning strike,' the knight said. 'It will take you to the Abbey by a more direct route, and you can avoid the main road to St Omer. There are certain to be men on it looking for you.'

They all nodded gratefully as the knight continued.

'The way is marshy and treacherous, but if you keep to the track you will be safe. There is a ferry that will take you over to the island. The Bear will not know of the road.'

'Thank you, Sir Falconer,' Thomas said.

'You are most welcome, Brother Christian.' The knight smirked again and bade them good day, walking off with his bird and hound.

'I pray his catch is good,' said the Archbishop.

'Let us get off this road quickly,' said Hywel. 'If we take the track he told of it would be better. We draw far too much attention to ourselves.'

They hurried quickly to the fork in the path and took the road less travelled to the Abbey. They had gone a few miles down the path when three stocky ruffians stepped out of the bushes. All of them were armed with long daggers and wore leather hauberks.

'Kill the servants; take the Archbishop,' said one with a grey bonnet on his head.

Hywel drew his sword and stepped forward as Osbern pulled his knife from his belt. The Rabbit was terrified but would fight if his life depended upon it. Thomas stepped back and leaned on his staff. He was forbidden from fighting with a blade as a priest, but part of him yearned for battle again.

'I was a warrior once,' said Thomas sadly to himself.

The first two men came at Hywel from both sides with their daggers, but the wily old Welshman was too quick for them. He stepped forward and slashed one across the belly, whilst dodging the other's blade. The cut man screamed at the wound, but Osbern stabbed him in the back and silenced his cries.

Grey Bonnet went for Thomas himself as the servants fought.

'Give it up, Cheapside,' said the man. 'Count Matthew wants you.'

'Your Count Matthew can bugger off,' said Thomas, surprising himself with the coarse language. He did not like to be reminded of his common birth, but he still remembered the streets.

The man tried to grab at his robes with one hand, holding a dagger in his other, but Thomas stepped back and swung his staff at the man's head. He struck the man on the left temple, taking him completely by surprise and knocking him down senseless.

'I was a warrior once,' he said to the unconscious body.

The last man facing Hywel down had seen one man killed and his leader knocked out. He turned and ran rather than face the old crusader's blade. Osbern and the Welshman turned to their

Lord. Thomas was stood with a wide grin on his face, flushed with victory over the prone bandit.

'I rather enjoyed that,' he told them.

'I did not,' said Osbern.

'You were a hero, Rabbit,' Thomas assured him.

Hywel finished off Grey Bonnet with a cut to the throat and searched the two bodies but found nothing of interest, not even some coin.

'They were the Count of Boulogne's men,' said the Welshman, as he cleaned his blade. 'Not English or Norman at any rate.' He looked to Thomas. 'It would be best if we find the abbey soon, Lord. We need sanctuary before more of them come for us.'

'Do you think the falconer knew they were waiting?' asked Osbern.

Hywel shook his head. 'He had a sword and hound. If he had wanted to hold us he would have. I think the falconer sent us this way in good faith.'

Thomas nodded at that. He had liked the young knight.

'Come,' said Hywel. 'It cannot be far now.'

The Abbey of Clairmarais was just outside St Omer on an island in the marshes. A new establishment, but it was isolated enough that Thomas and his companions would be safe. A lay brother transported them in his punt over to the abbey. It was obvious he knew who his bedraggled passengers were, but he said nothing. They all sat in silence as he pushed them through the brown reeds.

Herbert of Bosham saw the three of them disembark from the punt and was shocked into silence. The tall, slender, fastidious archbishop was haggard and bent by the journey, his thin face drawn and the skin tight to the skull around his mouth and eyes. He was dressed in a rough dirty habit and looked next to collapse.

He looks like a walking corpse, thought Herbert, but he rushed to greet them.

'Well met, your grace, well met indeed. Come in, come in. I have news for you but not much coin, I fear.'

***

King Louis of France had been thoroughly enjoying the news of Thomas's confrontation with Henry and escape from Northampton. Louis had become morose since the victory at Toulouse. His second wife had died and his third marriage had thus far proven as barren as his first two. That his first wife Eleanor was now married to Henry and would be just as furious about the rebel Archbishop's flight to France was another fillip to the scandal. Eleanor had already given the English King more heirs than she had ever given him. Still, the woman was a shrew, far too clever for her own good, and he was lucky to be shot of her. Louis held up his hand and the English herald fell silent.

'I will consider your duke's request.'

The herald grimaced at that. Henry was king only in England as far as Louis was concerned. In France he was a duke at best. It showed which way the wind was blowing with the French King. The herald was dismissed and retreated out of the hall.

'Where is he?' Louis turned to the clutch of men at his side.

'The Abbey of Clairmarais, Highness,' said one of his gentlemen. 'I met them hawking and spoke to the Archbishop and his companions myself. I set them on a path that would avoid FitzUrse and his men.'

Thomas's old friend John of Salisbury bowed before Louis. 'I cannot thank you enough, Highness. Without your help the Archbishop would be back in England already.'

'Henri's envoy says he is Archbishop no more, but they cannot seemingly tell me who deposed him.' Louis gave a sly grin. 'They splutter and foam as if they have eaten foul fish. It is most amusing.'

John of Salisbury said nothing while Louis debated with himself. He knew the politics of the situation were precarious and the French King's mood could be changeable. While Louis was clearly overjoyed at Henry's problems, he had no wish to bring them on himself. Nor was he prepared to go to war over a recalcitrant priest. Nevertheless, the French King decided, with the pope in Sens it would be wise to grant the rebel safe passage to the pontiff.

'Let the pope decide in this matter,' he declared.

Thomas of Canterbury was, if nothing else, a troublesome character for anyone who got involved with him, Louis thought to himself. *I doubt the pope will thank me for the decision, but such are the trials and tribulations of rank.*

'I will meet with Thomas of Canterbury in Soissons,' Louis told John. 'And let us see then which way the land lies.'

John of Salisbury bowed. That was much more than he or Herbert had hoped for. Wherever FitzUrse was, he could not now strike at Thomas without bringing the French down on himself.

'Checkmate,' said John of Salisbury to himself and hurried to send word to Thomas.

***

'Charge!' FitzUrse yelled at his men. 'Kill them all!'

They all drew their swords and spurred their horses into a run, sweeping down the road in a tight wedge towards the French knights blocking their way. The Bear cursed that he only wore leathers – the Frenchmen had mail coats and open faced helms – but FitzUrse had more men.

The grinning fool who had refused them passage came straight for the Bear with his sword and hacked at his head. FitzUrse swayed back and the blow missed his face by inches. He cut at the man's sword arm, trying to disarm him, but the horses flashed past each other. FitzUrse had to yank on the reins and turn the beast to face him again. A dismounted man grabbed at his stirrups, but he kicked him away.

'Where is the fop?' He asked himself.

The other men were fighting in a tangle of men and beasts. There were horses with no riders, some men had been dismounted. At least one body was lying on the floor. FitzUrse took it all in. This fight was not going well for his leather clad men. He cursed again. The fool had needled him into this fight and now he was losing it. Then he saw him again hacking down at one of his unhorsed men. The Bear spurred his horse to attack the French knight.

The Frenchman saw him coming and grinned; he held his shield steady and kicked his own horse into a run to meet the Bear. The two of them came together in a great crash. FitzUrse hammered a blow into the man's heater, sending splinters flying and splitting the wood with a groan. At the same time, the Frenchman slashed at the Bear's head, stunning him with a blow to the helm. Both of them turned their animals to face each other again.

FitzUrse shook his head trying to clear it, and noted that the other men had stopped fighting. They were all looking down the road, behind the Bear so FitzUrse turned. There were more knights, more horses, all in shining mail coats and enclosed helms coming down the road towards the skirmish. They were bearing banners and lances. At the front of the grand procession, held aloft by an armoured knight on a white charger, was the blue and gold fleur-de-lis banner of the King of France. If FitzUrse continued this battle he would be outnumbered and overwhelmed. Henry would not thank him for starting a war; he would punish him if he then lost it the same day.

'Perhaps you can ask my liege if he will change his mind?' said the knight, breathing heavily from the fight.

The man was baiting him again, but FitzUrse knew better than to fall for his taunts. Starting a fight with King Louis himself was a fool's design.

'What is your name, sir? So that I may seek you out one day and give you a lesson in manners,' said the Bear, trying to regain some semblance of control.

The Frenchman burst out laughing.

'You are hardly a refined courtier, FitzUrse. I am Ademar de Champfleury. I look forward to your pedagogy. Will it be Socratic?'

This man knew exactly where to stick the needle. He mocked the Bear for being uncultured and coarse; it infuriated FitzUrse because he knew the man was right.

'You are nephew to the Bishop of Soissons, Chancellor of France?'

'Uncle Hugh is such a generous benefactor.'

The French royal train was getting closer, FitzUrse and his men would have to move out of the way to let it pass or cause a scene. The Bear wanted so much to finish this fight but he knew Henry would not thank him for it.

'We go back to Normandy, for now.' He told his men, and then turned back to De Champfleury.

'We shall meet again, Sir Jester.'

'I shall look forward to it, Sir Bear.' De Champfleury smiled nonchalantly.

That just infuriated the Bear more, but he pulled his men off the road away from Louis retinue and watched as the French King passed down the road to Soissons. Thomas would be waiting for him there; waiting, ready to betray his king. He kicked his horse into a trot and turned north back to Henry's lands. His band of ruffians and hedge knights followed him. King Henry was not going to be pleased.

***

King Louis of France met with Thomas at an Augustinian abbey just outside the town of Soissons. John of Salisbury joined Thomas and the others there beforehand, bringing word of his meeting with Louis in Paris. Osbern managed to scrabble together robes and vestments for the Archbishop, but there was little of the splendour Thomas usually exuded. His normally fastidious master had grown old in these last weeks. The flight from Northampton, the colitis in his stomach, the lack of food; all of it had conspired to break Thomas physically, but still his master endured. Thomas kept to the hair shirt he took on before Northampton. It scratched his skin and was louse ridden and filthy. Osbern had begged Thomas to take it off, certain it was making him ill, but the Archbishop had refused, covering the smell with perfume. It was his penance, it focussed his mind. None of the excuses Thomas gave made any sense to Osbern.

'You shall have to bear the cross in front of me, little Rabbit,' said Thomas with a wan smile. 'I have no clerks or attendants, and it would not be seemly for Herbert or John to bear.'

'The French monks should provide you with a retinue,' said Osbern. 'It is outrageous that they do not honour you, Lord.'

'They wait to see how King Louis will treat me. It is not so shocking when you think about it.'

It is the very same reason that we are here, thought Osbern. When it is all boiled down; who rules, King or God? But he said nothing to his master.

'Louis will give you support,' said John of Salisbury. 'But only so far; he will not go to war for you.'

'What did he tell you?' asked Herbert.

'He will grant us sanctuary in his realm and an allowance, but little more of value. He wants to annoy Henry, but not provoke him. If he can bring about a reconciliation he would be just as pleased, and our King just as furious.'

'The Lord reigneth, he is clothed with majesty; the Lord is clothed with strength, wherewith he hath girded himself: the world also is established, that it cannot be moved,' Thomas remarked.

Herbert and John nodded sagely at the line from the scriptures, but Hywel and Osbern both shared a look and shook their heads in despair.

King Louis was shocked when Thomas was shown into the Abbey Hall for his audience. The cultured urbane cleric, who had studied in Paris in his youth and charmed everyone as Chancellor of England, was replaced with a broken old man. Thomas was gaunt and emaciated from his trials, his hair thinning and turned grey, the beard scraggly and unkempt. Louis turned to his own Chancellor, Bishop Hughes de Champfleury, who sat beside the King on cushions. The French Chancellor was plump, jolly and red-faced. He was the very opposite of Thomas of Canterbury.

'Do you see what happens to Henri of Anjou's bishops and chancellors?' said Louis. 'Be thankful you have me as Lord and master.'

'I thank Saint Denis every day for your favour, Lord,' said de Champfleury with a grin. 'He looks a different man, does he not?'

Thomas approached the dais with little Osbern holding a cross before him. Then he knelt before the seated King Louis, shuffling forward to kiss his hand. The King stood and helped the broken Archbishop up as Thomas struggled to his feet, kissing him in turn on both cheeks.

'You have my good will and my favour, your grace' said King Louis. 'We shall give you safe passage to His Holiness in Sens. Ademar will guard your way.' The King gestured to one of the men of the court.

Thomas, Osbern, and Hywel all started with surprise when they noted the King's man. It was the knight they had met hawking over a week before; the man who had sent them on a safe path to avoid the pursuing Bear. Ademar de Champfleury gave them all a wide grin and threw a deep bow.

'It is an honour to meet you all,' he said.

'Well met again, Sir Falconer,' said Thomas. 'Well met indeed.'

8.

Pope Alexander was not a happy man, and the Archbishop of England had only made his problems worse. He met with the English bishops in the newly built choir of Sens cathedral with his own Italian cardinals and bishops in attendance. It was cold with the high vaulted roof and no fire. The red-robed conclave sat on hard benches along the walls their breaths steaming, as the English made their arguments to the bored pontiff on his dais. Alexander huddled in his robes and surveyed the deputation of King Henry's bishops and royal heralds with utter disdain. He curled his thick lips as they pontificated to their pontiff on Thomas's insults to their king and rank. They were already too late.

Alexander had met with Thomas's companion Herbert of Bosham the night before, and heard the Archbishop's version of events. He saw through the self-serving graspers before him, but, his own position was precarious and Henry of England was a powerful enemy. The Holy Roman Emperor had set up two German antipopes forcing Alexander out of Rome and into exile in France. It made the pontiff sympathetic to Thomas's plight, but cautious of making even more royal enemies.

'As you can see,' Gilbert Foliot said. 'Thomas of London is vain and stubborn and his refusal to submit to King Henry brings us all to disaster. The King's authority is paramount in all his realms. We must, after all, render unto Caesar what is his.'

'My oh my,' chuckled Alexander at the pompous rhetoric. 'You are overflowing with a surfeit of spite, Foliot.'

The Bishop of London went red in the face at that comment, flustered and unsure what to say next. He looked at his fellow Englishmen for help. Hilary, the Bishop of Chichester, stepped forward and started to monologue in overly theatrical Latin about Thomas's perfidy, his insults to the king, his unsuitability for the role of priest, his vanity, his stubborn nature, all of it poured out in cod Latin. Alexander merely grimaced at the basic errors in grammar, but the assembled conclave of cardinals and abbots fell about laughing.

'It's amatum not amavi,' called one, to roars from the red robed ranks.

Hilary of Chichester was no less flustered than Foliot as his pomposity was pricked by men with real Latin scholarship rather than his assumed superiority. He was not used to being laughed at.

'One so foolish he does not understand how foolish he is,' said another Italian bishop.

'These will wage war against the Lamb, and the Lamb will overcome them, because He is Lord of lords and King of kings, and those who are with Him are the called and chosen and faithful,' said Alexander.

He grinned at his cardinals as he saw the Bishop of Chichester struggle to translate the perfect Latin.

'*Asinus asinum fricat*,' he said, and then translated into French for the bemused Hilary. 'The jackass rubs the jackass, no?'

The mission was not going well for the English deputation. They knew that King Henry would not be pleased if their mission failed but Alexander supported the rebel Thomas. Each approach they made to the Pope merely seemed to drive a wedge further between them.

'Sycophants to their English sovereign,' said the Bishop of Arles.

You are no less a sycophant to yours, thought Alexander, but said nothing. He needed the French priesthood more than he needed the English bishops. At least Louis of France had some piety. Henry of Anjou was an untamed beast whose line was spawned by the devil.

Roger of Pont L'Évêque, the Archbishop of York, fared little better with the papal conclave when he stepped forward, but he was wise enough to hedge his accusations and condemnations. Roger had seen Herbert of Bosham in the court, and realised that Thomas's agent had got to the Pope first and dripped poison into his ear about the King. Once he had finished with his soliloquy, the Pope waved for them to be dismissed. The

English party retreated from the cathedral, and gathered at the wayside inn they had made their base. The Bear was waiting for them with his band of ruffians.

'We could take him on the road,' said FitzUrse to Roger. 'There is word that the rebel will arrive tomorrow. I can attack the party, kill them, and that would be an end to it.'

Roger shook his head at the Bear.

'That would bring down all of Louis vassals on us, the Pope would excommunicate you and probably us, and the King would tear out our hearts with his bare hands. Anyway, there is word that he travels with knights and priests in his train. Since he saw Louis in Soissons they have heaped coin and attendants and honours upon him. You would not get to him now.'

FitzUrse grunted. The Bear's claws had been pulled.

'I saw Bosham at the court,' Roger continued. 'I fear the Pope will judge in Thomas's favour.'

'The King will be furious,' said Hilary of Chichester.

Gilbert Foliot and some of the others nodded forlornly at that. None of them wanted to face Henry in failure. One of them poked Hilary of Chichester.

'No more of your cod Latin. It makes us look like amateurs to these Italians and Frenchmen.'

'I do not understand why they were laughing.'

Roger shook his head in despair. It was little wonder that Thomas was able to outwit such fools at every step. Only he had the wisdom to defeat the rebel.

'What do we do now?' Hilary asked him.

'Now we pack our bags and go back to the King, and pray he does not take it against us that Thomas has escaped his justice. Now the Pope must decide.'

***

Thomas repeated the words that his friend Arnuld of Lisieux had sent to him: 'In King Henry, we are dealing with a man whose cunning frightens distant nations,' he said. 'His power overawes his neighbours, even Louis of France, and his stubbornness terrifies his own subjects. We all know his rage, but he is clever cold and calculating when the need arises. He is ever dangerous.'

'The Pope will be kind to you,' said Herbert. 'Henry's embassy has made things worse. They insulted Alexander and made a mockery of the court. They turned the cardinals against the King.'

Osbern gave a sly smile at that. Word of the cardinals openly laughing and mocking the English bishops had given their spirits a distinct lift after the flight from England.

'Thank God for Hilary's ignorance and Roger's arrogance,' said Thomas. 'They have always been our greatest gifts of providence in this matter. If Henry had competent sycophants we would be in trouble.' The irony that he had once been the King's competent sycophant was not lost on Thomas.

'We would be in even more trouble, Lord,' said Osbern.

There had been word that the King would make their families suffer if Thomas did not submit. The King had threatened to break anyone associated with the rebel Archbishop. Hywel's welsh clan were out of Henry's reach, and the Welsh prince cared little for them anyway, but the Rabbit's father was in Dover. He worried about his family left to Henry's mercy. Thomas had assured him that Canterbury would take care of its own but Osbern was unsure of that. Even Thomas's sister would be under threat and she was in Holy Orders as a nun, what hope was there for a rude wine merchant?

The exiles' condition was much improved since the meeting with King Louis in Soissons. The French had provided new robes, coin, and lodged them well. A retinue of knights and priests had followed them to Sens. The three original fugitives had been joined by the most loyal of Thomas's followers from Canterbury. Alexander Llewellyn had turned up with some smuggled coin and books, and some twenty other attendants including Adam of Ely were lodged around Sens. Adam had taken the first boat to France after his release from Dover. He had given an account of his trials, gleefully mocking the Bear's impotence.

The support of his usual retinue and fastidious dress sense gave some gravitas to Thomas's party that belied their rebel status. He made Osbern re-shave his tonsure and chin, and had eaten egg possets that settled his stomach and gave him back strength after the journey. All of their spirits had cheered.

They waited for Henry's bishops to leave for England before making their final entrance in to the cathedral town. Thomas had been lent a white stallion by the Bishop Miles of Therouanne to make his arrival in Sens. The French Kingdom had become a sanctuary for exiled priests, the Bishop had told him. And he had never warmed to the Angevin.

Osbern watched his master climb into the saddle with Alexander Llewellyn in front carrying the Archbishop's cross. A procession of chanting monks followed behind, whilst an escort of armed men under the command of Ademar de Champfleury watched in case the Bear or his men tried to stop Thomas meeting the Pope.

'It is less than two months since we did the same in Northampton, but in that time the world has completely changed. I do not like change,' Osbern muttered to himself. 'It always leads to trouble.'

Hywel looked at him 'Thomas is a catalyst for trouble, friend. Have you not yet realised that. He adores the confusion and the drama. He would be bored without it and when he is bored he becomes overly sanguine.'

Osbern nodded at the Welshman's words. John of Salisbury had one said something similar.

'It is all or nothing with Thomas, he knows no other way,' he said.

Thomas's entrance into the cathedral was better received by the conclave of cardinals and Pope. They all leaned forward as the rebel Archbishop came into the choir to hear his words. The events in Northampton and the fight to France was the talk of every household, both high and lowborn. Thomas of Canterbury stood before the Conclave and bowed his head, waiting for the Pope to give him leave to speak. After a moment, Alexander gestured for him to begin.

Thomas had practiced the speech in his mind the night before, but now the moment had come he was riddled with nerves. Everything depended on the Pope's decision. He gave an honest account of himself and his actions. Quietly at first, stilted, but his soft voice grew in strength as he listed the complaints and arguments between him and Henry. He was honest even when it came to his own failings.

'I lament that the liberty of the church was gradually destroyed and its rights dispersed to the avarice of princes,' said Thomas to the assembled conclave. 'I believe that the coming assault must be resisted.' He bowed his head, as if in supplication, as his words echoed through the vaulted ceiling.

The cardinals and bishops were all grave and intent on his words. They could see the threat to their own position should the English King succeed in corrupting the English Church. Christendom would become the plaything of princes. Who rules, God or King?

'It is Henry's advisors who are at fault in this matter,' Thomas continued. 'They mislead him into becoming a tyrant. I was left with no choice but to resist in the name of the mother church.'

John of Salisbury had advised him to blame the King's advisors, even though both of them knew this conflict was all of Henry and Thomas's own stubborn making. It gave the King a way to save his face, and Henry would need that if he was to make peace. Thomas hammered the point home. It was the advisors and faithless bishops that were at fault.

Unlike Hilary of Chichester the day before, Thomas's grammar and diction was perfect. The red robed cardinals were nodding along sagely at his words.

The Archbishop of York had set FitzUrse to watch the conclave and report back to the King on the result. The Bear could see which way the wind was blowing. The rebel Archbishop had been welcomed with kisses and his honour and body restored by the French. FitzUrse turned and stalked out of the cathedral choir. He did not need to hear anymore of the audience. The Pope had already decided, and King Henry would not be pleased.

Ademar watched him go and had some of his men follow. The Bear was a dangerous foe, and King Louis did not want any unfortunate accidents to happen to Thomas. The Archbishop of

Canterbury was a thorn in the Angevin's side that Louis meant to twist and stick until Henry bled.

'I am unsurprised by the actions of the untamed beasts at court that deceive the King.' Thomas was summing up his argument. 'But I am stunned by the perfidy of the bishops and priests who have sided with such vacuous courtiers. None of this should be imputed to the King, for he is the servant of their conspiracy not its author.'

Thomas fell to his knees as he finished his speech, and begged the Pope and conclave for forgiveness for his sins with genuine tears in his eyes. It had been a perfect piece of theatre for the assembled audience, and the Archbishop had played his part perfectly. Pope Alexander got out of his throne and raised Thomas to his feet, kissing both his cheeks.

'You are welcome, Brother. We shall discuss the matter further,' the Pope assured him.

The remaining English contingent, including the Bear, set out for London later that afternoon in low spirits. At the same time, Thomas met with the Pope secretly in a small chamber at the cathedral. Only two of his clerks newly arrived from Canterbury were in attendance, as Thomas confessed everything to Alexander.

'It is all my own wretched fault,' he ruefully admitted to the Pope. 'I did not want the honour of this rank; the King forced me to take it. Nevertheless, it would be an evil precedent for me to renounce the jurisdiction of the Archbishop in matters clerical without your Holiness' favour. I recognise my appointment was far from canonical or seemly and hence I resign into your hands my Archbishopric.'

Thomas tugged the heavy archbishop's ring off his finger and offered it up to the Pope with a zealot's fire in his eyes. Alexander viewed it with horror. That was the last thing he wanted. He knew that some of his cardinals, fearful of Henry's might, would want him to take the ring and banish Thomas to settle the matter, but the Pope refused it.

'Now at last, Brother, it is plain to us what zeal you have shown, and still show, for the house of the Lord God,' said

Alexander. 'As you are a loyal son to the mother church, so the church will always be loyal to you.'

The pope would not accept his resignation and confirmed him in all his rights and actions. That single act meant that Thomas had trumped King Henry. The English Church would not bow to the English King. However, there was no safe way for Thomas to return to his seat in Canterbury. Henry would see him killed, papal protection or not. Instead, Thomas would have to go into exile until peace could be made between the recalcitrant monarch and his rebel archbishop. A place would be made for him and his closest companions and attendants at the Abbey of Pontigny.

Thomas could hardly believe it. He had won.

***

'It is nothing but a building site,' said Herbert of Bosham. 'Some victory if this is our prize.'

They could all see The Abbey as they crossed the rickety wooden bridge. It was, as Herbert pointed out, still under construction. Wooden scaffolding teemed with men hammering and hauling. Great limestone blocks were being lifted into place by wooden A frame cranes, and everywhere there was rubble and dross. The Cistercian brothers lived in austere conditions that horrified Herbert. Thomas was more circumspect.

'We have safety and solitude. I am quite looking forward to it.'

Herbert did not respond as they rode up to their new home. He planned on going to Auxerre as soon as possible to find some good food and wine, and not plain Cistercian fare that made him fart. Word had been already sent ahead by Champfleury that he would bring the Archbishop to sanctuary. John of Salisbury had told Thomas that the abbot was a good man. Both Osbern and Herbert both noted that John preferred to stay in his lodgings in Paris rather than follow Thomas to Pontigny.

'Dull, dull, dull,' John had told Osbern. 'I would die of boredom if I had to stay there. My books are here and I am more use to the cause close to King Louis.'

The Rabbit had followed his master into exile and would stay with him at the abbey. He would be happy enough living in solitude, but Hywel had gone home to the Welsh to settle a family matter. With both Thomas and King Henry stubborn as mules, all of them realised that their exile was going to be a long one. Allusions to the Israelites in Egypt or the Holy Family's flight from Herod had been bandied about by the party, but Osbern just wanted to rest. He planned on sleeping for a week now they had finally stopped running.

'I shall go to the Holy Land soon,' said Sir Ademar. 'Your Welshman had some tales of Jerusalem.'

Osbern remembered the promise he had made on the stormy crossing from England.

'So shall I one day,' he said. 'But not till this matter is settled. I am sworn to the Archbishop.'

The abbot was waiting for them at the porch to the great building as they arrived. A group of white robed brothers with him; all were smiling and happy to see their famous guest. Abbot Guichard was a tall grey-haired man, thin-faced with an aquiline nose that dominated his features. Thomas dismounted and bowed before his host.

'You are most welcome, your grace,' said the Abbot. 'I am afraid it is a bit rough and ready, but cells have been found for you and your companions.'

'Cells just like a prison,' muttered Herbert.

That is rich thought Osbern. You have egged my master on in this matter, always urging the most extreme course of action, and now you complain about the consequences. He hoped that Herbert would take off to Auxerre sooner rather than later, and leave them in peace from his whining.

'It is going to be a long time in exile,' said the Rabbit.

Historical Note.

The confrontation in Northampton in 1164 set off a train of events that would culminate in Thomas Becket's murder in 1170. Henry II's determination to break Thomas at the trial left the Archbishop with few options. He could have submitted, as many of the assembled bishops hoped and expected, and would have probably been sent into exile and deprived of his clerical rank. Instead Thomas took the most radical path left open to him. He confronted Henry's authority and stunned the court.

The escape was recorded in excruciating detail during Thomas's lifetime, before the hagiographers warped the record, and the rebel archbishop's words and actions were discussed throughout the royal courts of Europe. Where possible (and it is more possible with Thomas than any other 12th Century figure), I have used the words spoken by individuals as recorded in the histories of the day. Thomas really was the scandal of the age.

Henry II was completely thrown by Becket at Northampton. Despite their close association the King could not conceive that Thomas would dare defy him in such a manner. The King's refusal to face Becket in person demonstrated just how terrified he was of the spiritual power of excommunication. It is something that modern readers often find difficult to understand. The reality of heaven and hell was unquestioned to the medieval mind, and the church's power to sever a man from grace feared by everyone. Henry was left desperate to capture the fugitive archbishop, without alienating the English Church's generally supportive leadership. It was a difficult balancing act that he only managed because of Becket's personal animosity to some of the most important bishops. Henry also did not want to antagonise Louis of France into openly supporting Becket. Once Thomas had escalated the situation, Henry was left with little choice but to play catch up. It was, without question, the first real time the Angevin monarch saw his will challenged. He did not react well, Henry was bewildered by the change in his friend, but as the dispute dragged on made genuine attempts to reconcile with Thomas. However their personalities were such that the two men, archbishop and king, would find it utterly impossible to compromise their positions.

Louis of France supported Becket in his struggle with Henry as much through spite as anything else. The papal schism had seen Louis support Pope Alexander over the German anti-pope, and his undeniable piety gave him authority in the dispute between Thomas and Henry. However, Louis' support for Becket only went so far. He allowed Thomas sanctuary in his realm but urged reconciliation with Henry. It was an urging that Thomas steadfastly and frustratingly refused. Louis would discover, as Henry had before him, that Thomas was stubborn beyond most normal men. The recalcitrant Archbishop's exile would stretch into six long years with no compromise between him and Henry.

The issue of the hair shirt and when Thomas started wearing it is contentious. Most of the chroniclers and hagiographies have Thomas wearing the shirt from his consecration as Archbishop onwards. However, Frank Barlow asserts that it is not until later, most probably during his exile in Pontigny, that he started wearing it. That is today generally accepted by most modern historians. Certainly Thomas's first few months in exile at the abbey were marked by heavy fasting and scourging that made his health worse, and concerned Thomas's companions so much that the Abbot had to intervene. Perhaps the only person other than Thomas who would have known the truth was Osbern. For the purposes of the story, I have kept to the chroniclers account rather than the modern interpretation.

Pope Alexander III had succeeded the only English Pope (Adrian IV) in 1159, but his accession to the papal see was disputed. Whilst most of the cardinals supported Alexander, a small section supported the anti-pope Victor IV. The German Holy Roman Emperor Fredrick Barbarossa, with his own ambitions and lands in Italy, wanted to control the papacy through Victor and initially had the support of most of the crowned heads of Europe. The conflict between church and state was much wider than the arguments between Thomas and Henry. As Fredrick Barbarossa's power alienated and terrified other states, Alexander III slowly gained support among Europe's Kings and Princes. This was strengthened after Geza II of Hungary recognised his authority in 1161, and with support from Louis of France. By 1164, Alexander was in a much stronger position to deal with Thomas's rebellion against Henry. The first anti-pope had died and whilst Barbarossa had immediately installed another one, support for Alexander was growing. Only a year later he would be secure enough to leave his French exile and return (if only for a short time) to Rome, although the conflict with Barbarossa would continue until Fredrick's defeat at the Battle of Legnano in1176.

Ademar de Champfleury is partially fictional. Certainly the incident and conversation with the young knight hawking was recorded at the time. Thomas was incapable of staying disguised and his love of falconry was well known. I merely gave that individual a name and personality beyond his conversation with the Archbishop, and tied him into the real French Chancellor.

Midwives in the medieval period had a difficult relationship with both the church and the male dominated medical profession. However, they fulfilled a vital role that put most churchmen in a quandary. The right for midwives to give the sacrament of baptism or last rites when infant mortality and death in childbirth was at a hideous rate was impossible to suppress. However, it certainly challenged the patriarchal church society. Ultimately it was believed that the Holy Spirit actually gave the sacraments in an emergency, rather than the person delivering them. At the Lateran Council in 1215 the long held tradition was confirmed, after initially being formally established by Pope Urban II (rather more famous for starting the Crusades in 1095). Even so, the church was merely recognising a long held tradition with midwives rather than inventing it.

All of these primary sources for Becket are available digitised and transcribed through Early English Books Online, which you can access for free at your local library or educational institution. John Guy, Frank Barlow, and Anne Duggan's biographies are all essential reading for the early period of

Becket's life, whilst William Urry's investigation into his last month is an outstanding piece of micro-history.

As always I must give my wholehearted thanks to James Smallwood and Nigel Williams for advice and inspiration, and everyone at Sharpe Books for their support. All the mistakes are mine!

Thomas will return in Becket: Martyr.

Jemahl Evans is the author of the critically acclaimed Blandford Candy series set during the Seventeenth Century and available from Sharpe Books. You can follow Jemahl on twitter @Temulkar

Becket: Martyr

Jemahl Evans

1

Dover, Advent Sunday November 1170.

Osbern the Rabbit sniffed at the air. Dover stunk, it had always stunk. He was glad to be home. Osbern had been born in Dover, but wished he could have returned under better circumstances.

'If wishes were fishes all the world would be fed,' he said to himself.

The Rabbit was of middling age, slight and small. His short sight gave him an odd squint, and nobody would claim he was a great thinker. As a youth, by fluke and fortune, he had found himself in the household of Thomas of London, the Chancellor of England. When Thomas had been elevated to Archbishop by King Henry, Osbern had followed him to Canterbury. The King and Archbishop, once the best of friends, had divided in bitter acrimony, and Osbern had fled with his master to France. He had served him for six years in exile. Now, by Thomas's command, he was home, but he rather suspected there was to be no joyous welcome.

Osbern paused at the carved oaken doors to settle his nerves. The Church of St Peter in Dover – on the north side of the marketplace – was only yards from the quays and was his first stop. It was the centre of the town's community. Built of local flint with stone dressings, the building dominated the square. A curfew bell in the tower rang out the daily life in Dover, and the Rabbit had grown up with its peals. Osbern had disembarked from the French ship only an hour before, and found his quarry in the church with surprising ease. None of the townsfolk had recognised him as the Archbishop's servant. He had been away far too long. It was a clear sign of God's favour in his task, Osbern decided. He was going to need all of the divine favour that he could get. He whispered a prayer to Saint Peter, promising not to bear false witness, pushed the church door open quietly and stepped inside.

St Peter's was filled to the rafters with congregation and clerics. The foul Archbishop of York stood at the high altar delivering his sermon to the masses. Here was Osbern's first mark; here was Osbern's moment.

'Archbishop!' He called out.

The words echoed around the vaulted rafters loud enough for all to hear. The congregation turned to see who disturbed the service: a shabby, short, sandy haired serving man. Some nudged each other and whispered – this was an unexpected spectacle for the gossipmongers.

Thomas had drilled the words he would say next into Osbern, making the servant repeat them time and time again until he was satisfied, but Osbern was still worried he would forget his speech at the critical moment. There was a hush as he walked up the central aisle. Communion was already finished and at the dais the lean Archbishop of York was chanting the end of the service, but every eye was on the Rabbit as he approached the altar.

'*May we receive, O Lord, thy mercy in the midst of thy temple, that we may prepare with due honour for the approaching feast of our redemption. Through our Lord Jesus Christ, thy son who lives and reigns with thee in the unity of the Holy Spirit...*'

Roger of Pont Eveque, The Archbishop of York, was a tall man, lean and muscular under his vestments. He was in his fifties, with dark hair only just turning grey at the temple. He prided himself on keeping trim, and still rode to the hunt regularly. His black eyes fixed on the intruder stalking up the aisle. He stuttered to silence when he noted the Rabbit holding a piece of parchment, and beckoned Osbern forward. The Archbishop of York recognised Thomas's servant even if nobody else did. The congregation watched on in a hushed fascination. A common servant daring to approach the Archbishop in his service was unheard of, particularly when it was such a dirty, scruffy commoner as Osbern.

The Rabbit could feel everyone's eyes on him as he walked steadily towards the waiting prelate.

'Why, it is Osbern the Rabbit,' came a voice from the audience. 'I have not seen him these past years.'

'Who?'

'Thomas of Canterbury's man.'

Those whispers rippled around the congregation. The Archbishop leaned forward on the wooden altar, gesturing to the parchment that Osbern clutched in his hands. The Rabbit ignored him and instead recited Thomas's words to the Archbishop of York.

'The Pope sends you by me such a greeting as you deserve, Lord. Here, read this letter which His Holiness hath sent you.' Osbern now handed the parchment over to the stunned archbishop who took it in silence. 'You are cut off from all appeal and from your sacred calling.'

Roger of Pont Eveque fell back, shocked into silence. One of his attendant clerics caught him as Osbern turned to run. There was uproar in the church. The Archbishop of York had been excommunicated, expelled from the church of God, damned by the Pope in Rome. This could only be Thomas of Canterbury's doing, a studied insult; the exile had sent a commoner to deliver the devastating blow. The Archbishop of York's servants made to hold the Rabbit.

'Grab him,' shouted one, pointing to Osbern.

'Oh bugger,' said the Rabbit.

Osbern took to his heels and ran down the aisle, boots slapping on the cold stone, his rabbit moniker had been earned by the dash as much as his stature. None of the congregation moved among the shouting to stop his escape, and he charged out of the church at full pelt into the market square. His mission was not yet finished. Osbern was breathing heavily and sweating in the cold air outside, but there were other letters of excommunication to deliver. He ran hard and fast, he did not have much time. Soon the whole of Dover would be roused against him.

Osbern had been Thomas of Canterbury's faithful servant for over ten years, and Thomas had chosen his messenger well. Osbern was honest, if sometimes pompous of his position with the other servants, and loyal to Thomas above all men. He was a commoner and a layman and as such, would be the last person suspected of carrying letters of excommunication from the Pope in Rome via the exiled Archbishop of Canterbury. It was a studied insult to Thomas's clerical enemies to send a common born English servant with the Papal interdict.

'I am getting too old for this,' he said to himself.

Osbern ran on to the small chapel on the other side of the marketplace first; his next victim was inside also delivering a sermon. News of Roger's damning predicament and the uproar in St Peter's had sent the port town into a tumult. Crowds were gathering on the streets shouting, some for Thomas some against. Sailors had climbed to the mast tops of their boats to see the spectacle, cheering at the Rabbit as he ran. Osbern caught fat Bishop Gilbert Foliot of London outside the chapel just after his service had finished. Foliot was completely oblivious to the confrontation across the square, and confused by the shouting crowds. The Bishop struggling with his fat frame mounted a horse, and made ready for his return to the castle that glowered over the town. There was a rich feast waiting and Foliot was looking forward to it. None of his staff or any of the watching monks stopped Osbern as he pushed past and thrust the Pope's letter into the Bishop's hand.

'Take this, my lord. It expels you from the community of the church!'

Gilbert Foliot, the fat Bishop of London, looked down at the parchment in shock. He saw the seal of St Peter affixed to it. Foliot was damned, cut off from all sacraments, destined to burn in hell for eternity. Gilbert almost collapsed from his horse and had to be kept in his seat by servants. It was a devastating and unexpected sentence.

A dolorous stroke, thought the Rabbit as he ran on. Osbern was blowing now, and there were armed men coming out onto the streets beating the crowd into submission. St Peter's curfew bell was ringing and the marketplace clearing of bystanders. It was at this point Osbern realised he might be in serious trouble if he was caught. Yet, he kept grimly on with his task, running on to St James where he did and said the same to the understandably annoyed Bishop of Salisbury.

In less than an hour since arriving in Dover, Osbern had delivered his three letters: three of the most eminent churchmen in England had been cast out of the faith; the town was in uproar, and there were armed men in the streets out for his blood. This was the most difficult part of his task – escape with his own head secure – but he had been born in Dover and knew the streets and alleys below the castle better than his pursuers. Osbern cut down a side alley, and headed to the one place he would be almost certain of sanctuary – his father.

'I hope the miserable old sod shows a welcome.'

Two streets down and up the alleyway he had known as a child. He prayed his father still lived, prayed he still lived here, and prayed that Pater Rabbit had forgiven his son all the trouble he had caused.

'Particularly as I am bringing him some more.'

Trouble is a currency rarely in demand. The house looked smaller, shabbier, a sign of his father's fallen status. Osbern hammered on the door to his old home, near shaking it off the leather hinges. He could hear men shouting nearby; they were close to the alleyway. The door opened and his old father peered out at the interloper.

Richard of Dover was like a shrunken withered version of his son, the same slight stature and buck teeth. He recognised his son despite his poor eyesight and ten years of absence. His boy Osbern, exiled with the troublesome Archbishop of Canterbury, was a man of such impenetrable stupidity that giving him into service in the church had been the only place for him. How Osbern had managed to rise in the Archbishop's service was beyond the old man, but he wanted no more trouble because of it.

'No thank you,' he said, and slammed the door in Osbern's face.

'Pa!' Osbern hammered at the door again. 'Pa!'

The shouting pursuit was getting closer; there were men at the corner of the alley. Osbern began to panic, his heart pumping. If they caught him, he was dead. The door opened once more and his father's little hand reached out, grabbed Osbern by the collar and yanked him inside the crumbling building. The door slammed shut behind him, and Osbern breathed a sigh of relief. He was home.

The broken down building was just as Osbern remembered from his youth: one dark room with a bed in the eaves. In bygone days the warehouse next door had been filled with imported wine that Richard of Dover brought from Gascony, but his industry had been strangled when the arguments between King and Archbishop began. Now he mended fishing nets for his keep. Osbern took it all in: a pair of stools and table; nets and twines, bone needles and hooks, all of his father's tools and trade. There was a single rush candle and glowing embers in the fireplace that cast a pitiful orange light. His father could at least afford some coal. Osbern studied the old man: he was more wizened, more crooked, whiter hair.

'You would bring disaster on my house,' his father grunted. 'What have you done this time?'

Osbern opened his arms wide. He was unsure what to do next. There had been no instruction beyond deliver his messages, escape and wait for the return of his master.

'I still serve the Archbishop of Canterbury, Pa.'

You serve a crooked-nosed knave, oh witless spawn of my loins. Your Archbishop is a hedge-born coxcomb grown too proud for his station, and you are a fool. Why are you here? They will put out my eyes for harbouring you.'

'I am exiled no longer, Pa. There is peace between the King and Archbishop. I saw them kiss in friendship in front of all. It happened not one month past. The Archbishop is coming home.'

'Peace you say? You dung-headed fustilugs. Why are there armed men hunting you then? I should have let them take you, but your ma would not have forgiven me.'

Mother Rabbit was some twenty years deceased.

A great hammering started up on the door to the hovel. The hunters had run their quarry to ground. Osbern looked at his father in desperation. The old man could easily hand him over to them, wash his hands like Pontius Pilate as they dragged him away. Richard sighed.

'Your Ma would never forgive me. Get up in the eaves.'

Osbern clambered up to the bedding high in the roof pulled himself onto the dirty straw mattress and pulled nets and blankets over himself. He peered out of the crack as his father went to answer the door. There were men in metal armour and bearing weapons. Osbern's actions that day had sent the town into uproar, and once he had been recognised it was not long before warriors were sent to his father's house. Richard gulped at the sight of the mail clad men.

'Where is he?' asked a man at arms.

'Who?'

'Your son, Richard, where is your traitor son?'

'In exile with Thomas, his traitor master. You all know that.'

The armed men pushed past Richard, silencing him with their weapons as they filled the small room. Osbern could feel his heart hammering, so loud he could swear they would hear it and discover him in his hiding place, but not one of them looked up to the rafters.

'He is not here?' The man at arms was persistent.

'My son is in France, and I disowned him long ago.'

'Your son has returned, Richard. If he comes here, bring him to the castle. There will be a reward in it for you from the De Brocs.'

Osbern gulped under the covers. His father was ever the parsimonious soul; he would only require a few silver pennies not thirty to expose his son, and the De Brocs were a wild clan that had exploited the Archbishop's absence for profits. They had seized Saltwood Castle nearby, raided Canterbury Cathedral's lands, stolen the priests' goods and sworn enmity to the Archbishop. They would not hesitate to slay Osbern.

'You can be sure that I will, if I see him,' said Osbern's father. 'You can be sure that I will.'

Osbern was certain his father gave a sly glance at his hiding place when he uttered those words. The sooner his master came home to England the better, thought the hiding servant. Then all this would be settled - and he would at least be protected from the King and his supporters. Osbern had been puffed up with pride when Thomas had first chosen him for this task. He had leaped at the chance to come home after so many years away. Now, he wished he had stayed supping ale in the kitchens and avoiding any hard work.

The men-at-arms tramped noisily out of the hovel, just as they had tramped noisily in, with Richard following on behind. Osbern heard them admonish his father again at the doorstep, and heard his father promise to betray him at the first opportunity. Then the door slammed shut. There was a pause and Father Rabbit came back to the room.

'Come down then, my son.'

Osbern peeked out from his hiding place. Only his old father was in the room. He breathed a sigh of relief, and whispered a prayer of thanks.

'What have you done?' asked his father.

Osbern told Richard all he knew: that the Archbishop had made peace with the King (Osbern was there, Osbern had seen it), but Thomas's enemies in England still sought only to do him harm. His Holiness the Pope had agreed and the interdict against Thomas's enemies had been sent in good faith.

'Good faith?' said his father. 'You still have problems when things involve thinking, I see. There are armed men all over the town seeking you out to kill you. That is not peace in good faith. Get out of Dover, get yourself to Canterbury, and pray that your foolborn master comes soon to rescue you. That is your only hope for survival.'

They were wise words, and Osbern knew his father was in the right, but he also knew his master was coming home. He would not be a fugitive for long.

'He is coming home, Pa. Thomas is coming home. Tomorrow or the day after at the latest. They were waiting for a boat when I left. He is finally coming home.'

'Then God help us all,' said Richard to his son. 'For the De Brocs will not stand for it.'

2

Archbishop Thomas of Canterbury shivered as an icy blast of wind swept along the cobbled jetty. Wissant was a small village near Calais, boats for England left regularly to make the short voyage to Dover. Soon he would make the crossing back home. His tall slender frame was crooked and bent; his once dark hair almost completely white, and the smooth royal courtier's face was now lined and creased with worries and age. He had grown old in his long years of exile. When he saw his face in a glass he could hardly recognise the wizened crone that stared back. Thomas pulled his cloak close as he stared across the slate grey waves to England. The cold reached into his bones. Homeward bound after six years in exile; a tenuous peace brokered between the Archbishop and King by the Pope and King of France.

'Henry will not keep the peace,' Thomas muttered to himself. 'His word is worthless. Even if he wanted to the others would poison him against me.'

'Your Grace! Your Grace! There is an English ship coming!'

Thomas's young clerk, Gunter of Winchester, came running down the cobbles. 'Master Herbert has gone to speak with the master.' Herbert of Bosham was one of Thomas's closest advisors. 'There will be news from home.'

Thomas smiled at the lad and turned back to his distant destination. On a clear day one could see the English coast in the distance, white cliffs rising out from the slate grey waves, but not today. He wondered what the reception would be when he finally returned. He had too many enemies, and knew could not trust in Henry's capricious nature. It was why he had sent Osbern on ahead. Thomas meant to bring the conflict to a head, to lance the boil, whatever the consequences.

'I have been too proud of my station,' he said to himself. 'I confess it. I have been vain and stubborn, and betrayed my calling at Clarendon. Perhaps I could have bowed before him. Perhaps I could have bent my knee. He is the King, after all, but it was not my vanity or pride that stopped me. I loved him, he was my brother, but Henry is not my master. He cannot be. I am servant only to Jesus Christ our Lord and no mortal monarch may bind my soul nor turn me away from my duty again. I told him not to make me Archbishop. I warned him all those years ago.' There were steps on the cobbles behind him. 'I would have been happy to stay but his chancellor and friend.' The last came out in a whisper.

'Come this way, make sure to doff when you meet the Archbishop.'

Thomas could hear Herbert warning the ship's master as they approached. Herbert of Bosham was one of Thomas's most trusted advisors. He had been in exile with the Archbishop and had endured the same hardships (even if he was constantly complaining about them and making sure to have luxuries delivered to the austere abbey they were stuck in to rot). Herbert was well versed in the gospels and theological arguments, and he had studied with John of Salisbury in Paris. He had stiffened Thomas's resolve in the fight with King Henry and always urged the most radical of actions in defence of the church's rights. Thomas's manservant Osbern and Herbert despised each other, the Rabbit considered Bosham to be nought but a zealot, but the Archbishop relied upon them both and Osbern was an ill educated commoner not a clever cleric. Herbert brought the ship's master before Thomas.

'What is your name, master?' asked Thomas, smiling at the dirty fellow.

The man doffed his bonnet and bowed. 'My name is Jakes, Lord. Master of this tub. We run wool from home and take back wines.'

'What is the news from Dover?'

'Fortune does not smile upon you, Lord. There are knights in the port, vassals of the De Brocs, ready to set about you when you make land.'

Thomas had expected that news, but young Gunter went pale. The boy had hoped that the peace between King and Archbishop would hold, but Thomas seemed determined to antagonise the King whilst Henry was sly and duplicitous and certain to break any promise he made. In many ways the two men, archbishop and monarch, were alike as two peas in the pod.

'You have made everyone furious,' Jakes continued. 'Especially the King's men, what with your excommunication and suspension of these bishops. When we left Dover the town was in chaos and they were hunting your man. The clergy and clever men are saying that this is Advent time, a good time for the world, and things ought to be peaceful. But you have upset everything.'

Herbert was outraged at the man's impudence, but Thomas thanked him and gave him a silver penny for his trouble. The news from Dover did not surprise Thomas. He had understood the effect Osbern's actions would have on the De Brocs and his other enemies. He prayed the Rabbit was safe, but trusted his ingenuity to escape. Osbern is as slippery as an eel, he thought. Thomas also expected that there were messengers hurrying to Bayeux with word of his acts to complain to King Henry. The King was certain to explode in a fury. Thomas shrugged, his plans were set. There was no turning away now.

Herbert of Bosham was similarly unconcerned by the news of warriors in Dover, but Timorous Gunter was dismayed.

'If the country is upset like this, your grace,' he said when the captain had left. 'Then what is it going to be like when the King finds out?' His voice cracked with fear.

'Be silent,' said Bosham.

Thomas touched the boy's arm to calm him. 'Gunter, we will be home soon,' said Thomas. With God's help I mean to cross. I well know that the time of my suffering is very close, but if we keep our trust in the Lord we shall be redeemed.'

The young clerk nodded sadly. He did not want any part of this, but he was bound by his loyalty to the Archbishop.

'Is there a boat that will carry us?' Thomas asked Herbert.

'Yes, your grace. We can depart on tomorrow morning's tide, god willing and the winds permitting.'

'It is the feast day of Saint Andrew tomorrow?'

Bosham nodded. He was far more steeped in theology and cannon than Thomas who had spent most of his life as a courtier and clerk.

'Saint Andrew was a fisherman and a sailor,' said Thomas. 'His boat carried the saviour himself across the waves. It is somewhat fitting that we sail for home on his feast day.'

'Yes, your Grace,' said Herbert with a smile.

Andrew ended up being martyred, thought Gunter to himself, but he said nothing.

It was two days before the boat was ready to take them across the channel to England. The crossing was short with a brisk wind behind them billowing the sails and speeding them over the waves. Thomas huddled in the prow of the boat under the cold winter's sun, his eyes fixed upon their destination.

'The fair wind is a sign of God's blessing,' John of Salisbury told his fellow passengers.

With word that the De Brocs were in Dover, the helmsman set course for Sandwich instead. The small town was held by the monks of Canterbury, and Thomas would hopefully find safe landing and friends there. The Archbishop and his party crowded into the prow of the boat as they rounded the headland at Deal and started the run up to the harbour. They were all desperate to see their homeland. Six years was far too long an absence. Other boats slowly moving along the coast with them towards the port, carrying goods and passengers, hailed their boat as tacked into the shore. Thomas smiled to himself and turned to Gunter.

'Set up my cross at the front,' he said. 'Let everyone see that we are coming home.'

Gunter scrambled to set the cross high up in the prow where it could be seen by the other ships and watchers on the shore. By the time the boat reached the quayside at Sandwich, the quayside was heaving with townsfolk ready to welcome their exiled archbishop home. The boat grounded short of the quays on the muddy foreshore and the common people rushed out to carry Thomas and his companions to dry land, stripping off their hose and tucking their tunics between their legs, and hoisting the priests on their shoulders. There were cheers and cries of Hosanna when the crowd spied Thomas in the boat. Two burly apprentices carried him took him off the craft and carried him high above their heads in a chair, and deposited him on the quay's cobbles. Everyone surrounding the party was cheering and weeping for joy at Thomas's return. There was a crush as people reached out to touch the long absent Archbishop. They had to fight through the crowds. It was the very welcome home that Thomas had dreamed of. The Archbishop and his party took lodgings in a building owned by the Canterbury monks, just off from the boats. It was tall stone building with four or five black robed monks waiting at the threshold to welcome them. They entered and Gunter closed the door behind him and breathed a sigh of relief.

'We are home,' said Thomas.

'Is there any wine?' asked John of Salisbury.

***

'Smash down the door!'

Four heavily set men in leather jerkins picked up a bench and began hammering it into the wood, shaking the door off its hinges with only a couple of blows.

'Find him.'

The men nodded and rushed into the dark hovel.

Ranulf De Broc was running out of time. News that Thomas was returning to England had reached him in Kent. He had been squeezing every last coin out of church lands in the Archbishop's absence. Thomas's homecoming was certain to lead to trouble for him, and the loss of valuable incomes that he and his cousin Robert relied upon. Neither of those prospects enthralled Ranulf De Broc. A coarse brutish individual, broad shouldered with dark untidily cut hair. De Broc had a reputation for violence and terror.

His four men dragged Richard of Dover from the building; the poor old man was weeping and wailing at their rough treatment.

'Where is he?' De Broc demanded of the man.

'Where is who, Lord?'

De Broc slammed Pater Rabbit around the mouth with his mailed fist, knocking him to the ground.

'Where is your son? Where is Osbern the Rabbit?'

'He has already departed for Canterbury, Lord,' Osbern's father said with no hesitation, spitting blood. 'I would not harbour him, Lord and sent him on his way.'

De Broc could believe that; the former Vintner was a weasel, but his son was the Archbishop's closest servant and trusted messenger. The angry baron wanted to find Osbern and cut his fingers off after the events in Dover. He wanted to know where the Archbishop was, when he was expected to return, and where he was going to land. Osbern's father knew none of the answers and was dragged off to Saltwood Castle to wait on the De Broc's pleasure. Father Rabbit protested his innocence all the way to the dank dungeons, all to no avail.

'What now?' Asked Gervase.

De Broc paused before answering. Gervase Cornhill was the Sherriff of Kent. De Broc would need him if he was to neuter Thomas. He could not simply bully the man.

'We need to find the Archbishop. Kill him or cow him, one or the other.'

'He will not be cowed,' said Gervase.

'Then we shall deal with it,' said De Broc firmly.

Word of Thomas's landing in Sandwich finally reached them in Saltwood Castle that afternoon. De Broc led a part of knights to Sandwich to confront the Archbishop as soon as he heard the news. He took Gervase with him to provide some façade of royal authority. De Broc had murder on his mind, but Cornhill urged restraint.

'We cannot just kill him out of hand,' he told De Broc as they rode. 'There has to be some legality to our actions, else the King will hold it against us.'

'The King is as sick of the upstart as we are,' De Broc retorted. 'He has the perfidy to make peace with the King only a month ago, to starting up a new war as soon as he returns.'

The old Roman road took them straight to Sandwich where the Archbishop and companions still rested after their channel crossing. De Broc planned to go straight to the monks' house on the quayside and deal with Thomas, but they were met outside Sandwich by the King's clerk – John of Oxford.

'What are you doing?' Oxford cried out when he saw their blades and armour. 'The man is under the King's protection.'

'We mean to do for him once and for all,' De Broc told him.

'You would have the whole of Kent in uproar,' said Oxford. 'I have been in Sandwich. The townsfolk will take up arms to defend him, if you try to use force. You will have a revolt on your hands.'

'That trumped De Broc's hand. The King would not forgive him if the people rose up.

'I still want to see him,' said De Broc. 'I want to know what he about.'

'Do you have messages from Young Henry? That might persuade them.'

'The King's son sent us to act,' Gervase lied to the King's clerk. 'I have the Young King's authority as Sherriff of Kent.'

John of Oxford knew that for a falsehood but he merely nodded.

'Then I will take you to the Archbishop,' he said. 'You will have to leave aside your arms before meeting with him. The monks will not stand for mail shirts and blades in their house.'

De Broc knew then that he could not simply murder Thomas and be done with it - no matter how much he wanted to – but he could put the fear of God into the man, send him scurrying back into exile. John of Oxford took them to Sandwich where Thomas and his companions rested. They were watched grimly by the townsfolk as they passed. There was a threatening silence and sullen glances from the crowds as they dismounted and entered the building. De Broc glowered at the insolent peasants, but knew he could not risk a revolt. Gunter, the young clerk, showed them into a chamber where Thomas waited, but the Archbishop did not rise to greet the barons.

De Broc was shocked when he was taken before Thomas. The cultured urbane courtier that Ranulf remembered had been transformed into a wizened, broken, old man. His crown was bald and the beard white and deep furrows marked his face giving him a mournful countenance.

'You have come with fire and sword, excommunicating the King's bishops,' said De Broc, wasting no time on pleasantries or introductions. 'The Archbishop of York had done nothing but the King's command in crowning Young Henry. If you do not take better counsel something might happen which we all regret.'

De Broc glared at Herbert of Bosham, another snake that needed to be dealt with and John of Salisbury. All of them were upstarts who needed to be put down. John of Salisbury went white but Bosham simply glared back. Everyone knew what De Broc meant by his words, but Thomas refused to be cowed.

The Archbishop knew exactly how De Broc had acted during his long exile. They had stolen and looted Canterbury's wealth and terrorised the townsfolk. The De Brocs had armed men guarding the gates to the cathedral town; monks were beaten in the street, harvests taken with no recompense, goods destined for the priory or the cathedral robbed by the De Broc men. Thomas's deer had been poached, his wine stolen, and his hunting dogs taken, his woodland cut down and his tenants terrorised, but now was not the time for his revenge. He spoke calmly and clearly in response.

'I do not wish to deprive Young Henry of his English Crown; rather I would see him wear four crowns.' Thomas gave a wry smile at that. 'But the coronation of the King's son was performed unjustly and against the dignity of God and the Church of Canterbury. The Archbishop of York understood that, and will have to answer to Pope Alexander for his actions.'

'What of the other bishops?' said De Broc with barely concealed fury at Thomas's calm words.

'I would do what I can for the others, what is in my power, that is. I will need to think on it.'

He smiled at them and it pulled a thorn. The knights had been expecting stubborn resistance in all matters, but Thomas's reasonable demeanour flustered them.

'Come back tomorrow,' said the Archbishop. 'I will have decided the matter by then.'

His clerks ushered the dumbfounded knights from the room and into the courtyard outside before they could offer any protests.

'What now?' Gervaise asked De Broc as the stood on the cobbles with the horses.

'We go back to Saltwood and send word to Young Henry.'

'The boy likes Thomas; he spent time in his household.'

'He likes his crown more.'

They took to their horses, clattering back down the road to Saltwood Castle.

***

Osbern could see down to the city's west gate from the hill above Canterbury. A smoke haze hanged over the red tiled rooftops. The cathedral shimmered in the winter sunlight, dominating the town. There would be monks in the Bishop's Palace who would help; monks who would be waiting for word of their prelate's return. The problem for Osbern was the guards who were set on each gate into the town. De Broc had men everywhere and they were all seeking the Rabbit. He had to get into Canterbury to get to the cathedral, but the coarse ruffians and hedge knights in service to his enemies stood between Osbern and safety.He scrambled down the slope and into a copse of woodland and waited. The daylight would not last much longer.

'I am going to get wet and cold,' he said to himself.

As night fell, Osbern crept down to the banks of the Stour. There were guards on the stone bridge checking any who wished to enter the town, but Osbern knew a way to avoid them. He crept down to the river, trying to hide in the shadows, but slipped in the mud and slid down to the water's edge. He held his breath and looked up at the men illuminated by torchlight above him on the bridge. They had not heard him. He looked back to the icy black water and paused.

'Please Lord let it not be too cold. I could catch my death in this season.'

He slipped into the water, the shock of cold stealing his breath, and waded across half-paddling-half wading. On the other side, he followed the river bank to the town's outer wall, There was an iron grill where the water entered Canterbury, but

Osbern knew of a loose bar that could be taken out to let someone enter or leave the town unseen. He had used it often enough in the past to escape curfew. Shivering from the cold and wet through, he finally located the rusted iron bar and tugged. It did not budge.

'Please, St Augustine, help me.' Osbern appealed to Canterbury's patron saint, and heaved at the bar again. It came free with a great groan. Osbern froze, convinced that De Broc's men must have heard the noise this time, but there were no cries of alarm, no shouts or notice.

'Thank you Saint Augustine,' he said quietly.

The Rabbit slipped past the grill and replaced the bar. Crawling, wading, and shivering through the water tunnel into the city. The water was freezing and fetid, and he gagged at the stench. When he finally clambered up the stone steps out of the waterway onto the cobbles by Hopper's Mill, he was shivering uncontrollably from the cold, panting hard like dog.

There will still a few people about in the narrow streets, but none of them took any notice of the dripping Osbern. Nevertheless, he kept to the shadows as he made his way quickly down Blackfriars to the cathedral compound. He waited until there was nobody on the street and took a run to the wall. Up and over the flint stones in a leap and a scramble, scratching his arse and ripping his wet breeches as he went over the top and landed on the other side.

'I am far too old to be playing such games,' he said, standing up and patting himself down. 'It's been six years since I had to sneak back in here.'

Osbern had used this way into the compound often enough when Thomas had been resident in the cathedral town. Whenever he wanted to visit the wine merchants and troubadours of the town, he would go over the walls to avoid monkish disapproval or his master's disappointment.

'And they never caught me,' he smirked to himself despite the cold.

A blow to the head sent him spinning to the grass, his eyes went black at the edges for a moment, and then he rolled to avoid another blow from a cudgel.

'Damn scoundrels stealing our plate, we shall have no more of it!' screamed a chubby monk at Osbern. 'Get back to De Broc and tell him the Archbishop is coming home and you and the rest of your scoundrels will be turned out.'

The friar kicked Osbern with a sandaled foot, catching him just under the jaw, making him bite his tongue.

'God's teeth, friar, I am no servant of the De Brocs, he squealed. 'I come from the very Archbishop himself.'

The monk paused with his cudgel held ready to deliver another blow as Osbern cringed.

'Who are you?' asked the friar.

'Osbern of Dover, I am Lord Thomas's manservant.'

'Osbern the Rabbit?'

'Yes.' He winced as he climbed to his feet. His mouth was bleeding.

'Where is the Archbishop? When is he coming?' the desperation in the man's voice was palpable.

'Please, Friar, I am cold and wet and hungry and have travelled a long way in a short time. Can I at least get some warmth before answering all the questions?'

The man sniffed at that.

'One thing is true,' said Osbern to placate the friar. 'Archbishop Thomas is coming home. He may well have already landed.'

'He is truly coming home?'

'Yes.'

3

Cheering crowds lined the road from Sandwich to Canterbury as Thomas passed in procession to the cathedral. His clerks and attendants had rushed to the port as soon as Osbern brought word of Thomas's return. All of them had been shocked at the white-haired stooped old man that Thomas had become in his years of exile, but they took their places with happy smiles; happy that their lord was home. Alexander Llewellyn, Thomas's cross bearer, rode at the head displaying the Archbishop's tall cross to the world, holding it high and with a big grin on his face. Following on behind was Thomas on his white horse and dressed in full regalia. There were others on horses and walking alongside, monks and priests and common folk delighted at the spectacle. Carts of luggage brought from France, and books and all the baggage of a prince of the church, followed on behind.

'He is enjoying this,' John of Salisbury told Herbert as they rode sturdy sumpter horses in Thomas's wake.

'He is home to tend his flock,' said Herbert sanctimoniously. 'What true priest would not be overjoyed at returning to his calling?'

John rolled his eyes. He thanked God for keeping Herbert in the abbey whilst his exile had been in the wine shops of Paris. For all his devotion, Bosham was a sanctimonious irritant.

Thomas waved at the poor who flocked to catch a glimpse of their rebel archbishop. There were screams and yells wherever he came into view. Cries of hosanna and cheering that rolled along with their party as the trod the straight road to Canterbury. As they reached St Martin's Hill, and finally looked down on their destination, the people started throwing garments of clothing before them, so they walked on a road of cloth. Parish priests and monks sang out with the people to welcome Thomas home.

'Blessed is he that comes in the name of the Lord.'

'Hosanna in the Highest.'

Osbern was waiting for his master at the top of the hill utterly dismayed by the spectacle. For all his father's taunts, Rabbit was not completely witless and he had served Thomas through his time as Chancellor and Archbishop. He had seen the ways of the Royal Court and he knew the King's temper firsthand. He knew of the cruel men who served the Angevin Lion, men like FitzUrse the Bear; men like the De Brocs.

'The King is going to be furious when he hears of this.'

'The King is ever furious about something,' said Friar Timothy blithely.

'There is no need to antagonise him.'

Friar Timothy nodded at those words. The ruddy cheeked priest and the Rabbit had spent the previous evening in their cups, once word of Thomas's return was given to the Prior. Both of them were somewhat worse for the wear the morning afterwards.

'Best I go down to him,' said Osbern.

Osbern knew his master's vanity would run away with him in such a situation. Thomas ever adored the spectacle of it all. He made his way down to the procession, pushing past the cheering onlookers. Alexander Llewellyn saw him and nodded as Osbern stepped in beside Thomas's white horse. The Archbishop smiled down at the Rabbit.

'And you feared we would not meet again, when I last saw you, Rabbit?'

'God's grace is good, Lord.'

'You have a blackened eye?'

'I was accosted breaking into the compound, Lord. They stopped once they realised who I was.'

Thomas smiled at those words.

'You are getting old, Osbern. You used to be able to do it unseen and unknown even when you were in your cups.'

'There were fewer guards in those days, Lord. De Broc's men were everywhere yesterday.'

'And now?'

'They have gone, Lord, to who knows where. There are too many people here for them to assault us.' Osbern gestured at the exultant crowd.

As they approached the city, even more of the townsfolk and monks from the cathedral came out to meet them. It was already getting dark by the time Thomas passed through the gates into Canterbury. There was a fanfare of trumpets and the cathedral bells rang out. A festival atmosphere had overtaken them all. Thomas passed out gifts for the poor from his baggage. The procession crawled down St George's with people hanging out of windows and cheering, monks chanting and singing, the heavy smell of incense engulfed them all as the party turned into Mercery Street and approached the cathedral compound. Osbern took a flask of wine from Friar Timothy and swigged at it.

'Christ conquers! Christ reigns!' chanted the crowd.

'It is like the messiah's entrance into Jerusalem,' said the friar.

'Christ conquers! Christ commands!'

At the cathedral gate Thomas dismounted, took off his shoes and prostrated himself before the temple of Christ. Then he stood and walked barefooted into the compound, making his way through the monks and priests to the high altar of the cathedral. He prostrated himself once more, his lips moving in silent prayer as he gave thanks for his return, and begged for strength in the coming days. Finally, he stood and walked to the Archbishop's throne set behind the high altar.

Taking his place on the cold stone, he called them watching clerics to him. Most came with tears of joy in their eyes, giving their lord the kiss of peace, but there were some who held back, whispered in corners. Osbern noted them. The Archbishop's return was not welcomed by all.

'He has snubbed Prior Odo,' said Timothy.

'Odo is one of the King's men,' said Osbern.

Odo is popular with the others and he performs his duties diligently. The Archbishop does not want to alienate everybody as soon as he returns.'

Osbern burst out laughing and looked at his new friend.

'Why, Friar Timothy, that is exactly what he intends on doing. You are either with him or against him.'

Timothy sighed and took his place to give Thomas the kiss of peace and welcome his return. The Archbishop smiled and took the friar's hand.

'You gave my Rabbit a beating?'

'My apologies, your grace, I did not recognise him.'

'I am certain he will not hold it against you.'

Thomas nodded and Timothy moved on as the next supplicant took his place. He returned to Osbern waiting in the choir.

'What now?'

'Now, I think I am going to have some more of that wine,' said Osbern. 'In the calm before the storm.'

***

Ranulf De Broc arrived in Canterbury the next morning with his knights, furious that Thomas had left Sandwich and determined to press his case with the Archbishop. Thomas, seated in his throne in the palace hall, held out his hand with the bishop's ring for De Broc to kiss and make obeisance, but the broad baron studiously ignored it.

'So, you have returned, and your first act is to break the peace and excommunicate the king's bishops?'

De Broc was prepared for the confrontation. It was the same argument as the previous days but delivered with new venom. Thomas tried to defuse the tempers.

'It was on the Pope's authority that they were condemned not mine.'

'You did it!' De Broc jabbed his finger at Thomas.

'The bishops of London and Salisbury are within my jurisdiction,' said Thomas. 'If they submit to my spiritual authority, I will redeem them. I have no authority over the Archbishop of York and cannot undo what His Holiness the Pope has done.'

'He only did it on your connivance!' The barons with De Broc could barely conceal their anger.

'It was a circular argument, and De Broc could see he was not getting anywhere with it. Thomas's return threatened the De

Brocs' power in Kent, and their finances. He paused before the recalcitrant archbishop, in decision.

'You have authorised this in contempt of our lord King,' he stated coldly. 'And in violation of the customs of his realm. You fixed today for us to come and hear your words, so what is your answer?' He gestured contemptuously at the seated archbishop. 'If you don't restore them to their offices.' De Broc's voice dropped almost to a whisper. 'If you don't restore them to office, some unheard of evil, something pretty wonderful to relate, will come of it.' He left the open threat hang in the air for a moment. 'What kind of peace do you promise when you are waving about your axe at us? Think hard on what you are doing.'

He simply does not care, thought Osbern. He has no fear and these bullies are not used to that. They expect him to cower in terror, instead he smiles and lectures. This is not going to end well, and he doesn't care. In fact I think he welcomes it.

Thomas listened to the monologue in silence with a wry smile on his face. He had heard it all before. He gestured for De Broc to carry on with his speech; he had no other answers to give the baron.

'You are eliminating the King's supporters all about; will you take his crown from him too? I am warning you. Absolve the bishops.'

Thomas rolled his eyes at the ridiculous suggestion and opened his arms like a haggling trader.

'What Rome has bound, we at a lower level cannot unbind. If they submit, perhaps I can abrogate some of His Holiness's authority, perhaps; perhaps I can intercede on their behalf with him, perhaps. If they submit...' he left the last hanging.

De Broc knew when he was beaten. He could not bully or bluster the archbishop and force him to absolve the bishops. He could not physically assault him before witnesses and within the confines of the cathedral. That was a sin too far even for Ranulf De Broc, but he could find others who cared less about their souls and more about their purses.

'You will be sorry,' he snarled at Thomas, and stalked out followed by his retainers and supporters.

Osbern breathed a sigh of relief and rushed to his master with the cordial to settle his stomach. Thomas smiled at him, completely unperturbed by the confrontation.

'They thirst for you blood, Master.'

Thomas gave a wan grin, for a moment looking years younger.

'Let them drink it, said the Archbishop. 'They will choke.'

De Broc and his men galloped down the Dover Road after leaving Thomas. He sent his clerks to the excommunicated bishops waiting at a house by the quayside and retired to Saltwood to plot. The clerks gave a full account of the meeting with Thomas, and his offers to intercede if they submitted. The bishops, coddled together waiting for a boat to France, were dismayed at the turn of events.

'This has gone too far, Roger,' fat Gilbert of London said. 'We cannot stand against the Pope himself. You know how much I despise the actor archbishop, but there is only so far we can go.'

Bishop Jocelyn of Salisbury nodded his agreement at those words. 'We submit to him and then let the King deal with it all.'

Roger of York cursed the day had ever met Thomas; the arrogance, the conceit, the sycophancy. The man had been raised high on little merit whilst others, like Roger, had to strive for everything. Even as boys, Thomas had been insufferably smug and arrogant and always the favourite.

'I have the King and Pope in my pocket,' Roger told the other two firmly. 'In my treasury I have eight thousand pounds, and I will spend every penny to break his pride and arrogance. York can match Canterbury in coin. Come, let us cross over to the King and plead our case.'

Gilbert and Jocelyn looked unsure.

'If you side with Thomas in this dispute, Henry will hold it against you.' Roger pressed that point. Fear of the King was as great for the two bishops as fear of their Pope. 'Henry will think of you both as turncoats. He will take your possessions and leave you destitute and begging in the gutter.'

The loss of their fortunes and benefices finally convinced the reluctant two priests. They both nodded their agreement, and

Roger turned to one of his clerks before they could change their minds. He would keep stiffening their resolve until the matter was settled, but settled it would be. Of that the Archbishop of York was determined.

'Find us a boat for Normandy, as quick as you can,' he told the clerk.

***

FitzUrse the Bear watched the column wind its way down the valley from the ridge. There was only a small escort of perhaps twenty armed men, guarding two carts laden with riches from the Abbey of Montmarte. The Bear had men concealed in the tree line - archers and spearmen – and he had his horsemen hidden behind him. When the party was half way across the ford, he would spring the trap. In his late twenties, broad, tall and muscular, with a shock of dark hair and beard; the Bear was one of King Henry's trusted bullyboys. FitzUrse had a fearsome reputation and a dark temper to match. He was not a grasping baron or polished courtier; the Bear was who Henry turned to for the darker missions. The coarse knight had been in the King's household since childhood and was a loyal dog to his master.

'They have no idea we are here,' said Brito to the Bear in a hushed tone.

The young sandy-haired knight lying next to FitzUrse was nervous, not as used to this raiding as the older Bear. The two Norman warriors watched their prey, waiting patiently. The French party had reached the ford and some of the riders were splashing across the swollen river whist others had dismounted to help the wagons across.

'Now?' Brito asked.

'Not yet.'

Some of the enemy riders were crossing the river. Others were milling around at the rear watching the treasure laden carts.

'Now,' said FitzUrse, and raised his hand.

One of the horsemen hidden behind lifted a horn to his mouth and blew a high pitched tone that echoed down the valley. The

French party crossing the river heard it and started to panic. Arrows started to rain down on them from Brito's hidden archers in the trees. Horses and men were struck by the cruel barbs, falling into the river. English spearmen suddenly appeared from the woods all around them. The ambush had taken them completely unawares.

FitzUrse mounted up on his destrier and charged down to the carts, leading his horsemen to cut off any flight by the French. A small clutch of French horsemen at the rear of the column saw them coming and tried to rally themselves to face the new threat. FitzUrse and Brito careered into them at full pace followed by their men at arms. The Bear hacked left and right with his heavy mace, battering his enemies, breaking bones and crushing skulls. Brito was beside him, swinging his sword and stabbing at the Frenchmen as they tried to escape. The Bear caved one man's head in, splattering grey brain and blood as the skull shattered under the force of the blow. His spearmen were dragging others from their horses, stabbing them. The carters were slaughtered where they sat. Their bodies dragged down and thrown into the water with no ceremony.

'Kill them all!' shouted FitzUrse. 'No mercy.'

There was to be no survivors, no ransoms, nobody to tell of the attack. The King had been quite insistent on that point. There were only a few of them left now, all trying to run.

Brito saw a mounted knight making his escape, one of the few Frenchmen in a mail coat and wearing a helm. He kicked his horse up into a gallop to catch the man, soon overtaking and swinging a sword blow at his head. The blow missed as horse and riderflashed past. Brito yanked on his stallion's reins, turning him on a sixpence, and raised his shield as the Frenchman tried to slash him in turn with his blade. The enemy's sword cracked Brito's shield, splitting the wood and sending sparks up from the iron rim. The English knight withstood the force of the blow, and stabbed at the man's leg as they wheeled their horses around each other. Both of the knights were panting, but continued to hack away at each other with their broadswords. Neither could break the other's defence. The rest of the column had already been finished off. Men were looting the French corpses.

The Bear watched the combat for a few seconds and then told an archer to bring down the Frenchman's horse. The man put three arrows into the horse's side in short order. It fell screaming to the floor, trapping its rider. The French knight was swiftly killed by a couple of men who thrust their spears into his body, silencing his cries.

Brito was furious. 'It was a duel,' he complained to FitzUrse. 'And I had him beat.'

The Bear quickly disabused the youth of that notion.

'We are here for coin, not honour.'

The French escort had been butchered in short time, their corpses stripped naked and dumped into the river. The laden carts they had died to defend were hauled out of the river.

'Let us see what we have then,' said Brito. He was unhappy at the Bear's dishonourable acts, but just as greedy for the gold.

FitzUrse nodded. He wanted to see the riches that the Abbot had sent to King Louis of France. It was wealth that the French King would have used to attack the English and Normans in the Vexin. The loss of the coin would be a severe blow to Louis' plans for next year's campaigning.

The chests were broken open and the lids flipped back. The men all gasped at the sight of the precious plate and gold. There were bales of silks from Cathay, and rich embroidered tapestries depicting scenes from the bible on one of the carts. Brito reached out to touch one of the exquisitely sewn peacocks. The cost to bring silk from the east was enormous.

'This is a fortune indeed,' he said.

The Bear nodded. 'Louis of France will be spitting blood when he hears that the convoy has been lost.'

'He will know it is us.'

'He will know, but he has no proof.'

'They looked again at the riches.'

'It is a good Christmas gift for the King,' said the Bear.

They turned their horses back to Normandy and Bayeux where their King would be waiting for news of the raid. Had they been caught or beaten, Henry would have denied all knowledge of their actions. That they were successful meant the King would be pleased and generous, but he would still deny it to Louis when the complaints came from Paris. The King liked his plausible deniability.

4

The arrival of the three excommunicated bishops at Bayeux set the court into uproar. The Archbishop of York had sent messengers on ahead with a highly charged account of Thomas's actions that sent Henry into apoplexy. It was the Bishops personal testimonies, delivered with all the spite they could muster in front of the assembled barons and knights of Henry's personal retinue, that put the final nail in Thomas's coffin.

'He challenged your son's coronation,' said Roger of York. 'He threatens the succession.' The last accusation was given in a low snake's hiss.

There were mutters from the barons and Roger's words. The Archbishop gestured to the assembly, noting the reaction.

Henry could hardly believe that Thomas had betrayed him again. Only a month before, the two of them had given each other the kiss of peace and settled their differences. Now Thomas had declared war once more on the crown. Henry was stunned by the treason.

'I believed him,' he said, so quietly none of them heard. 'I truly believed him.' This final betrayal cut Henry deeply.

'Take counsel from your barons and knights, Lord King,' said Roger of York, slyly. 'It is not for us priests to advise your course of action.'

Henry nodded at the words, turning red in the face and fuming. He could not understand why Thomas had done this thing. Why would he threaten his son's succession? It was beyond the King's comprehension. Thomas liked the lad, why would he steal his crown away? For nearly a decade, the man he loved most, a man he had raised to the highest office, had become his fiercest enemy. The rebel Archbishop of Canterbury had cost him more coin and castles than the King of France ever had. This new treachery was the bitterest betrayal after everything had been settled, but Henry was King and Lord. He ruled in England, not Thomas, not the Pope in Rome, and certainly not Louis of France. Henry was God's anointed.

'Thomas has declared war upon me,' said Henry. 'In spite of everything we agreed at Freteval last month.'

There was a nodded agreement from the courtiers at Henry's words. The settlement between the Archbishop of Canterbury and the King of England had been drawn out and torturous, and Henry had to finally admit defeat, under pressure from the Pope and the French King. This news from England, these new interdicts set on his supporters, it simply reignited the old arguments. This was beyond base treachery by Thomas; it was a repudiation of the carefully constructed peace agreed only a month before.

'This Thomas is a dangerous man, Lord,' said the Earl of Leicester. 'He should be outlawed.'

'The only way to deal with such a man,' croaked the ancient Igelram de Bohun. 'Is to hang him on a gibbet.'

The Archbishop of York allowed himself a sly grin at the decrepit old man's words. This was turning out better than he could have hoped. Thomas had excommunicated De Bohun's nephew along with the Bishops and his other opponents, and that had outraged the old man's sensibilities. Others in the court were not so easily persuaded to murder. Making Thomas outlaw and exile was one thing. Killing a priest, even a recalcitrant rebel, was an entirely different matter. A Breton lord, eager to make his name at the Angevin court, spoke up at the noble mutters.

'When I returned from Jerusalem,' he said, clearly so everyone could hear. 'I passed through Rome. Whilst there, I asked my host about the popes, amongst other things, and he told me that one Pope had recently been killed for his insolence and intolerable impudence by the Roman mob.'

That was true enough: older men nodded recalling Pope Lucius' untimely demise, but to actually wield the dagger oneself would be a curse for eternity. There were few men who would do such work.

'My Lord,' Gilbert Foliot butted in. 'While Thomas lives you will have neither peace nor quiet, nor see good days.'

Henry bristled at the Bishop of London's words. He had started to calm down as the barons discussed the matter, but Foliot's comment pricked the bubble of reason and sent him into apoplexy once more. Henry went red in the face again and stood up, fists clenched and bellowed aloud.

'What miserable drones and traitors have I nurtured and promoted in my household!' he screamed, waving his fists at the barons. 'Who let their lord be treated with such shameful contempt by a low-born cleric!' Henry was looking directly at FizUrse the Bear. 'Who shall deliver me from this turbulent priest?'

FitzUrse had been drinking heavily, his good mood at the raid dissipated at the King's anger. He was just as shocked as Henry at Thomas's behaviour. The Bear remembered Thomas on the Toulouse campaign. He had been proud to follow the man as Chancellor of England. Thomas had been witty, urbane, prepared to get his hands dirty in battle. The Bear had happily sworn oaths of loyalty to Thomas back then, but as Archbishop the man had become a constant rebel against royal justice; a constant rebel against his King. Stung by Henry's words, the Bear sat back flushed but said nothing. Instead, he began to formulate a plan to deal with Thomas of Canterbury.

'More wine,' he told a servant, who hurried away.

The King retired after his outburst to make his decision. He was still shocked at Thomas's acts, and a part of him still loved the man, but the threat to his dynasty could not be tolerated. His son Young Henry would inherit the crown of England. That was everything to the King. Henry had lived through the anarchy caused by the death of his grandfather's heir on the White Ship. It had been Henry's own coronation that had put an end to decades of civil war. England and Normandy had been torn apart by the fighting. The King could not risk that happening to his realm again. Securing the Angevin line was everything. His sons were the future of the dynasty, the future of his crown. He fell back into his bedchamber, furious and calculating.

'It is only a month since I last saw him,' Henry said to himself. 'I believed him and he has betrayed me. In only a month…'

***

The peace had seemingly been agreed with ease at Freteval, at first. Henry had welcomed Thomas like a long lost friend, which in truth he was. The King held his rebel Archbishop in a bear hug and kissed both his cheeks. The two of them had seemed like brothers once again, after so many years of bitter recrimination. They sat late into the night talking together of old times, old campaigns and victories, laughing together at old jests and forgotten friends. The next morning, they rode out together watching the hawks hunting, and it seemed that the hard years of conflict were forgotten and forgiven on both sides. There was just one sticking point between the two men.

'The bishops of London, Salisbury, and York are mine to remonstrate, Lord,' said Thomas to the King as they rode along. 'Only I may crown a King of England. That is an established precedent. The three of them have usurped my rights as prelate of Canterbury in their exceedingly bold and blind ambition. They knew exactly what they did.'

Henry bristled at that. His young son's coronation was the final piece in the puzzle to secure his line and reputation. He would not let England fall back into the anarchy of the past. He pulled a piece of rich parchment from his tunic. Henry had expected Thomas's complaint about the bishops, but quite literally had a surprise up his sleeve.

'I have this instruction from His Holiness himself giving me the rights to have my son crowned, as I saw fit.'

Thomas was stunned at those words; the Pope had told him nothing of it. He took the parchment from Henry and scanned it.

We command you, that whenever the king shall request it, you shall place upon the head of his aforesaid son the crown on the authority of the apostolic see, and that what therein shall be done to you we decree to remain valid and firm.

Pope Alexander's seal was affixed to the parchment. Thomas briefly wondered if it could be a forgery, but reasoned that even Henry would not stoop so far. It could be too easily proven false and the consequences for the King would be dire indeed.

Thomas remembered something Henry had once said to him in better days, before their falling out.

'Were you not accustomed to once say that you would prefer your son to be beheaded rather than this aforesaid Archbishop of York,' Thomas spat the last out. 'Should place his heretic hands upon young Henry's head?'

Henry sat bolt upright in his saddle and flushed at Thomas's words. The Archbishop realised that he had gone too far. Thomas silently cursed his mistake. He had brought the Young King into the argument instead of focussing his complaints on the bishops.

'I mean no disrespect to your son,' Thomas added hastily. 'We desire only his success and the enlargement of his renown, and we shall labour in the Lord to bring it about.'

'If you love my son, you have a twofold duty to do what you are bound to,' sniffed the King. 'I myself gave him to you as a son to take into your own household, and you received him from my own hand.' Henry paused and gave a sad sigh. 'The boy loves you with such great affection that he refuses to see any of your enemies in a true light. And he would have destroyed them already if I had not prevented it.'

'But what of the bishops?' Thomas pushed the point again. He could not stand for his subordinates' insubordination.

Henry sighed again, he knew Thomas was as stubborn as a mule, and the two of them could argue this point for years, but he needed the matter settled.

'I know that you shall avenge yourself on them even more harshly when you have the opportunity,' said the King. 'On the other hand, to those that have betrayed us both, by God's providence I shall pay them all back as the base traitors they are.'

Thomas smiled. That was all the reassurance that he wanted and craved. He pulled the up his white palfrey and dismounted, prostrating himself in the mud before his King. Henry dismounted in turn, raised him to his feet, and they kissed each other on the cheeks.

You have made your robes dirty, said Henry, and the two of them fell about laughing like a pair of fools.

The King helped his prelate back into the saddle with wide grins all around. The gentlemen, clerks and courtiers that rode with the two men relaxed. There would be peace after all.

***

The four of them huddled in a corner of the great hall in Bayeux, and hatched their murderous plot in the firelight. FitzUrse the Bear was the leader, but the other three knights were all eager to please their King. All of them had their grudges against Thomas of Canterbury, but Henry's angry words had stung them. Miserable drones indeed. Now they would act on the royal command.

'We shall travel separately,' said FitzUrse. 'If we all leave tomorrow we can be together in Saltwood Castle in three days. The De Brocs will give us welcome.'

'What then?' asked Brito.

The Bear tried to give a reassuring smile. Brito was the youngest and most nervous about the plot.

'The De Brocs have men at the castle, perhaps one of them will be there,' he told the lad. Once we are back in England, we can see how the land lies.'

'Perhaps Thomas will have submitted.'

'Not if I know the Archbishop,' said De Moreville. 'He is a lowborn villein and base traitor to defy the king and break the peace, yet again. He took my estate from me when he was chancellor, now we shall take his head.'

De Moreville was from the north, his father was Constable of Scotland. He was brusque and brutal, but a good warrior and eager to make a name with the King of England.

Brito paled at De Moreville's words, but it was too late for him to back out. The others would hold it against him and he needed friends at court. Brito was the least of the conspirators, the youngest and landless.

'What then?' the young knight asked again.

The last knight, William De Tracy, had been silent as the plans were laid out, simply nodding his agreement at the Bear's words. He had his own grudges against Thomas of Canterbury they all did. Now, he leaned forward to stiffen young Brito's resolve.

'When it is done, the King will reward us all for the unpleasant task.' He slapped Brito on the back. 'You will have your own fine estate instead of being a beggar at court.'

'It is still murder.'

'He is a traitor. It is no murder, it is the dispensing of justice,' De Moreville told him forcefully.

The King's words had been quite clear, and the way he fixed FitzUrse with his gaze when he issued the command was easy enough to interpret. There was no confusion in the Bear's mind, or De Tracy and De Moreville. The King wanted his rebel archbishop dead and the task, unpleasant as it was, had fallen to them. Roger of York had promised the Bear funds to travel and would send a message onto the Brocs in Kent. Brito finally nodded his agreement at their words and FitzUrse called for wine to seal the bargain. They swore their oath together.

The next morning, in the twilight before dawn, all four left Bayeux and set out for the Kent coast and England. The Bear and Brito would travel together, and had a boat waiting on a long beach two miles to the north of the town. De Tracy would ride east to Honfleur, whilst De Moreville was set for Cherbourg. They would meet up again in three days at Saltwood Castle.

'We can be thankful that the weather is with us,' said Brito.

'God is on our side,' said the Bear. 'Archbishop Thomas offends our Lord with his treason.'

FitzUrse had decided to keep Brito close when they travelled to England. De Moreville and De Tracy were both wise enough and bold enough and could be trusted, but Brito was nervous. He could spook too easily at the bloody task ahead. The Bear did not want him taking fright and giving the plot away. He did not want to give Thomas warning and the chance to escape. The Archbishop had slipped from FitzUrse's grasp in Northampton six years previously. This time the Bear would run him into the ground if he tried to escape. Speed and secrecy were their greatest weapons. Once it was all over, the King could soothe any ruffled priestly feathers and quietly reward the four knights with the land they all desired. The Bear had served Henry nearly all his life, and he knew how the King played his games.

The longboat was pulled up on the sandy beach waiting for them in the cold winter sunlight. They clambered aboard, leaving their horses to be taken back to Bayeux.

'We shall find others in Dover,' the Bear assured Brito.

The channel was calm, with a fresh wind that would blow them to England. The boat was owned by the De Brocs of Saltwood. Their factor in Rouen had provided the transport for the Bear. FitzUrse knew the Kentish barons were threatened by Thomas's return to Canterbury. He knew that the De Brocs would be his allies in this. They had spent the last six years looting Kent in the Archbishop's absence. They would use any excuse to put the Archbishop down. Thomas had made far too many enemies for the peace to last, but excommunicating everyone left and right had set England ablaze.

'He knows what he is doing,' said FitzUrse, to himself. 'He always knows what he is doing.'

'What? Who does?' asked Brito.

'It is of no matter,' said the Bear. He did not want to worry the young knight.

They sat in the prow of the longboat as sailors dragged it out onto the water and clambered dripping aboard. They set the sails and the master turned the prow north towards the Kent coast. The wind caught the sails, billowing them out, and skimming them across the waves. By nightfall they would be in Hythe and at Saltwood Castle early the next morning. The other two would not be far behind.

5

Thomas only rested for a couple of days in Canterbury. Osbern did not call it rest. The Archbishop was busy sending letters to the Young King in Winchester or to his supporters across England. Word of Thomas's return had set the country into an uproar. Osbern made ready for Thomas to travel in procession to London. The Archbishop had first hoped to visit Young Henry, the King's eldest son. He had known the boy since he was a babe in arms, and had brought him up in his own household as Chancellor of England. Young Henry's advisors would have none of it. They were more worried about the old king's temper than his son's old acquaintance. They would not let Thomas anywhere near the boy.

Thomas had not expected to be refused access to the boy. He was the Archbishop of Canterbury and had every right to demand an audience with Young Henry. It came as a complete surprise to him to be denied such. A flash of disappointment crossed his face as Prior Richard told him of the audience with Young Henry, and the boy's hostile councillors. Thomas sat back and sighed deeply. His enemies would be spinning tales to the boy about his return and to the King across the sea in Normandy. Their tales would be dripping poison into everyone's ears.

'We shall travel to London instead,' said Thomas after a pause. 'I should receive some welcome there at the least.'

Travel, travel, travel, thought the Rabbit. That is all we have done for days. I just want to sleep.

'I want everything ready for Tuesday,' Thomas continued. 'We shall see to our lands and tenants that have been looted by De Broc these past years, and then we will travel onto the capital. The Aldermen will welcome me.'

The clerics and monks all nodded at his words, and rushed to make their arrangements. Thomas retired to his chambers, and beckoned Osbern to follow him. The Archbishop's private chambers in the palace at Canterbury were well furnished, despite the ravages of the past years, and there was a hot bath waiting fresh drawn by the servants. The Rabbit helped Thomas out of his priestly heavy robes, and stripped off the goat's hair trousers and shirt that his master insisted on wearing underneath. He cast them to the floor viewing the lice riddled garment with distaste. The hair shirt moved with the fleas that infested it.

'It is swarming with vermin, Lord. You should not wear it; it will only make you ill.'

'Behold, blessed is the one whom God reproves, therefore despise not the discipline of the Almighty,' intoned Thomas. 'For he wounds, but he binds up, he shatters, but his hands heal.'

Osbern rolled his eyes behind Thomas's back, and bathed the bites and festering sores with vinegar to clean away the infection, but the whole torso was dappled and bruised from the scratching. Thomas shivered as Osbern lathered his back with a cake of rich soap and then washed it away with warm water.

'Why do you do this, Lord? We could have come home in peace.'

'The King would not keep the peace, Rabbit. I know him too well. The time would come when he would take from the church what it rightfully owns. I am God's servant, not Henry's.'

You are just as stubborn as the King, thought Osbern, but said nothing more as he cleaned and bound up the wounds. When he was done, Thomas poured a cup of hot wine for himself and sat in a cushioned chair.

'You will tell none of the hair shirt, Rabbit.'

'I gave you my word, Lord, I have told none of it these past years, although I still think it a fool's vanity.

'That is bold.' Thomas giggled to himself. 'I am an old crone now and have little to be vain about, only my duty, but perhaps I am still a fool.'

It is not your duty to antagonise everybody, thought Osbern.

'May I be dismissed, Lord,' he said. 'I have things to make ready if we are to travel to London on Tuesday.'

Osbern could barely hide the disapproval in his voice, but Thomas ignored it and waved him away. He headed out to the Westgate; there was a tavern for travellers on the London Road, and Friar Timothy was waiting for him with a jug of ale. Osbern wanted to ask about the mortification shirt that his master had worn for so long, but he had given his promise to Thomas and said nothing.

'We're off to London now,' he told the friar instead.

'There is good ale in London.'

'It's freezing, hardly the weather for travelling halfway across England.'

'Oh, you are a dour fellow, Rabbit, said the Friar. You are finally home, and it is only right that the Archbishop sees the depredations De Broc has wreaked upon us in your absence.'

'You have been too long in your cups,' Osbern told him. 'I know my master. This is only going to cause more trouble. He is set on it.'

***

It was a grand procession that set out from Canterbury for London the following Tuesday. Thomas travelled on his customary white steed in full robes and regalia. A jewelled cross was carried before him by Alexander Llewellyn, Thomas's loyal bearer. Others had flocked to his retune at their Archbishop's return. Thomas's temporal vassals were in his train, knights bearing arms, as were a host of clerics, and monks, and priests, baggage, and servants. There was a festival atmosphere as they set out from Canterbury in the winter sunlight. Osbern was glum as he mounted a grey mule for the journey. The knights in armour would be spun to King Henry as an armed insurrection, it would be used against him, but Thomas seemed completely oblivious to the danger.

Not oblivious, decided Osbern, he is relishing it.

He likes the spectacle of it, but it must be uncomfortable riding so laden down in robes, said Friar Timothy.

Osbern smiled at the cleric. 'My master's spectacle always has a purpose, Brother, even if I rarely understand them. It does not diminish his private devotion.' The hair shirt was still on Osbern's mind.

'Oh I meant no recrimination, merely an observation, and I too like a show.'

The party made good time travelling the sixty miles to the capital, stopping at Newington at midday, but moving on swiftly in the afternoon. The bright winter sunlight and hard ground made the going easy. At Rochester, they were met by more monks and cheering lay folk who were delighted at Thomas's return. From there on, every step was greeted with singing crowds growing ever bigger as they drew close to the outskirts of London.

'Te Deum laudamus!' The crowd hailed Thomas, singing out the hosannas.

He bowed his head at their praises in a display of humility, but Osbern saw a sly smile of pleasure cross his master's face.

'He's enjoying this.'

'He has been away for too long,' said Timothy. 'The people support him; the people have missed him.'

'The people do not have long swords.'

A group of poor London scholars approached Thomas on the road, reminding him of his time in the city. The crowd around them was growing vaster by the minute. They were still some miles distant from the city, but could not force their way through all the well wishers who clamoured for Thomas's attention.

'Blessed be the Lord God of Israel!' The crowd chanted.

Osbern noticed an old woman standing on the crossroads as they rode past. She was dressed in rags, with wild white hair, her face lined and with whiskers on her chin. The crone was the only dissenting voice amidst the praise.

'Archbishop!' the crone called out. 'Archbishop!'

Thomas turned at her shout.

'Beware the blade,' she cried, and gave a sharp cutting motion at her throat.

Thomas went pale at the face with her words, but she was swept away in the crowds before they could stop and question her.

'This is getting out of hand,' Osbern said. 'The King will be incandescent with rage when he hears.'

Even the portly, jolly, friar Timothy agreed.

They paused their journey, and took up residence at a house belonging to the Bishop of Salisbury, another studied insult to the Archbishop's adversary. Thomas and his party dismounted to the rapturous applause of the crowds, and led the beasts into the courtyard where servants rushed to stable them. Thomas walked slowly to the Bishop's house, exhausted after the long ride and the cheering crowd, but he waved away help. He did not want the crowds to think he was weak or ill. Once inside and out of view, Thomas nearly collapsed into a chair brought for him by a monk. Osbern rushed to make his master's cordial as their beds were made up. It was the only think that could settle the Archbishop's stomach.

'Thank you, Osbern,' Thomas said taking the drink when it was ready.

'The King will not thank you for today's display, nor will Young Henry, Lord.'

'I know,' said Thomas, sipping his wine.

The next morning proved all of Osbern's fears correct. Two emissaries from the Young King arrived at the house in Southwark. They were dressed in armour and flushed with anger by the time the monks showed them into the Archbishop. They gave no genuflections or polite introductions; instead, coldly informing Thomas that he was barred from entry into London, and any other of the King's towns or castles.

Thomas sat up in his chair at their words, stung by the sentence. He had not expected such a response.

'What?' he cried. 'Does the King repudiate my allegiance freely given at Freteval?'

'Certainly not,' said the one of the men. 'But you have opposed him too often, and now you go about the country with armed men to try and take the crown from the Young King's head. That is rebellion.'

Osbern grimaced at their words. He had known that the paltry number of knights in Thomas's retinue would be spun into a fearsome army by the time word was relayed to the King.

'I am trying to do no such thing,' said Thomas. 'That is slander.'

'The King requires that you absolve his bishops, to whom you have ever done great wrong,' said the baron.

Thomas sighed. He was tired of the same argument, tired of giving the same old reply.

'I cannot and will not undo what His Holiness the Pope has done,' he said, waving his hand dismissively.

That infuriated the assembled men.

'If you do not obey the King's orders he will make you pay for it, and dearly to.' One of them pointed his finger at the Archbishop to gasps from the watching monks and clerics. Thomas was unconcerned.

'As I have said countless times before, if the Bishops of London and Salisbury come to me I will intercede with the Pope on their behalf. Of Roger of York I can do nothing, I have no authority over him.' He sniffed, his contempt for Roger evident to all.

'Since you refuse to absolve them, you are forbidden entry into the King's towns and castles,' said the baron. 'Get you back to Canterbury to do your business there.'

'How can I minister to my flock if I am forbidden to attend them?'

'We came to give orders not to debate them.'

At those words the two barons and their attendants stalked out, leaving the priests in despair.

Thomas was more than despondent at the failure of his plans. He had hoped to see Young Henry and had been thwarted. He had pinned his hopes on the long friendship with the boy. But was denied. Then, he had planned to enter London, but that was now barred to him – no matter how much the common people hailed him. Word that Robert De Broc had stolen a ship containing expensive wines brought from France for Canterbury only added to the sense of gloom that had fallen over the party. Thomas sighed deeply.

'This sport of theirs will not endure for long,' he said finally. 'It is but the mockery.' He turned to the Rabbit. 'Osbern, my cordial, bring it to me please.'

'Yes, Lord.'

Osbern hurried to get the posset made up in the kitchens. He knew Thomas well enough to see the disappointment at the barons' words, but he also knew it would pass and be replaced with bitter determination to carry on regardless. The friar was in the kitchen supping late. Osbern had spent more time with the man on the journey; he enjoyed the jolly friar's company.

'It is a rising tide that washes everything away, Brother' he told Timothy, as he stirred the egg into a wooden cup.

'It is all the Lord God's divine plan,' said Friar Timothy. 'Do you read?'

'Not well,' admitted Osbern.

'You should try more.'

'So he keeps telling me.'

The friar laughed and slapped Osbern on the back, as if the whole day had been a jest.

I am cursed with clerics who think nothing of trouble only of God. This is not going to end well. The King will be furious. He took the drink back to his master.

***

The young clerk gulped in fear at the sight of King Henry in full fury pounding down the flagstones towards him. The broad muscular monarch was a fearsome sight at the best of times but terrifying in a rage. The King was holding a small jewelled dagger in his left hand, and a trail of worried white-faced attendants followed in his wake.

'You!'

The clerk bowed his head. 'My, Lord.' What have I done? He thought.

'Pen and ink, take this down.'

The clerk breathed a sigh of relief when he realised the King merely wanted his services, and hurriedly dipped his quill into the inkpot.

'To His Holiness Pope Alexander, the third of that name. Bishop of Rome, etcetera, etcetera, etcetera,' Henry began. 'Fill in the usual honorific.'

The clerk nodded and left some space, praying he had enough to fit everybody's titles in.

'Honoured, Father, I have been devoted to you from the moment of your elevation,' said the King. 'A point which may have slipped your memory.' He turned to the flunkeys. 'Let us remind him that there is still a German Pope out there to support if he is not accommodating. Do not write that!' he bawled at the clerk.

The clerk took out his knife and scraped away the last words, as the King glared at him and continued with his speech.

'At the least, Holiness, you must bear in mind that I have complied to all of your recent requirements. Nevertheless, this man is an insufferable enemy to me and it is impossible to live in the same kingdom with him. He is hard at work all the time setting traps and scheming to do me down.'

The flunkeys and attendants all nodded at Henry's words, as the clerk scribbled furiously to keep up with the King's fast monologue.

'Then there are these men of his who have been travelling all over, slandering me behind my back. I submitted to you,' Henry concluded. 'And I let him back in peace and protected the very people who have caused me injury. It is for you to decide if I am to be rewarded with evil for my good.'

The clerk finished writing out the words and risked a glance at the King. Henry was lost in thought for a moment. Then he smiled to himself as if the decision was made.

'Make an appeal for the excommunications and suspensions to be lifted by the Pope,' Henry said, and then affixed his seal to the document. 'Get that finished and sent off to the Pope today,' he told the clerk. 'That will trim Thomas's sails,' he said to his courtiers. 'I shall have the every Bishop and priest in my realms write to the Pope of Thomas's insufferable vanity and perfidy.'

The clerk nodded and completed the document in silence as the King returned to his chambers. Once the parchment was completed and the royal seal affixed, it was sent on to Rome at speed.

'It will all be over by the time it reaches its destination,' the clerk said to himself. 'There is murder in the air.'

***

The next day, Thomas and a small group took the road from Southwark to Harrow. The Archbishop had an estate there, and he planned to rest and see if the Young King could be persuaded to meet. The weather had turned; a wet sleet and dark ominous clouds above had dispersed the cold sun of the previous day. They crossed the Thames at Lambeth, avoiding the city, and headed north. The mood in the party was sombre and glum to match the weather. Thomas's manor at Harrow on the Hill was a modest stone built affair: a large hall and kitchens on the ground floor, with wooden steps up to bedchambers and a private chapel on the second storey. There were stables and outhouses as part of the complex, and the servants rushed to take their long absent master's horse and bring him refreshments. The hearty welcome lifted the party somewhat, and Thomas was soon relaxed in front of a roaring fire in the hall.

'Do you think we shall rest here long?' Friar Timothy asked Osbern.

The Rabbit shook his head. 'He has sent messengers to the Young King. The lad is in Windsor now, it is not so far.'

'He still hopes to see him?'

Osbern poured himself a cup of ale, then poured it back into the jug and helped himself to some of the friar's wine instead.

'I avoid the grape mostly as you know,' he said in explanation. 'But it has been a very long journey. I feel as if I have not stopped running since leaving France.'

'You did not answer my question?'

'Any hopes he had with Young Henry are surely fading now. I do not think we shall tarry here long before returning to Canterbury.'

The arrival of two messengers from Windsor soon gave truth to that statement. They warmed themselves before the fire and told Thomas what they had found at Young Henry's court.

'They promised restitution, Lord, for the goods taken by De Broc's bully boys, but nothing more. You are still forbidden to enter any of the King's towns or cities.'

Thomas nodded sadly.

The other man was Thomas's personal physician. The Archbishop had sent him in secret to the Earl of Cornwall and to see if there was anything that could be done to bring about a meeting.

'I aided him with his fistula, your grace, but I was recognised by some at the Young King's court. The Earl gave me fair warning.'

'What did he say?'

The man paused before answering, nervously twitching his cloak. 'He says you must flee, Lord. Those about the Young King have only one idea for you, and Master John.' The physician nodded to John of Salisbury, Thomas's tubby long time companion sitting at the Archbishop's side. 'And your other bosom companions.'

'What is their design?' Thomas leaned forward in his chair, gripping the cup of wine in his hand so tight the knuckles whitened.

'Wherever you are found you will be put to the sword.'

Thomas sat back with a soft smile on his face as John of Salisbury burst into tears and started wailing.

'I knew it. I damn well knew it,' said Osbern to himself.

The Archbishop turned to John, reaching out and touching him on the arm to calm him.

'You have no need to fear, old friend.' Thomas tapped his own neck twice. 'Here, here, the knaves will strike me.'

I think he wants to die, thought the Rabbit.

6

Saltwood castle lies on a small rise on the edge of Romney Marsh above the town of Hythe. A simple square keep and curtain wall built of local stone enclosed a large bailey with stables, storehouses, bakeries, kitchens, houses, and quarters for the garrison. The stronghold was owned by the Archbishop as part of Canterbury's fiefs, but it had been seized by Ranulf De Broc when Thomas had fled to France. De Broc and his cousin had expelled the Canterbury castellan with the King's connivance and taken up residence there. The De Brocs used Saltwood as the base of their terrorism of the local population. Thomas's return would mean his officers would demand the castle's return, eventually. They would be forced to give it all back.

Ranulf De Broc, and his cousin Robert, had spent the last six years looting and pillaging the cathedral's lands and wealth. They had grown wealthy on their stolen profits, powerful at court, and they were determined not to lose it all on the whim of an arrogant cleric.

'Set men on every gate and alley in Canterbury,' Ranulf told his captains as they rode out. 'Let none of the monks move without my say so. I want every monastic, priest, or clerk in the city terrified of us.'

'The Archbishop will take it ill,' said one his men. 'He is certain to react in some way.'

'I want him to,' said De Broc. 'I want him to react; I want him to make some fool move, and then we will have our justification.'

De Broc's words hanged in the air. None of the men asked what they needed to be justified. Everyone knew that Thomas's return threatened their livelihoods. Only his head on a platter would suffice, if they meant to save their fortunes.

'Where is he?' De Broc asked another of his men.

'They have left Harrow and return with a retinue to Canterbury.'

'We could take them on the road,' said his cousin Robert.

'No,' said De Broc. 'Let him twist in the wind for now. It is almost Christmas. We shall cause his tenants some trouble for the season instead, and send them all running to the Archbishop with complaints.'

They left Saltwood in a great party of armed men, and rode onto some of Thomas's estates around Canterbury. They burned out four small holdings in short order, turned out the Archbishop's tenants, pillaged their winter stores and left them all to flock to Canterbury to protest to Thomas. The next victim was but a small manor with apple and pear orchards and a cider press. The tenants had fled at the arrival of the armed men. Word of the De Brocs raiding was spreading throughout Kent.

'Burn it down! Burn it to the ground!' Ranlph De Broc screamed at his men.

His cousin Robert, sat alongside him on a destrier, smiled as two spearmen took torches and started fires in the thatch. The flames quickly took hold and soon the whole building was engulfed.

'The Archbishop shall have no perry for Christmas,' said Robert.

'He shall have no damned cheer at all,' his cousin responded.

The evicted tenants watched on aghast from the trees as the warriors destroyed their home. There was no arguing with the armed men; the De Brocs would brook no disobedience. Had they tried to stop the men ruining the holding, they would have been cut down and killed. Instead, they would go to Canterbury and seek restitution from their Archbishop. It was exactly what Ranulf De Broc wanted.

'On to another of the Archbishop's holdings?' said Robert

Ranulf nodded.

'Soon he will not know which way to turn. I know Thomas of Cheapside, he is a base coward, and will flee back to Louis of France when he understands that he has no power here.'

Robert De Broc was more thoughtful than his brash cousin but just as mendacious. Their clan's wealth was dependant on the Archbishop's absence. The great quarrel between church and state had been quite lucrative for the De Broc family.

Neither of them saw a need to settle the matter and restore good governance to the region.

'Where next?' Robert asked his cousin.

'Blean, then around the city to Stuppingtonn. There are timber stores at Blean. I want them to build some more houses, and the foolborn miller is another of Thomas's loyal men.'

The Archbishop had already complained to the Young King and De Broc about the theft of rich woods that had been used to build a rich new house in Canterbury, and the wines stolen in port. The De Broc retainers in the city had been contemptuous of the Archbishop's summons, and had been consequently excommunicated in turn for their insolence to the church. Thomas cast out interdicts like eggs at mummers, but to ever decreasing effect.

'Soon he will have excommunicated us all.'

'He is a fool; his punishments carry no weight.'

They rode on to the storehouses at Blean. Tall well built halls filled to the brim with coppiced woods and sawn planks. More of De Broc's retainers arrived with bullock carts and ropes to strip the building of anything of value.

'He is going to be livid,' said Robert.

'I know.' Ranulf grinned widely. 'I only wish I could be there to see it.'

From Blean it was south around the cathedral city to Knockholt Mill. A tall wooden tower, perhaps forty foot high with great woollen sails that powered the mechanism. The miller and his family had already fled as word of the De Brocs approach, but the looters did not care. Sacks of grain and milled flour were stolen from storehouses and loaded onto wagons.

'Do we burn it, Lord?'

Burning down a mill would have the whole country in uproar. It was only Thomas that Ranulf wanted to bait, not start a rebellion. If the peasants could not grind their grain they had no bread, then they would start a riot.

'No leave it stand, we can come back again when we need some free flour.'

His men laughed at the jest and once the place was stripped of anything of value the carts were sent down the coast road

206

towards Saltwood. De Broc and his cousin slowly rode on ahead with a couple of guards. As they approached the coast, both men turned in their saddles at a shout. One of Ranulf's men from the castle was waiting for them on the road. The man bowed and blurted out his message.

'My Lord, there is word from the Archbishop of York in France.'

'What word do they bring?'

'There are men coming, Lord, sent by the King. The Archbishop says they will come to capture the Archbishop and take him in chains to the King. If he will not come they will kill him. On the King's orders, so the Archbishop's missive says.'

Ranulf De Broc stood up in his stirrups and yelled to the sky in triumph. There was no escape for the Archbishop now.

'Let us away to Saltwood to await these knights, and see what they are about,' he said to Robert.

Ranulf turned his horse to the coast road and kicked it into a run. His cousin nodded and followed down the road towards Hythe, but he did not share the exultation. Thomas would not go down without a struggle; would these men murder him in the cathedral? Surely none would dare commit such a sin. No matter how hateful the archbishop was, to kill on hallowed ground was beyond the pale. It was to be cursed for eternity. What kind of men would even consider such a crime?

***

It had been a miserable procession from Harrow to Maidstone. The King's ban on Thomas entering any town or city meant they had to cross the Thames away from the main fords and bridges. That had made the going harder than usual. A couple of priests had taken a dunking when they crossed the river in a leaking ferry, and had complained all the way to the manor at Wrotham. A poor place, it was held by one of the five near destitute knights who had come to guard the Archbishop. It was a sorry estate to guest such a party. Their host was constantly apologising for the lack of facilities and the coarse furnishings and foodstuffs, but Thomas merely smiled and waved his protests away. He had been born in Cheapside, he understood poverty.

Osbern did not care much about their rude lodgings either. He was just grateful to catch some sleep. They would be in Canterbury on the morrow and then it would be Christmas. Once the feast days were over, perhaps peace could be restored. He served the archbishop his cordial in the small hall, with Thomas's other close companions at hand. The rushes on the floor stank and smoke from the fire blew out into the hall making their eyes water. The priests were all miserable, but the Thomas was in good cheer. He behaved as if the weight of the last years had been lifted. News that he was to be killed had seen a serene calm descend over the tired Archbishop.

'There is a priest at the door,' a servant announced. 'He begs audience with you, your grace.'

'Let him in, let him in,' said Thomas. 'I will not hide away in fear.'

The servant brought a poor greybeard from the local church in, shabby torn robes and a badly shaved tonsure. He is nought but a poor parish priest, thought Osbern, and relaxed.

'Come in, Brother,' said Thomas. 'What is it that you seek of me?'

The poor priest bowed as low as he could and stuttered out a response.

'I have brought relics for your blessing, your grace. True relics of Saint Cicely and Saint Vincenza: a finger bone from the former and a lock of hair off the latter.'

'Oh really,' said Thomas, with a wry smile on his face.

John of Salisbury was grinning for the first time in days. He and Thomas both knew how many false relics and false purveyors of such crawled all over Christendom. The Archbishop had expelled priests for peddling their fake idols in the past. It was a lucrative trade that attracted the very worst type of mendicant, but this man was too poor to be selling the items for gain. John leaned forward to peruse the relics.

'They are real, your grace,' the priest said defensively. 'Saint Lawrence himself came to me and told me to bring them to you.'

Thomas sat back in his chair and reached into his robe to scratch at his hair shirt and smiled.

'Did the blessed saint tell you anything else?'

He told me that the hair shirt you wear was torn but it is now fixed.'

Thomas went pale with shock and Osbern gasped. Only a few knew of Thomas's shirt, all of them were in the room and none had ever spoken to the priest before. Herbert of Bosham crossed himself as they all looked at each other in disbelief.

'Nobody is to know of that,' said Thomas.

'I give you my word, your grace, I will tell none.'

'As long as I live,' said Thomas.

'As long as you live, your grace.'

He must have seen Thomas reach in and scratch, thought Osbern. He is a priest and will understand all about these shirts, this mortification. He is just observant, that is all. It is not a miracle. Still there was a nagging doubt, and he crossed himself.

Thomas blessed the priest's relics and the man departed happily back to his parish leaving a bewildered party of clerics behind.

'They struck Saint Cicely three times on the neck,' said John of Salisbury. 'Three times, yet she lived on for three days.'

'Three times,' said Thomas quietly touching his own neck.

The evening drew to a close in silence after that. Osbern helped his lord out of the hair shirt, and cleaned the sores, as he did every night. Once his master had retired to bed, the Rabbit curled up in front of the fire in the hall. Friar Timothy was already snoring.

'We will be home tomorrow,' Osbern said to himself.

The next morning they set out on the final leg for Canterbury. The weather was foul, sleet and muddy roads made the going hard, even for Thomas on his rich white horse. Yet, at each stop he blessed and baptised, christened and confirmed. The Archbishop took his duties seriously and cheerfully, in spite of his priests' complaints at the weather. The common people flocked to him. They been too long without an Archbishop in Canterbury in residence; there were still cheers and praises sung, but it was a sombre party that finally arrived back at the cathedral. De Broc's ruffians had not assaulted them on their return, allowing the party to retire unmolested through the West Gate, but fast riders were sent to Saltwood Castle to take word of Thomas's return to the De Brocs.

***

The Rabbit was set on getting drunk. The return to Canterbury had been blessed relief for Osbern, and Thomas had finally given him leave to enjoy himself. All the palace servants flocked around their archbishop at his return, doting on him, and Thomas turned to the his loyal man.

'Go,' said the Archbishop softly smiling. 'I have no need of you tonight, little one. Once my cordial is made up you are free until the morrow.'

'You will need to clean the sores, Lord.'

'Thomas waved him away. I do not think it matters so much for one night.'

Osbern did not argue; he needed the release. He skipped out of the palace compound in good spirits. It had been over six years since he had supped in The Tap opposite St Margaret's church but the old place had not changed. There was always a welcome for the Archbishop's man in the dark alehouse. Good food and good wines were served by pretty maids, and there was an escape from the cloistered confinement of the cathedral. He stepped over the cobbled courtyard to the main hall and pushed open the door. The hubbub of conversation inside died as he entered the taproom. Low hanging ceilings, hot and sweaty and a roaring fire. Osbern threw off his cloak, holding it over his arm, and nodded to the patrons. They turned back to their cups and conversations.

'Well, well, if it is not Master Osbern the Rabbit.' The innkeeper had a wide grin on his face. 'It has been many years since we have seen you here, Rabbit?'

'Too long.' Osbern pulled up a chair

The innkeeper tapped his nose.' I have something for you; if the Archbishop has given you leave?'

'He has.'

You cause one drunken scene over an Easter festival and everyone holds it against you, thought Osbern.

'I have had some wines arrived this very day from Paris.'

'I have drunk more French vintage these past years than I care for more.'

'Ah, then it will be Greek wine from Crete. The Emperor himself is said to sup it.'

Osbern laughed. 'You have not changed, old friend. The Cretan grape it is.'

'You do have the coin, Rabbit?'

Osbern reached into his purse and pulled out a cut ha'penny.

'Enough for a jug,' the man said.

'Enough for the first jug,' said Osbern.

The innkeeper hurried to get Rabbit his wine and Osbern turned to look around the taproom's clientele. It was mostly local tradesmen and apprentices at this late hour, breaking their fast after a long day at work. Canterbury was filled with industry for the cathedral: smiths of all types, bakers, tailors, chandlers, butchers, fishmongers, millers, merchants and grocers. There were almost as many merchants as monks in the city. The archbishop's return was the main topic of conversation in the room. Osbern heard Thomas's name mentioned more than once, and furtive glances cast his way.

'Here you are, Rabbit.'

The innkeeper brought him his wine. Osbern sipped at the sweet heavy liquid. The man had told the truth, it was an exceedingly good vintage.

'It is good,' he said.

'Only the best for the Archbishop's man.' He looked around the room. 'There are only friends here, but you should still have a care when you go back to the palace. The De Broc's men are all over.'

'He has excommunicated another one this very day,' said Osbern. 'The man stole his timber.'

'Aye, but they care little for that. The more people he severs from grace, the less the rest of the villains seem to care.'

Osbern nodded at those words; they were wise indeed. John of Salisbury had said something similar to his master, urging restraint, but Thomas was set on his design. Herbert of Bosham said it was a battle for the soul of the English church and the Archbishop could not surrender. The Rabbit had always disliked Herbert.

'Did you ever go on crusade to the Holy Land, Rabbit?'

'No,' Osbern replied. 'But I have thrice sworn to go when I am released from the Archbishop's service.'

'The way things are going that might not be long.'

Osbern gave him a quizzical glance.

'There is murder in the air, Rabbit. Men from Saltwood roam across the land denouncing your lord. They will not leave off at shouting.'

'I know,' said Osbern, sadly.

He was drunk by the time he returned to the Archbishop's compound. There was a late service in the cathedral for St Lucy. A festival of light that saw the building bright with hundreds of flickering candles. He peaked inside and saw that Thomas was by the altar delivering his sermon to the assembled monks and priests.

He looks so old and stooped, thought Osbern. His face is so lined and mournful, hair white and balding. The last six years have broken him. I do not think he cares how this ends anymore, only that it does end.

Thomas heaved a long sigh as he brought his sermon to a close. Christmas was at hand and he had relaxed his usual strict rules and regulations, as evidenced by Osbern's visit to the Tap.

'Beloved,' said Thomas. 'We bestow upon you this mercy beyond what might be expected or thought fitting. You are our creatures and are to keep remembrance, as you are bound to do, al that we have piously and generously conceded to you. May the Lord grant his blessing and grace upon you.'

'At least we shall have a proper Christmas feast on the morrow,' said Osbern, and headed for the kitchens.

7

It was cold in the cathedral. The mist from a thousand breaths steaming as the dull winter's sun from the arched windows cast a grey light into the nave. All of the townsfolk of Canterbury were gathered together to hear the Archbishop's Christmas sermon. Six years of long absence had swelled the crowd. Osbern was standing at the back with the other servants and scullions, perched on tiptoe and bobbing up and down trying to see the glistening glimmering display at the candlelit altar. The chanting of the monks soared through the vaulted ceiling, the Latin words ethereal and otherworldly to the congregation.

'What do the words mean?'

'Glory to you, who have shown us the light,' Friar Timothy chanted in French along with the Latin. 'Glory to God in the highest and on earth peace, good will to all people. We praise you, we bless you, we worship you, we glorify you; we give thanks to you for your great glory. Lord, King, heavenly God, Father, almighty; Lord, the only-begotten Son, Jesus Christ, and Holy Spirit.'

Osbern looked at the poor priest in shock. He had never met anyone who could translate Latin into French in such an instant way. Even scholars like John of Salisbury or Herbert of Bosham would struggle with such a feat of learning.

'How?'

'I have a gift for language,' Timothy told him. 'It is God's favour.' Then he tapped his nose. 'Best not to mention it, the Abbot thinks it is sinful.'

The congregation was swept up in the majesty and spectacle of the Christmas service. Thomas had made sure that the Lord's nativity would be celebrated in all its glory and pomp. Food and wine, ale and meats, had all been brought to the palace for the feast. More dark rumours and warnings had arrived at the Archbishop's court over the last few days. More talk of murder. Osbern had been privy to the meetings, privy to the whispered secrets, as he tended to his master's needs.

'You are faithful to the last, Rabbit,' Thomas had told him.

'I hope the end is far away yet, Lord,' said Osbern.

His master had merely given a wan smile and sipped at his cordial as the clerks and knights told their dire warnings.

The monkish singing was coming to an end, drawing Osbern back to the service. Every eye was fixed upon the altar as the Rabbit's crooked broken master climbed up the four steps to the pulpit. There were mutters and whispers from the townsfolk at the sight of the broken Archbishop, and then Thomas turned to face the assembled congregation.

He looked down at the sea of white faces that back stared up at him, waiting on his words, waiting on his sermon. Thomas had been nervous before the ceremony, but now he was fixed with proud determination. He would tend to his flock and do his duty to the Lord God. Come what may.

'Peace on earth and to all men goodwill,' Thomas began. 'In this time of the nativity of our Lord, let our woes be lifted by the grace of our saviour and father.'

His voice was clear, as if the years of worry and trials had fallen from him as he spoke to the lay folk from his pulpit. Even the Rabbit could see him speak, as he bobbed up and down at the back of the congregation. This was the Thomas of old, tall and slender, clear spoken and relishing the actor's performance. If it was to be his final scene, he would play his part to the bitter end. Thomas spoke at length on the history of the church fathers, the holy martyrs who had died in the service of their god. He could always transfix people with his words, when he wanted to. The audience was suitably enthralled, on the very edge of their seats gripped by his every word. At the end, as the sermon finished, Thomas turned to his cross bearer Alexander Llewellyn, loyal through all the years in exile, standing to one side of the pulpit.

'This church has one martyr already in Saint Alphage,' said Thomas loud enough that the congregation in the nave could hear. 'Soon it will have another in myself.'

Alexander Llewellyn looked surprised at Thomas's words, and there were cries of 'nay' from the congregation.

'What mean you, your grace?' Alexander asked.

'The time of my death is at hand,' said Thomas beginning to weep. 'Soon I shall be taken from this world.'

They were weeping along with him in the aisles, the Canterbury congregation sobbing along, and hushed whispers and groans at the Archbishop's words. Most of them realised he spoke of the De Brocs. A man stood up in the nave, looking about the pews. Osbern thought he was a local butcher, but could not be certain.

'Father, why are you leaving us so soon? Who are you going to leave to so desolate.' He waved at the weeping people around him.

Thomas straightened up and wiped his face with the sleeve of his robes. The tears were gone as soon as they appeared. Osbern wondered later if they had been planned, part of the act. He would not put it past his master. Thomas was a consummate actor.

'The De Broc's, snarled Thomas at the butcher. 'I excommunicate them.' He grabbed a bell from a monk and rang out a single clear tone. 'De Sackville, I excommunicate him. Geoffrey Ridel, usurper of the church at Oxford, I excommunicate him.' He rang the bell again and again. 'Roger of York, Joscelin of Salisbury, Gilbert of London. I excommunicate them all!' He had grown wild in anger, tearing at his robes as he shook the bell. He grabbed a tall candle, almost half his height and dripping with hot wax, and cast it crashing to the flagstone pavement.

'Christ Jesus curse them all!' He screamed at the top of his voice.

The congregation watched on in horror as the madman archbishop railed at his enemies. Osbern noted a couple of people slipping out of the cathedral. Word of this display would soon be with the De Brocs in Saltwood and the King in Normandy.

'Let their memories be erased from the Book of Life,' shouted Thomas to the rafters. And then, in a harsh whisper audible only to Alexander the Crossbearer. 'Expel them from the kingdom of the elect.'

With his final condemnation he led the conclusion of the Christmas High Mass in silence, all his energy exhausted in the rage. Afterwards, he was led away by his attendants to the palace barely able to speak. A feast for Christmas had been made ready for them all and was waiting in the palace hall. The monks and clerics happily gluttoned and guzzled the food at the Archbishop's command. Thomas had relaxed the rules on eating meat on Fridays in honour of Christ's birth. He even indulged himself a morsel of meat, until the fatty pork turned his stomach and he had to ask Osbern for his cordial. At the end of the meal, Thomas pulled Herbert of Bosham and Alexander Llewellyn to one side and gave them messages for the pope and King of France. Both were to leave on the morrow. That was a fact that Bosham bemoaned to Thomas, so intent was he on sharing the Archbishop's martyrdom and glory.

'Here I am surrounded by my enemies,' said Thomas. 'Let my friends know what has truly occurred here, for the King's men will spin tales and untruths.'

Herbert burst into tears at the thought of leaving Thomas at his darkest hour; he was determined to share in Thomas's trials. He sought it out. He wanted to be a hero of the church.

'I would stay with you, your grace. I would share in your martyrdom.'

Thomas held him in a long hug, weeping along with his old friend and advisor.

'Not so, my son, not so,' said Thomas, breaking away. 'You will not be cheated of your reward if you follow your lord's orders faithfully. You will not see me again in this life, but you must go because the King sees you as one of the principles in this matter.'

Osbern the Rabbit had never liked Herbert of Bosham. He thought him a zealot whose advice to Thomas had done more harm than good over the years, but the Rabbit could not fault the man's bravery or devotion. Osbern was confused, unsure of what to do next, unsure of what to say. Everyone seemed so resigned to the De Brocs doing murder to his master. Yet nobody was lifting a hand to stop it. Indeed they seemed to welcome it.

'The world has gone mad,' said the Rabbit.

***

FitzUrse and the others had arrived at Saltwood separately just after Christmas. Ranulf De Broc had immediately seen the advantage their arrival gave him. They would be his weapons in this matter. He welcomed the Bear and his comrades like old friends, gave them expensive wines to sup and good food to eat. Then he whispered murder in their ears. FitzUrse was wise enough in the ways of court to see what De Broc wanted and the King's words were still fresh in his mind. The Bear understood his duty.

'So we are decided?' he asked the other three.

De Moreville and De Tracy both nodded, their faces grim, but young Brito still looked unsure.

'What will the King say?' the boy asked.

'You heard the King in Bayeux. He wants this finished and there is only one way we can deliver that for him. He will reward us well, when we have fulfilled our task.'

Brito still looked unconvinced by the argument.

'That estate in Wiltshire you covet will be yours,' said FitzUrse.

He knew the boy's family. They had holdings near his lands in Somerset. The Wiltshire estate was one that the Britos had long eyed. That seemed to settle the matter with the lad. He nodded finally.

'We are agreed,' he said in a soft whisper.

'I will tell De Broc,' said FitzUrse, before the boy could change his mind. 'He has a priest who will show us the way.'

'Another priest? Can we trust him?' said De Moreville.

'Aye, he is no friend to Thomas. The Archbishop unfrocked him and insulted him.'

The others nodded at the Bear's words. Thomas antagonised everyone. They all knew that the step they were taking was unprecedented, but the King had been clear in his rage.

FitzUrse rose and left the hall to go to De Broc. The clear air of the bailey sobered him up. He had known Thomas for years:

the Bear had served Thomas on the Toulouse campaign. He remembered when the King and former Chancellor had been as close as brothers. He smiled as he remembered the Rabbit drunk in his cups at Cahors. Then frowned when he realised the little servant would still be with his master. He liked Osbern.

Everything was so simple back then.

Had we stood together, all of France would have been ours, thought the Bear. Instead, Thomas spent seven years creating problem after problem until the great divide consumed everything that Henry did. All the while Louis of France laughed into his cups and stirred the pot to keep the arguments bubbling. The only way to finish this was to finish Thomas, and then they would make the King of the Franks pay for his interference.

De Broc's chambers were in the keep. Guards nodded the Bear through the doors to a small private room in an upper floor. Ranulf was seated on a cushioned chair with a half-naked girl pouring wine for him in front of a roaring fire. Two of his captains and another in monk's robes that the Bear did not recognise were with him, cups in hand.

'You are all agreed?' asked De Broc

'Yes,' said the Bear. 'There is no other way to settle this.'

De Broc gave a wide smile.

'You will be well rewarded for this, FitzUrse.'

'I do not do it for reward,' the Bear growled back.' I do it for my Lord's honour which this troublesome cleric insults. Who is this creature?' He waved at the dark haired monk in the corner.

The monk stood up and gave a short bow at FitzUrse's curt tone. 'I am Hugh of Horsea and well known here.'

'He is my cousin's chaplain,' said De Broc in explanation. 'The Archbishop has long been his enemy, and he will be of assistance to us in this matter.'

'How so?'

'I know the ways of the cathedral and of the city,' said Hugh. 'Thomas will not be able to hide or to flee from me.'

'You will guide us to the palace?' asked the Bear.

The cleric nodded and De Broc sat up in his chair.

'I have men watching the ports here and in Normandy, more around Canterbury and on the roads. He will not escape this time.

FitzUrse remembered Thomas's escape from Northampton years before. They would not be fooled again.

'Then we are all agreed,' said the Bear.

***

There was an air of forced joviality in the court at Bayeux. The King had spared no expense on the feasting. Cattle had been slaughtered, fresh vintages brought from Gascony, sweetmeats, nuts, and candied fruits galore were passed about for the revellers to nibble on. A troop of Jongleurs had arrived from the German Emperor to entertain and delight the courtiers with juggling and sleight of hand. Henry had observed the Advent fast only sporadically, but he had been determined to celebrate the feast of the Nativity. Thomas's actions in England had brought that good mood crashing down. Whilst others played and japed for him, Henry of Anjou sat glowering on his carved wooden throne. The quarrel with the archbishop had tainted everything, now it threatened his son's succession and his dynasty's future. He could not let everything fall back into anarchy on the whims of an upstart priest.

'It is only a month and he has betrayed me,' said Henry to himself.

The dwarf acrobats were clambering all over each other to build a tower, tossing wooden balls up and down; most of the audience was transfixed by the display. Henry thought it dull.

'In only a month, he has torn England apart.'

'Your pardon, Lord?' One of the flunkeys had heard his whispered thoughts.

'Bring me more wine,' said Henry, and sat back.

It had been Christmas when I made Thomas chancellor, after the celebrations in Bermondsey, thought the King.

The old Archbishop had persuaded Henry that Thomas would be the most loyal advisor. That he would proved good advice and deal with the administration.

And I trusted him, thought the King. I loved him.

Thomas had been cultured and urbane, with soft white hands like a girl's, but a good horseman. Henry chuckled to himself. He was not as good as me, and it rankled with him even then. They had played chess and sat late into the night talking. Henry would settle the realm with Thomas at his side. They became as close as brothers, two minds fixed upon one single design: to order England, to secure the line, to break the King of France.

'Where did it go wrong? Everything was in our grasp after Toulouse. Where did it all go wrong?'

Henry knew the answer. It went wrong when he made the foolborn Cheapside peasant a priest; he raised him so high that the man's vanity had puffed him out. Everything Thomas had, he had from the King, but the man thought it was all on his own meagre talents. Well, Henry was going to disabuse him of that notion.

The dwarf acrobats had collapsed into a heap to the delight of the onlookers, coloured balls bouncing left and right. Their leader looked to the King, to see if their display had raised his spirits – or at the very least not made them worse. Henry smiled benevolently and cast a small purse to the man. He would not take his frustrations out on poor entertainers. It was Thomas's blood Henry wanted. It was only Thomas's head on a silver platter that would suffice.

'Be careful what you wish for, Salome,' Henry whispered quietly to himself and drained his cup.

The King stood up in silence and stalked out of the hall, leaving the court to their celebrations. He fell back into his own private chambers and called for more wine from a servant.

This matter must be settled, his son's crown must be secured that was all that counted, thought the King. Else my whole life's work would be for nothing. With Young Henry in England, Richard in Aquitaine, and Geoffrey in Brittany, even little John in Ireland, Angevin writ would stretch across half of Europe. Henry would become a new Charlemagne; an emperor to match the Germans, perhaps even the Romans of Constantinople. The French Capetians would be destroyed and their lands taken.

'Now a treasonous priest threatens it all,' he said to himself. 'This matter must be settled.'

Henry would send officers to arrest Thomas, he decided. They would drag the rebel Archbishop to Rouen to face his King, as long as Thomas came quietly.

He will not come quietly, thought the King.

***

The four knights had risen early and broken their fast as the castle garrison made ready. The De Brocs had feasted them late into the night, a St Stephen's day celebration to fortify their spirits for the task ahead, and all of them had thick heads. The castle was being stripped of its men, and more were sent for before they were ready to leave. De Broc was intent on taking an army to the cathedral. He was determined that none would stand in his way.

They were quiet as they mounted their horses and made ready. All of them were pondering the day ahead. The Bear kept an eye on Brito; the lad was too nervous. FitzUrse did not need him taking fright when the task got bloody.

'Are you well?' he asked the white-faced young knight.

Brito simply nodded and swung himself up into the saddle.

'We go to avenge our king's shame,' the Bear reminded him.

'I know,' said Brito.

Most of the party were dressed for war, with mail shirts under their tunics and surcoats and open faced helms, but De Tracy had dressed as if he was riding to a winter's fair in a bottle green jerkin and multicoloured cloak.

'He thinks he is Joseph,' said De Moreville with a grunt.

'We go to put down a dog, not do battle with a warrior.'

The Bear smiled at those words. He remembered Cahors; he remembered Toulouse. He remembered Thomas unseating a French champion in the Vexin.

'Thomas is brave and he is wily, and he knows how to use a lance. Do not underestimate the man, William,' he told De Tracy. 'He got away from me in Northampton and has resisted our king all these years. He is no easy mark.'

'You sound as if you admire him.'

'I did, once, but the priest must die.'

De Tracy spat to ward off evil at the Bear's words. Whatever his bravado; they all knew what they were doing.

They were silent after that as De Broc led them up the roman road to Canterbury. It was but an hour's gentle riding to the city. More and more knights and men-at-arms joined them as they rode along. De Broc's summons and indignant anger at Thomas's return poured a cold fire into the men's hearts. All of them were steeled to murder the Archbishop. There was no question of backing down.

The road ran straight as an arrow towards its destination, only on the last leg twisting and turning as they descended from the Kent downs towards the city. They could see the towers of the cathedral in the distance. On the outskirts of the town they were met by two local citizens, the only Canterbury men to join the party.

'Where are the rest?' demanded De Broc. He had expected tens of men.

'Not coming,' said one of the townsmen.

The citizens and aldermen of Canterbury had refused De Broc's command to assemble. Ranulf cursed at few supporters. Instead of headings straight into the city, the party turned towards St Augustine's Abbey outside the old Roman walls and set in its own compound.

'Where are we going?' asked Brito as they turned away from the cathedral.

'Clarembald is there,' De Broc told him in explanation.

Abbot Clarembald was notorious. A tubby dissolute drunkard and womaniser, utterly unsuited to any priestly rank. It was rumoured that he had fathered seventeen illegitimate children, but none were certain of the true number, even Clarembald himself. The King had given him the title, and rents, of the abbey as a reward for his service as a courtier clerk. Unlike Thomas who had been gifted Canterbury in similar circumstances, Clarembald had little interest in serving God. He had not even bothered to have his shock of unruly blonde hair cut into a tonsure, and the Abbey's monks had spent years complaining and trying to have him removed. There was no love between the coarse Abbot and proud Archbishop.

Abbot Clarembald welcomed them into his house and fed them and served them wine. De Broc sent some men on into the city with orders to secure the gates and make ready. They would confront the rebel Archbishop that day.

'Is he there?'

'He is there,' Clarembald told them. 'Eating his supper and waiting like a lamb for the slaughter.'

FitzUrse and the others all took strong wine to fortify themselves. Brito's hands were shaking, but he could not back down. The Archbishop had to die. It was the King's command. Henry had been quite clear when he called them miserable drones.

'Are you ready?' said De Broc.

They left on their tunics to conceal the armour underneath but girded their swords. De Broc led them into the town, to one of the Canterbury men's house. Abbot Clarembald waved them off with a wide grin, sending some of his men with them. The Archbishop was finally going to pay for his crimes. The renegade priest Hugh was with them as they marched into the city through the Burgate, to a house of one of the Brocs' supporters. A whole crowd were gathered there waiting; horses tethered in the street, and even more men in mail shirts waiting in the courtyard. It was getting dark; the short winter's afternoon was already drawing to a close.

Hugh the renegade priest would lead the four knights into the cathedral, dressed in his monk's habit and sandals. De Broc and the others would wait at the house, wait for news. If things went awry, if Thomas had taken fright and run for the coast, they would be after him. There was to be no escape for the Archbishop.

'It is time,' said the Bear.

8

There was a commotion at the doors to the Archbishop's hall; shouting and angry voices. Thomas looked up from his plate and quietly whispered a prayer. A nervous young lay clerk rushed past the diners to the high table. Thomas could see his robes were too short, nearly halfway up his legs; the boy was growing fast, and the tonsure cut into the lad's thick brown hair needed to be shaved.

'There are four knights, my lord. They demand to see you.'

'God thank you, Henry.' Thomas prided himself on remembering even the lowliest lay clerk's name, even though he had only been back in England a few short weeks. 'They can wait until the hall is cleared.'

Servants were already removing platters and pottery. It was nearly time for vespers. Thomas had promised to attend the service.

'They are most insistent, Archbishop.' Young Henry sounded scared.

'They can wait, Henry.' Thomas's voice was calm but firm. He waved for the servants to continue clearing the tables.

The young clerk returned to the doorway but the shouting continued, growing louder, angrier. The monks, priests, and clerics in the hall all looked to Thomas; he could see that they were scared, whispering among themselves. With a sigh, he stood up and walked to the threshold of the palace hall. Osbern hurried to attend to the Archbishop, wiping his hands clean on his habit before taking his place behind his master.

The threshold was darker than the torch-lit hall. Five men wreathed in the shadows stood with angry eyes; their lips twisted into snarls as they swore and damned the young clerk. The knights were unarmed, not dressed for battle. Osbern breathed an audible sigh of relief as he noted that.

Thomas recognised the men, so did the Rabbit. They were the worst of the King's dogs: Reginald FitzUrse, the one they called The Bear, a cruel vindictive bully and whoremonger to the

King. He was hulking in size, towering over the others, with wild hair and beard. Hugh de Moreville was another; William de Tracy was with him, and Richard Brito. Thomas knew them all well, FitzUrse, de Moreville, and de Tracy had sworn oaths of fealty to him when he was the King's chancellor, and young Brito was a godless sycophant to the King's brother. The fifth was that renegade priest Hugh, who Thomas had disciplined and exiled from Canterbury. These cursed creatures had not come to receive the blessings of the season. Thomas knew that, Osbern knew that. Everybody in the hall had heard the murderous talk of the last few days. Would they murder him here and now in front of everybody?

FitzUrse saw the Archbishop first, pushing himself to the front to address Thomas. The others let The Bear speak for them, standing tongue-tied in silence behind his giant frame.

'God help you,' said The Bear. 'We have brought a message from the King Will you hear it in public or private?'

'Whichever you choose,' said Thomas, opening his arms

The monks and clerks, scared of the angry warriors at the doors, began slipping out of the Archbishop's hall.

'Cowards,' sniffed the Rabbit.

Thomas called them back. John of Salisbury, Thomas's friend for decades, tried to calm the situation. John knew these nights could kill, armoured or not, and he knew the Archbishop was too rash and too swift to speak his mind. It was, thought John, the greater problem between Archbishop and King: they were too alike. Now, however, even the tubby scholar's life was on the line.

'My Lord,' he said to Thomas. 'Let us converse in private.' John gestured to the appalled watchers in the hall. The priests and clerics all terrified of the Bear.

Thomas smiled at his old friend but shook his head. He wanted witnesses to the encounter.

'That would serve no good purpose, John. Such things should be spoken in public not in private chambers.' He turned back to face the knights.

The Bear jabbed a finger at him. 'When the King made peace with you he sent you back to Canterbury, but you have broken the peace and in your obstinate pride excommunicated bishops who crowned the King's son. You would take away Young Henry's crown too if you had the strength!'

'Never would I do such, FitzUrse,' said Thomas quietly. 'As God is my witness, I would not deprive the King's son nor diminish his power. It was by the Pope's command that the bishops were excommunicated, not mine.'

'You were behind it all.' snarled the Bear.

'I do not deny that it was done by my hand, but the sentence was that of my superior the Pope, and not in my power to change,' said Thomas. 'I made fair offer to the bishops of London and Salisbury, if they repented and accepted the Pope's verdict, but they rejected my offer.' He shrugged. 'The Archbishop of York is beyond my jurisdiction.'

The Bear was enraged by Thomas's answers, as were the other knights. It was the same conversation Thomas had been having since his return.

'The King's orders are that you and yours depart this realm,' the Bear said. 'There can never be peace with you for you have broken the peace.'

'Do not threaten me, Reginald.' Thomas gave FitzUrse a cold stare. 'My faith is in the King of Heaven. I will not leave this place. Once I fled from you like a timid priest, but I have returned to my church in obedience to the Pope, and I will not flee again. Any who want me can find me here.' Thomas half-turned but the Bear grabbed at his robe. 'The Lord King himself admitted me into his peace and gave me safe conduct, Reginald. You were there when he did it, all of you.' Thomas shook himself free. 'You did not object to me then?'

'From whom do you hold your authority?' said the Bear, ignoring Thomas's question.

'My spiritual authority I hold from God and the Pope. My material possessions I hold from the King.'

'You hold everything from the King,' snarled FitzUrse. His hands clenched in fury, white at the knuckles. He could hardly bear the insult to Henry.

'I render unto Caesar what is Caesar's and to God the things that are God's.' Thomas was uncowed.

'I am telling you what the King says,' said the Bear, going red in the face. 'You excommunicated royal officers. You should have respected the King's majesty – submitted yourself to his judgement.'

Thomas stood tall against them. 'Your threats are in vain,' he said. 'Even if all the swords in England were pointed at my head, they would not move me from my observance of God's justice and my obedience to the Pope.'

The four knights started to jostle the archbishop, pushing at him, grabbing his robes, but Thomas shook himself free again as Osbern and the others watched on in horrified silence.

'I tell you now,' said Thomas loud enough for all in the hall to hear. 'I shall strike any who violates the rights of the Pope or Christ's church. I will not spare him; I will not delay in imposing sentence upon him.'

'You risk your head saying that,' said Brito softly, speaking for the first time.

'Are you come to slay me then?' said Thomas, mockingly. 'If so I shall commit myself to the great judge of mankind.' They did not move to strike and he shook his head at them, like a disapproving schoolmaster with naughty pupils. 'I am not moved by your threats; find someone else to frighten.' Thomas turned away from the knights to return to the hall and prepare for vespers.

'We are the King's men!' shouted FitzUrse at the Archbishop's back. 'Seize him!' he screamed at the monks. Seeing that the stunned clerics did not move, the Bear grabbed one by the robes and dragged the man out of the hall. Brito did the same with another – taking the two as hostage. Thomas turned back at that, raising his voice for the first time in anger.

'Release them, FitzUrse! I command you in God's name! Release them!'

The knights took no notice, contemptuously dismissing the Archbishop, pulling the two prisoner monks outside into the dark night.

Thomas could hear the cries of 'King's men! King's men!' coming from the courtyard. There were more of De Broc's men out there. He turned back to his terrified clerks and attendants.

They crowded around their Archbishop, and Osbern barricaded the door against the knights' return.

'Fear not,' said Thomas, smiling, trying to reassure everyone with his calm presence.

'They were drunk,' said a monk. 'We are protected here by the King's peace.' Some of the others nodded at that.

John of Salisbury stood forward and touched Thomas on the arm.

'Look you, Thomas, you are doing what you always do,' John said to his old friend. 'Acting and speaking on impulse, never asking advice, always saying just what you like. What need is there to exasperate and inflame those butchers?'

Thomas reached out to John and touched his arm in turn. He gave his friend a sad smile. The old scholar was not suited to this confrontation. John was born for the library, for deep conversations over cups of wine, not for this battle. Thomas knew why the knights had come. Pacifying them would not have helped; the end would be the same. Sometimes you have to stand firm in the storm. He shook his head firmly.

'My counsel is now all taken,' he said.

'Pray God that it may turn out well,' said John, despairing.

'May God's will be done.'

This is madness, thought Osbern. We can still escape. There are passages and tunnels. They would not find us. But the Rabbit said nothing, just stayed close to his master's side.

A great hammering started up on the doors to the hall. The knights had returned girded for war. They had stripped off their tunics to reveal mail coats and their bright swords were unsheathed. The monks panicked, terrified of what was coming, rushing about in distress. They begged the Archbishop to flee, but Thomas would have none of it.

'You monks are too easily intimidated,' he told them. 'Do not be afraid.'

Then the vespers bell tolled.

The monks, seeing a chance to escape, tried to rush Thomas into the cathedral, into the sanctuary of the church, but he waited for young Henry to bear the cross in front of him. Osbern prayed they would have enough time. They hurried the

Archbishop to the cloister doors leading into the cathedral itself, only to find the bolt stuck fast in the freezing cold. Osbern stepped forward, waved his burning torch over the metal as John of Salisbury whispered a prayer. Once the iron was hot enough to melt the ice, Osbern shot the bolt back as if it were in liquid glue. Thomas smiled at his old servant as the monks bustled the Archbishop along the cloister. Their leather shoes slapped on the marble flagstones as they hurried; one priest even dared to grab the Archbishop's white robes and pull at him in desperate terror. The party entered the cathedral and Osbern turned to bolt the cloister door behind them, but Thomas stopped him.

'The church is a house of prayer,' he said. 'It is not a fortress.'

John of Salisbury sighed in despair and shot the Rabbit a look of utter desolation. Thomas is determined to die; they both thought the same. He could escape if he wanted to.

Thomas turned and slowly walked up the steps towards the high altar. Monks were chanting the vespers service in the choir as he ascended, but they hushed when they saw him appear. The Archbishop's attendants followed behind, step-by-step. Young Henry was leading the party bearing the cross in Alexander Llewellyn's absence.

The cloister door burst open behind them. The Bear stood there armed for war; the other knights were with him, naked blades to hand. They looked bigger in their armour, faceless metal demons exuding power and hatred. The sanctuary of the church was defiled. Priests, clerics and monks scattered in terror at the sight of the armed men. John of Salisbury ran and hid himself in the crypt rather than face the knights with Thomas. Even Osbern, so long Thomas's faithful servant, hid himself in the choir, peering out of the darkness to watch what happened. Only Edward Grim, a visiting scholar, and two others stood at the Archbishop's side at the knights' approach.

'Where is Thomas Becket traitor to the King and kingdom?' shouted The Bear.

He could have fled with his attendants; he could have saved himself, thought Osbern. It is too late now.

'Here I am,' said Thomas. 'What do you want from me? I am no traitor to the King but a priest.

The knights saw him, rushed at him brandishing their weapons. 'Absolve them,' they screamed at Thomas. 'Restore to communion those you have excommunicated; restore powers to those you have suspended.' Their voices boomed out in the great open space.

The Archbishop turned to face them down, holding onto a stone pillar as if for support.

'There has been no satisfaction, and I will not absolve them.' Thomas still spoke quietly and calmly in response to their shouts.

'Then you shall die,' said the Bear, 'and get what you deserve.'

'I am ready to die for my Lord,' said Thomas. 'In my blood the Church may obtain liberty and peace. But in the name of Almighty God, I forbid you to hurt my people whether clerk or lay.'

They grabbed at him again, trying to drag him from the pillar but Thomas would not yield. The Bear was frothing at the mouth in anger, spittle flying as he snarled, ripping at Thomas's raiment. The Archbishop pushed the Bear away.

'Whoremonger,' said Thomas. 'Touch me not, Reginald; you owe me fealty and subjection; you and your accomplices act like madmen.'

That sent the Bear into apoplexy. He waved his sword at Thomas's head, tipping off the Archbishop's cap.

'Neither faith, nor subjection do I owe you against my fealty to my lord the King!' FitzUrse spat in Thomas's face.

The Archbishop bowed his head and joined his hands together. He could see the high altar from where he stood. It was all lit up with candles, the glittering flames surrounded by halos of light in the darkness. He was still defiant, still proud, still determined to prove himself. His Lord was God not a mortal monarch. Thomas began to pray.

'I commend my cause and that of the church to God, to St. Mary, and to the blessed martyr Denys.'

FitzUrse struck out at Thomas with his sword. Edward Grim, one of the three who had stayed to watch over the Archbishop, reached out to stop the blow. The Bear's sword cut through the man's limb right to the bone. Grim fell back screaming, bleeding, mutilated, and the blade smashed on into Thomas's crown. There was blood streaming from the archbishop's head, staining his white robes red. Another knight slashed at Thomas's head but the Archbishop stood firm. At a third blow he fell to his knees, his lips still moving in prayer. Osbern, still frozen in terror in the choir, let out a low groan of despair as he saw his master struck down.

'For the name of Jesus and the protection of the church I am ready to embrace death,' the Archbishop was still whispering his prayer.

Young Roger Brito stepped forward and swung at the prone priest, striking Thomas so hard with his sword that sparks flew up and his blade shattered against the stone floor.

'Take that, for the love of my lord William, the king's brother!' shouted Brito.

Thomas's crown was cut from the back of his skull. He collapsed to the ground; a pool of dark blood spread out over the white marble. Hugh, the renegade priest who had long hated the Archbishop, stood on the dying man's neck. With the tip of his dagger he scraped out the brain and scattered it on the pavement.

'Let us away, knights,' he said when he finished the gruesome task. 'This one will rise no more.'

The knights fled then, white-faced and in terror, with a dawning realisation of what they had done that night; miserable drones that would be forever haunted by their act. Monks and clerics emerged from their hiding places at their departure and fell to the marble floor. Mopping up Thomas's blood with their clothes, scooping up brain and bone into vials and chalices. There would be no need to wash the body for burial. The martyr had been sanctified by his own sacrifice.

John of Salisbury understood that better than most of them. He stood there watching over Thomas's broken corpse; a witness to the horror. Watching as they bound up Becket's head and stripped off his torn bloodied white robes; watching as Grim was carried away; watching over young Henry of Auxerre struck dumb in shock. John realised that the King was beaten by Becket's sacrifice; the church was saved by his martyrdom. He saw the stricken Rabbit, sitting in silence in the choir, white at his master's murder. The tubby scholar took it all in, he would write about it later. When the attendants revealed the coarse hair shirt crawling with lice under the Archbishop's rich clothing and called him a saint, John finally wondered if he had not misjudged his old, reckless, friend.

***

The King's council were gathering together when news of murder in the cathedral arrived. Henry had summoned his barons and churchmen to the Castle of Argentan to discuss Thomas's interdicts and their response to the Pope in Rome. The King planned to overwhelm the Pope with a flurry of letters from all his loyal priests and barons. They would attest to Thomas's perfidy, as Henry commanded. He would tie Pope Alexander up in legal arguments and force the rebel Archbishop out of office.

Henry was perched in his carved wooden throne on a raised dais in the hall, a cup of wine in hand. The council chamber was a large space on the top floor of the keep, with a roaring fire and rich tapestries on the walls as you ascended from the great hall below. A small door led off to Henry's private apartments behind the dais with his bedchamber and wardrobes. Some of the barons were already seated around the room; some were still coming up the narrow stairs from the hall below. Sturdy wooden chairs were set up around the hall for each lord to rest, but without the King's cushions or opulence.

There was a hubbub of murmurs as each councillor presented himself to the King and walked to his seat. Roger of York and the other bishops were also in attendance, standing beside the dais and dripping poison about Thomas to any who would listen. Most of the barons happily listened to the bishops accusations. All of them knew Thomas was the enemy, and everyone wanted to please the King. Perhaps forty or more of the most important men in Henry's realms waited on their lord's command.

Humphrey de Bohun, one of the last to enter, was the first to hear the news of the killing. The Lord of Trowbridge was walking up the stairs to the council chamber when his blonde manservant tugged at his sleeve.

'What is it?'

'Riders have come from Caen, Lord, with bring dreadful word from home.'

The man was ashen as he whispered the horror to his master. The Archbishop had been murdered, butchered before the altar in his cathedral by the King's own men. The House of the Lord had been defiled and despoiled. Bohun was at the top of the stairs; he glanced inside the chamber. The King was smiling and welcoming his supporters as they entered. He cannot know, thought the lord. He nodded his manservant away and paused before going in. The King might take the news badly and Bohun was not popular at court, but better to speak up than to hide away. Besides, he had liked Thomas and had enjoyed his company before the great divide between King and Archbishop had started. De Bohun waited his turn and bowed deeply before the throne when he was called. The King smiled and told him to rise.

'My Lord,' he began when Henry welcomed him. 'I have just received word from England, from Canterbury...' Bohun stuttered to a halt, white at the dawning realisation at the gravity of the news; every eye in the chamber was upon him. 'Archbishop Thomas is dead, Lord, murdered two days ago in his own cathedral by FizUrse the Bear and three other knights of your household.'

There were gasps at the words around the chamber, an instant of shocked silence, and then everyone started talking – except the King.

Henry sat back in his throne and sighed. He had expected something like this, it had been building for weeks, but the detail of Thomas's killing still had him shocked to the core. He had sent officers to arrest him, to bring him to Normandy, but he knew there were others in the court more inclined to violence. Thomas was always stubborn, he would never sumit. He remembered his old friend as he had once been, before all of this anguish. Henry recalled Thomas's wan smile at his jesting, Thomas's cutting wit in the council chamber. He remembered the hawking and hunting together; the triumphant march to Toulouse; all their victories over the Franks. Thomas had been his brother in everything, until Henry had made the man a priest. It was a bitter mistake that the King had cursed every day for the past decade. He cursed Thomas's stubborn pride that had brought them to this. He should have kept him at his side as his chancellor and friend. Then none of this would have happened. Henry recalled that Thomas had once told him as much.

'That is one problem solved then, Lord,' said one of the barons.

Henry studiously ignored the man. He noted the look of triumph on the face of the Archbishop of York and his fellow churchmen. They had hated Thomas from the very start. Roger of York had despised Thomas since their youth together as clerks. None of these men were friends of the murdered Archbishop, but Henry had loved him once. Henry had trusted him in everything. Thomas had broken that faith with the King over the last ten years time and time again.

What choice was there? What else could I have done? Could I have saved him and kept my crown? Henry wondered to himself, but he still said nothing to his chattering lords. The King retired to his private chambers in silence, coldly ignoring his barons and bishops, and called for hot almond milk to settle his stomach. The news had sent the King's guts into a spin. A small pageboy brought the milk, looking utterly terrified, but Henry took the drink and waved him away without another word. The boy left, leaving Henry alone in the bedchamber. He sipped at the warm liquid and grimaced.

'This tastes foul,' he said to himself, mixed in a cup of wine and tasted it. 'That is better.'

'Father?'

His son Richard had come into the chamber. Only twelve years old but the boy was already tall and broad; already fearsome with a blade and a fine horseman. Richard had his father's red hair, slate grey eyes, and a temper to match Henry's. All of the King's brood had inherited his temper.

'What is it?'

'The council is in uproar, after you left so sudden and saying nothing.'

Henry smiled at his son. 'Sometimes it is better to be silent and sow confusion than to speak out and be despised.'

'I do not understand this lesson?'

The boy would be made Duke of Aquitaine before long, part of Henry's grand design to strangle the French crown. He clapped the boy on the back.

'You will understand soon enough. Go back to them, speak to the council; tell them how stricken I am at the killing. You have an easy way with the barons, it will help calm things.'

Richard still stood before the King, lips pursed, fists clenched, defiantly waiting to say something.

'Well?' asked his father.

'I rather liked him, Father... I liked Thomas.'

'So did I,' said Henry sadly. 'He was my brother.' He touched his son's cheek and smiled. 'Perhaps I shall go on Crusade soon. The Pope would like that. Perhaps I shall take you?'

The boy gave a wide grin. 'I would like that very much as well, Father.'

'Go to the lords then, keep them happy. We will need an army of barons to fight the Saracens.'

Richard returned to the council chamber. Henry turned to a small arched window, opened the wooden shutter, and looked out over the town of Argentan. It was snowing, a pristine shroud of white that blanketed the town. There were fires in the bailey; workmen building up the castle camped there. Every day, the town walls were strengthened and the defences improved. It was costing the King an absolute fortune in silver, but the town was important to Henry. Argentan was a key piece in his ongoing struggle with Louis of France. It was a strategic choke point on the road to Caen and the Norman coast. From Argentan, Henry could strike at the French interior and take his war to the gates of Paris. His sons would carry on his work: Young Henry in England, Geoffrey in Brittany, and boisterous Richard in Aquitaine. He would even find lands in Ireland for little John, his youngest and his favourite.

Thomas had threatened all those plans with his stubborn pride. A lifetime's work brought to ruin by an arrogant priest. Cheapside had spurned any and every attempt at reconciliation for six long years. Even when the King had agreed to everything in order to settle the matter, Thomas had attacked his officers once more. The rebel Archbishop threatened the future of Henry's dynasty by questioning his son's coronation. Thomas had humiliated Henry time and time again. He had forgiven him, made peace with him, and Thomas had started again. There could never be a true peace with such a man.

Henry's barons would have turned eventually. If an upstart lowborn cleric could challenge their King they all could. Thomas had made him look weak. He could not afford to look weak. Henry knew that the Pope would blame him; he knew his enemies would be circling now. He understood that it had been his taunting of Thomas that had sent the Bear off to Canterbury. The man would not have acted on his own initiative. The four of them would have to be exiled, sent off to the Holy Land on crusade. That might pacify the Pope, but the rest would still condemn his angry words that had caused the murder. Henry was no fool, he understood all of that, but he was not prepared for the miracles, or for the popular rush to visit the crypt in Canterbury by everyone and anyone. He still did not conceive that that his old, stubborn, vain, dearest beloved friend, could become a martyr and saint. All of that was still to come.

'I am not Herod,' whispered the King to himself. 'I had no choice. It was him or me.'

Epilogue.

Fifty Years Later.

The festivities roared through the city. Flags and banners set up on every house, dancing and troops of musicians, frothing ale flowed in rivers as the revellers supped and smiled and danced. The procession of the great, good, and guilty wound through the town to the cheers and cries of the onlookers. Canterbury was wild with adulation for their patron saint. The shrine of Saint Thomas of Canterbury, the martyred archbishop, was finally to be consecrated. It had taken years of arguments and planning and finally building. A new chapel had been constructed to replace the fire destroyed structure that the saint had known, but finally the spectacle was completed. The high and holy had come to show it to the world. Inside the new chapel was the shrine to the cathedral's martyr: a shrine to Saint Thomas of Canterbury. Osbern started to chuckle to himself.

'Are you well, Grandfather?

Osbern looked up at the boy and leaned on his cane. His blond grandson towered over him, tall and pretty. He has his father's looks, not his mother's he thought. His daughter had been dark haired and slight, not like this blonde bumpkin, but she had fallen in love with a tanner and he had no heart to stop it. Now there was a brood of fair-haired Wiltshire grandsons to look after him in his dotage. He smiled gappily at the boy.

'I am well enough but I think I shall be happy to go back to the inn afterwards.'

'You should be at the front with the other guests of honour. None of these others were with the saint.' The boy sniffed dismissively at the head of the procession.

Osbern noticed a poor friar selling lead vials of Thomas Water on a street corner. They said it was the saint's blood mixed with holy water blessed by the Archbishop himself. The current incumbent that was, not the saint. In death, Thomas's bones had proven quite lucrative to Christ Church. The monks made fortunes on his memory. They sent fragments, shards of bone, all around Christendom. His elbow was in the Kingdom of Hungary, so Osbern had been told. The Rabbit remembered Thomas's scepticism over such things, and laughed again at the irony of it all.

The procession crossed over Dean's Bridge and into the cathedral compound and the Rabbit and his grandson shuffled along with them. Osbern drank in all the changes: the new buildings towering over the old. Newly dressed stone carvings and adornments gave testimony to the growing wealth of the cathedral and the town.

'In death he made their fortunes, but so few of them cared when he was alive.'

'Grandfather?'

'It is of no matter,' said Osbern. 'I am merely being maudlin.' He pointed to the low wall that circled the compound. 'When I was your age, I would leap that wall in one bound to escape into the town for some ale.'

The boy smiled at him, hardly able to believe that his decrepit grandfather was ever young, but his mother had told him tales of saints and crusades, and a summons to this ceremony from the King's court carried by a royal knight proved the truth of the stories. He was proud of his hero grandfather.

'What would he say?' the boy asked.

Osbern did not need to ask who "he" was. Thomas was everybody's topic of conversation.

'He would be disappointed with me,' said Osbern with a toothless grin. 'His disappointment was worse to bear than any rage, although he could rage.'

After the murder, few had sought out Osbern the Rabbit to ask what he had known of his lord. The manservant had been overlooked in the scramble by everyone to prove how close they had been to the martyr. Rabbit had left England within months and taken himself off to the Holy Land to fulfil his thrice sworn oath. The pilgrim's badges were still proudly displayed on his cloak. Osbern had seen a cave that held the beds of Adam and Eve in Palestine, Lot's wife turned to salt, the garden of Gethsemane, Calvary, even the messiah's birthplace in

Bethlehem. He had watched d'Augbiny duel the Frank at the Pool of Siloam, visited Rome and Constantinople, and seen the fall of Holy Jerusalem to the Saracens, but in the fifty years since Thomas's murder he had not once returned to Canterbury. When the royal summons came, Osbern had nearly ignored it happy in his West Country retirement, but his daughter had insisted.

'People should know you were at the saint's side,' she had said.

'I ran and hid,' he told her.

They had reached the newly constructed Trinity chapel that contained Thomas's shrine. Fresh cut stone, sharp lines, and vaulted roofing.

'I will hold you, Grandfather.'

The boy helped him up the steps into chapel, built after Osbern's time and towering over the lost structure he remembered. There were a thousand candles burning inside as the crowd packed onto the marble pavement inside. Osbern gasped at the paved floor; that alone was of breathtaking quality. Italian marble, laid at enormous expense, with all the animals of the zodiac depicted in the stone. At the centre of the chapel, with its vaulted roof, was a canvas canopy covering the new shrine. The priests had already conducted their ceremonies; this display was for the townsfolk of Canterbury. It was for the commoners who flocked to the city to seek out Saint Thomas's favour, and the merchants and mongers who made their fortunes off the visitors. In death, Thomas was praised by those who had cursed him in life.

Thomas's successor stood before the canopy, he was speaking but Osbern could not hear the words.

'What is he saying?'

'He is thanking everyone for coming, thanking them for the gifts,' said his grandson.

'He needs to speak up,' Osbern grumbled. 'Thomas's voice was always clear.'

The boy smiled at him as some of the other guests shot the complaining deaf old man snide glances.

'They say this one is much like your Thomas,' said a finely dressed old man at their side. 'You are Osbern the Rabbit, Master?'

The Rabbit gave him a quizzical look, his eyesight was not good, but he did not think he recognised the man.

'My father used to own the brew house opposite St Margaret's,' said the man in explanation. 'I remember you, Master. When I was a boy I used to serve you Greek wine. I run the place now, and have sons of my own to follow me.'

'You have a good memory, friend. What is this one truly like?' He gestured to the still speaking Archbishop.

'Stubborn,' said the man, and Osbern chuckled. 'Langton did not like the old King, and talks of Thomas as his guide in all matters. You know he spent time in Pontigny in exile, just like the saint? They say he was much like your master in defending the church against the old king.' He repeated the last point.

The old king in question was John but nobody had liked him much, and Osbern remembered the exile in Pontigny: cold, wet, and miserable.

'There are none like my master,' he told the brewer.

Osbern turned back to the dais. Archbishop Langton was finishing his eulogy. With his last words Langton nodded to some waiting monks who hauled on ropes to lift the canopy and reveal the new shrine to the world. There was silence as the ropes tightened and the canvas slowly lifted. Marble pillars were exposed first. Until finally, to gasps of wonder from the crowd, a raised platform with a golden bejewelled sarcophagus that held the saint's relics was shown to their wonder. The golden screen that covered the stone coffin could be lifted to view the remains. It was a glorious gleaming construction. People fell to their knees praying to the Saint for his blessings, begging him for health and wealth.

The Rabbit stood alone, leaning heavily on his cane, unable to speak as he stared at the golden shrine with tears streaming down his face.

Historical Note.

The murder of Thomas Becket in Canterbury Cathedral was a seismic and defining event that has resounded down the centuries. It had a direct and immediate impact on Henry's continental ambitions and his battle with the church. In the longer term the murder marked a decisive turning point in his reign. Becket's sacrifice was a victory in the wider struggle between church and state that would culminate in the supremacy of Pope Innocent III in Western Europe forty years later. Since 1170, the murder has continued to hold an interest far beyond twelfth century. In death, Thomas became an icon of resistance to an overbearing state.

The dispute between Henry and Thomas was part of a wider struggle between local and national rulers, and the transnational church. After Thomas's murder, Henry would tread much more lightly with the church. At first he tried to front out the murder and even threatened his accusers, but the widespread universal and unequivocal condemnation across Christendom, and growing word of miracles at Canterbury completely confounded that stance. He would be forced to do penance for his words that sent FitzUrse to Canterbury, although Henry would always protest that it was unintended and there is no historical consensus on what exactly the King said to the four knights. In 1174, the King publicly renounced his sins and allowed the monks of Canterbury to beat him for his harsh words – given the amount of blows by over 80 individuals in total, one must conclude they were not overly enthusiastic in the admonishment. Henry also swore to go on crusade as penance, an oath he never fulfilled despite repeated urgings. The King was not above using Becket's memory for his own purposes. Also in 1174, he would claim success in putting down his sons' revolt was because of his public support for Becket's growing cult.

The struggle between church and state was mirrored between the Holy Roman Empire and the Papacy, as well as the Angevin

Empire. The growth of national states and the nature of the transnational church was always going to cause friction, but this early phase of conflict would ultimately be won by Rome and Thomas's death was a major victory for the Pope. The later reign of Innocent III saw the Papacy able to manipulate imperial elections and unseat Emperors. The Battle of Bouvines in 1214, established a temporary supremacy for the Roman Church over the secular rulers of Europe. Whilst it would not last, as the slow development of national states continued apace, it is not hard to draw a direct line from Thomas Becket's murder to the defeat of King John and his German ally 44 years later.

Henry II's hopes for the succession and his dynasty were dashed by his own intransigence after the murder. Young Henry, and his brothers Richard and Geoffrey, would in turn fight against him and each other, tearing the Angevin Empire apart. Young Henry would predecease his father and never take the crown as would Geoffrey, leaving Richard and John to carry on their father's legacy.

By the end of his reign, Henry II was widely unpopular and in open warfare with his two surviving sons and Louis of France. Even John, Henry's supposed favourite, had deserted his father at the last to support Richard. The Lionheart's long absence on crusade left the Angevin Empire at home rudderless. The French crown gradually reasserted its authority over Angevin territory even after Richard's return. Under Louis VII's successor, Phillip Augustus, it would rapidly retake much of France. In 1214, at the Battle of Bouvines, Angevin power in France was finally shattered and even Normandy (part of the English crown since 1066) was lost. It was a complete reversal in dynastic fortunes: Henry II mired in succession problems after Thomas's death, whilst his rival (and Thomas's ally) Louis VII's long years without a male heir were ended with the birth of a son. In succession, King John's abject failure as a monarch also contrasted with Philip Augustus's unprecedented success. The point was not lost on the monkish chroniclers. Thomas Becket's murder cast a long shadow over the Angevin kings.

The consecration of Becket's shrine in 1220 was Stephen Langton's triumph. Langton had, like his predecessor, been a leader of resistance to King John, and the dispute over his election had ended with the whole of England placed under Papal interdict by Innocent III and ultimately in Magna Carta. Langton would spend the first years after his election in exile, as John was determined to repeat his father's mistakes as well as adding some of his own. However, King John's catastrophic reign (and it was catastrophic despite some valid revisionism in the last century), put the seal on the Angevin dynasty's continental ambitions. John's son Henry III would prove more pious and malleable all around than his father, grandfather, or paternal uncles. Henry III would closely associate himself, and the now English Plantagenet dynasty, with Becket's growing cult.

The four knights soon realised that their actions would have terrible consequences. After the murder they fled to De Moreville's holdings in Westmoreland. Pope Alexander swiftly excommunicated them, and they were forced to depart for the Holy Land to serve out their days in penance – although the Bear took his time about it and took part in the Great Revolt by Henry's sons in 1173-4. Legend says the murderers were buried in the refectory of the Knights Templar, now the Al Aqsa Mosque in Jerusalem. FitzUrse is rumoured to have returned to Ireland in his last years, and there are other rumours attached to the killers returning, but there is no clear evidence of any of them actually coming home to Europe.

After the murder, Ranulf de Broc looted the Archbishop's palace, scouring it for incriminating documents that he sent on to the King in France. De Broc and his cousin mostly escaped the censure that fell on the four murderers, despite their prominent part in the killing, and Ranulf continued to serve Henry II loyally for the rest of his life. The three bishops eventually had their excommunications repealed by the Pope, and by 1172 were all restored to office. Roger of York, who had persuaded and funded the four knights, was the most reviled but even he would be restored to office. However, their church careers were ruined and reputations never rehabilitated.

It would be another royal Henry who had the last laugh over Thomas Becket. Henry VIII (a man very much in the mould of his Angevin ancestor) was caught up in his messy first divorce and saw Thomas as a symbol of Papist power that he was intent on defying. In 1538, he issued a proclamation that Becket was not a saint, his shrine was to be broken up and sold off, and his bones burnt and discarded. The proclamation described Thomas as a traitor to his king who had defied Henry II's honour. The amount of plate, gold bullion, and gemstones retrieved when the shrine was destroyed was estimated at £1 million - perhaps four hundred times that in today's terms. Saint smashing was lucrative business under the Tudor monarch. The Pope finally excommunicated Henry VIII after hearing about the shrine's despoiling, but Thomas's reputation was not to be rehabilitated in England under the Tudor monarchs who brushed off excommunication and numerous Catholic martyrdoms. The Seal of London that had born Thomas's image was quickly changed in 1539, as Thomas's home town chose crown over church.

In modern times, Thomas has been rehabilitated in film and books. My first exposure to the story was the Oscar winning film starring Richard Burton as Thomas and Peter O'Toole as Henry, followed by a school production of Eliot's Murder in the Cathedral and then studying the play for 'A' level literature. At University, I was fortunate enough to have Stephen Church as my tutor whose encyclopaedic understanding and boundless enthusiasm for the Angevins was infectious. Read his books, they are utterly brilliant and bring John's reign in particular to life. With 2020 being Thomas's triple anniversary: a millennium since his birth, 950 years since his death, and 900 years since the shrine's unveiling in Canterbury, it seemed apt to attempt a retelling of his career. Thomas Becket was a remarkable man, who lived in remarkable times. I hope I have done him justice.

All of the primary sources for Becket are available digitised and transcribed through Early English Books Online, which you can access for free at your local library or educational institution. John Guy, Frank Barlow, and Anne Duggan's biographies are all essential reading for the early period of Becket's life, whilst William Urry's investigation into Becket's last month is an outstanding piece of micro-history. As always I must give my wholehearted thanks to James Smallwood and Nigel Williams for advice and inspiration, and everyone at Sharpe Books for their support.

All the mistakes are mine!

Jemahl Evans, May 2020.

Jemahl is the author of the acclaimed Blandford Candy series set in the 17th Century and published by Sharpe Books. He holds an MA in Medieval History, and is a member of the Historical Writers Association. Jemahl lives in West Wales with his border collie.

You can follow him on Twitter @Temulkar
Facebook: https://www.facebook.com/TheLastRoundhead/
Website: https://jemahlevans.wixsite.com/jemahlevans

Printed in Great Britain
by Amazon

48855570R00151